Support Programs
for Ex-Offenders

*American POWs in World War II: Twelve Personal Accounts
of Captivity by Germany and Japan* (2009)

*Pearl Harbor Survivors:
An Oral History of 24 Servicemen* (2002)

*Prisoners of Nazis: Accounts by American POWs
in World War II* (1998)

American POWs in Korea: Sixteen Personal Accounts (1998)

*Scars of Vietnam: Personal Accounts by Veterans
and Their Families* (1994)

*Death Angel: A Vietnam Memoir of a Bearer
of Death Messages to Families* (1992)

Support Programs for Ex-Offenders

A State-by-State Directory

HARRY SPILLER

McFarland & Company, Inc., Publishers
Jefferson, North Carolina, and London

LIBRARY OF CONGRESS CATALOGUING-IN-PUBLICATION DATA

Spiller, Harry, 1945–
    Support programs for ex-offenders : a state-by-state directory /
Harry Spiller.
      p.   cm.

    ISBN 978-0-7864-4868-5
    softcover : 50# alkaline paper

    1. Ex-convicts — Rehabilitation — United States.
2. Ex-convicts — Rehabilitation — United States — States.
3. Charities — United States.   4. Charities — United States —
States. I. Title.
HV8987.S65   2011
364.8 — dc22   2010045076

British Library cataloguing data are available

Front cover images © 2011 Shutterstock

Manufactured in the United States of America

*McFarland & Company, Inc., Publishers
  Box 611, Jefferson, North Carolina 28640
  www.mcfarlandpub.com*

TABLE OF CONTENTS

INTRODUCTION

Incarceration in the United States is a concurrent power under the Constitution of the United States, which means that prisons are operated under strict authority of both the federal and state governments. Incarceration is one of the main forms of punishment for the commission of felony offenses in the United States.

The United States has the highest documented incarceration rate in the world. The U.S. incarceration rate on December 31, 2008, was 764 inmates per 100,000 U.S. residents. The U.S. also has the highest total documented prison and jail population in the world.

In 2008, 2,304,115 people were imprisoned in U.S. prisons. In addition, there were 92,854 persons held in juvenile facilities as of the 2006 census of juveniles in residential placement, conducted by the Office of Juvenile Justice and Delinquency Prevention.

From fiscal year 1998 to fiscal year 2010 state fund appropriations for adult corrections alone have increased 88 percent. Part of the crime rate problem is caused by ex-offenders committing new crimes after being released from prison. Roughly 40 of 100 inmates released from prison commit a new crime. Within three years roughly 26 of every 100 return to prison.

Part of the problem is that after years of living in fabricated environments, ex-offenders return to free society with no job, nowhere to live, and little money. They often find it extremely difficult to adjust to life on the outside.

Research has shown a clear link between crime and employment. Having a legitimate job lessens the chance of reoffending following release from prison. Also, the higher the wage, the less likely it is that returning prisoners will return to crime.

Although most prisoners had held a job before their incarceration, they confront many barriers to re-employment upon return to the community, such as low education levels, the stigma of prison, and loss of time in the labor force. Also, employers are more reluctant to hire former prisoners — job applicants with a criminal record are substantially less likely to be hired. Individuals with felony convictions are statutorily barred from many jobs. Additionally, the availability of criminal records online and changing public policies regarding access to those records make it easier for employers to conduct criminal background checks. The kinds of jobs for which employers have historically been more willing to hire individuals who were formerly incarcerated, blue-collar and manufacturing jobs, are diminishing in the national economy. To the extent that these issues present serious barriers to transitioning prisoners, they also present serious risk to the communities to which large numbers of prisoners return. The ability to find a stable and adequate source of income upon release from prison is an important factor in an individual's transition from prison back to the community. Further, former prisoners' employment prospects have direct and important implications for their abilities to contribute to the viability and stability of their families and communities.

Several factors about the prison experience contribute to reducing the employability of former offenders. A lack of education and vocational training contribute to the lessened ability to gain employment. Therefore, a key to finding and maintaining employment is developing certain basic skills such as reading and writing at more than basic levels to succeed in the labor market.

The circumstances surrounding the immediate days and weeks after release from prison are critical to the success of an inmate's reentry. From a workforce perspective, it is important to think about what can be done to increase the likelihood that a released prisoner is employed immediately following his or her release from prison.

Research suggests that well-conceptualized and strategically placed job training and placement interventions can be successful. The data also suggest that nontraditional interventions are required — a mix of traditional workforce development interventions along with supportive services to deal with issues of health, substance abuse, and housing during the time immediately following release from prison.

Ex-offenders frequently look first to their families to meet their needs for money, housing, and emotional support. Some adjustment to possible problems will be necessary. One issue involves struggles and renegotiation of roles. Ex-offenders who have been forced into dependency during their imprisonment may seek to assert their own power and control within their family upon return. However, women especially who gained independence and self-sufficiency during the time on their own may desire more egalitarian roles and struggle with their partner for control.

Another issue is dealing with resentment and negative emotions. Research indicates that fear, disappointment, and anger over past hurts are common of ex-offenders. Ex-offenders who have been accustomed to suppressing their emotions in prison, can feel the need to communicate intense feelings, especially if they are negative. Lack of contact during the incarceration can weaken bonds and impede healthy patterns of communications.

Reuniting partners often face many points of conflict including suspected infidelity, differences in how children should be raised, and the threat of new relationships women may have developed during their partner's absence. Conflict that occurs in conjunction with alcohol or drug use can easily escalate to violence. Perception of low self-efficacy in relationships have been linked to underemployment and unemployment, which is common among released prisoners

Although many ex-offenders rely on family when they are released, some individuals experience rejection from families and friends, as well as refusal of housing by private landlords and intensive screening for public housing. There are several types of nonprofits that are involved in housing ex-offenders. This is largely a function of their mission either to serve this population directly or indirectly.

Prisoners aid organizations are very familiar with the needs of ex-offenders and have long histories of serving their needs and advocating on their behalf. These agencies have significant strengths in service programs — such as employment training and placement, drug treatment and mental health care.

It is with this in mind that this directory is presented to assist ex-offenders in locating employment, housing, financial aid, food, clothing, and referrals to other helping organizations and support groups. They are familiar with the needs of ex-offenders and their families and will assist in any way they can. The organizations listed in this book include addresses, phone numbers, e-mail addresses, and websites.

The information contained in this directory came from federal and state agencies and through research by the author. The listing in the directory begins with the national government followed by state-by-state listings, including Puerto Rico, Virgin Islands, and Washington, D.C.

NATIONAL ORGANIZATIONS

Citizens United for Rehabilitation of
 Errants (CURE) National Office
P.O. Box 2310
National Capitol Station
Washington, D.C. 20013-2310
202-789-2126
http://www.curenational.org
  *A prisoner advocacy group with chapters in
all 50 states. Write for contact info for the
CURE chapter in your state.*

Conquest Offender Reintegration
 Ministries
P.O. Box 73873
Washington, D.C. 20056-3873
202-723-2014
  *Federal prisoners who want to be released
to Washington DC may write for an applica-
tion for transitional housing.*

Friends Outside
303 Tisch Way, Ste 507
San Jose, CA 95128
408-295-6033
friendsoutsideinscc.org
and
6116 Highway 9
Felton, CA 95018
831-336-9387
  *Chapters nationwide offering services to
currently and formerly incarcerated people.*

HIRE Network
www.hirenetwork.org

*National directory of employment services
geared towards those re-entering the community from prison.*

The National Center on Institutions
 and Alternatives
7222 Ambassador Rd.
Baltimore, MD 21244
410-265-1490
http://www.ncianet.org
  *NCIA offers parole advocacy services to in-
mates seeking parole, transfer between institutions, or death penalty mitigations.*

The Next Step
P.O. Box 19523
Shawnee Mission, KS 66285-9523
800-498-2207
www.thenextstep99.com
  *The Next Step is dedicated exclusively to
providing quality job opportunities to individual ex-offenders. They offer job placement
services specializing in the vital task of assisting
ex-offenders in their return to society. The Next
Step staff work to help ex-offenders find jobs
across the U.S.*

Northern California Service League
 (NCSL)
40 Boardman Place
San Francisco, CA 94103
415-863-2323
NCSL@NorCalServiceLeague.org
  Provides support service to current and former

prisoners in Northern California which include job training, life skills workshops, substance abuse counseling, parenting classes and legal referrals.

Phoenix House Foundation
800-DRUG-HELP
www.phoenixhouse.org

This organization provides comprehensive rehabilitation services to men, women, and children in more than 100 local centers in nine states (California, Florida, Texas, New York, Maine, Massachusetts, Rhode Island, New Hampshire, and Vermont). Services include transitional housing, vocational training, life skills development, drug and alcohol testing and psychosocial educational groups. Call to find out about regional and national offices.

Project Rebound
San Francisco State University
Department of Sociology
1600 Holloway Ave.
San Francisco, CA 94132
415-405-0954
rebound@sfsu.edu
Post release services.

Project Return
Director Bob Roberts
Tulane University Medical Center,
    School of Public Health and
    Tropical Medicine
2703 General de Gaulle Dr.
New Orleans, LA 70114-6222
504-263-8977
bob@projecttreturn.com
www.projecttreturn.com
Post release programs.

ORGANIZATIONS BY STATE

ALABAMA

Aid to Inmate Mothers
P.O. Box 956
Montgomery, AL 36101
800-679-0246 or 334-262-2245
www.inmatemoms.org

This organization provides services to promote the successful reintegration of women with criminal records by helping them become employed, obtain clothing, and secure housing.

CURE
P.O. Box 190504
Birmingham, AL 35219-0504
205-481-3991
Rosemarytc@bellsouth.net

CURE is a grassroots organization — from top to bottom. It does not hire professional leaders. Instead, its leaders come from the ranks of people formerly in prison and family members of friends of prisoners. The organization offers assistance to ex-offenders.

Re-entry Ministries, Inc.
P.O. Box 100461
Birmingham, AL 35219
205-320-2101
reentry@aol.com

This organization offers a variety of post-release services to former prisoners in Alabama. Programs include support groups for people

with criminal records and families of prisoners, church services, job assistance, and Alcoholics meetings. Write for detail.

One-Stop Career Centers

Alabaster Career Center
109 Plaza Circle
Alabaster, AL 35007
205-663-2542

Albertville Career Center
5920 US Highway 431 N
Albertville, AL 35950
256-878-3031

Alexander City Career Center
1675 Cherokee Rd.
Alexander City, AL 35010
256-215-4494

Andalusia Career Center
1000 Dannelly Ave.
LBW Community College
Andalusia, AL 36420
334-881-2304

Bay Minette Career Center
201 Faulkner Drive
Bay Minette, AL 36507
251-937-4161

Bessemer, T A Lawson State
1100 North Ave. SW
Lawson State Community College
Bessemer, AL 35022
205-428-6391

Birmingham Career Center
3440 3rd Ave. South
Birmingham, AL 35222
205-254-1300

Birmingham, T A Lawson State
3060 Wilson Rd.
Lawson State Community College
Birmingham, AL 35221
205-929-6301

Blountsville Career Center
68644 Min St., Suite 5
Blountsville, AL 35031

Brewton Career Center
1023 Douglas Ave., Suite 314
Brewton, AL 36426
251-867-3247

Center Point Career Center–Jeff State
   College
2601 Carson Rd.
Birmingham, AL 35215
205-856-8538

Cheaha Career Center
1721 Coleman Rd.
Anniston, AL 36207
256-832-0147

Cullman/Hanceville Career Center
801 Main St.
Wallace State Community College
Hanceville, AL 35077
256-734-4911

Decatur Career Center
1819 Bassett Ave., SE
Decatur, AL 35601
256-355-0142

Demopolis Career Center
1074 Bailey Drive

Demopolis, AL 36732
334-289-0202

Dothan Career Center
787 Ross Clark Circle
Dothan, AL 36303
334-347-0044

Eufaula Career Center
511 State Docks Rd.
Eufaula, AL 36027
334-687-8551

Fayette Career Center
2631 Temple Ave. North
Room 216
Fayette, AL 35555
205-932-3221 Ext. 5171

Foley Career Center
200 West Michigan Ave.
Foley, AL 36535
251-945-1575

Fort Wayne Career Center
2100 Jordan Rd. Southwest
Fort Wayne, AL 35968
256-854-1900

Gadsden Career Center
216 North 5th St.
Gadsden, AL 35901
256-546-4667

Greenville Career Center
117 West Commerce St.
Greenville, AL 36037
334-382-3128

Haleyville Career Center
2010 9th Ave.
Haleyville, AL 35565
205-486-4154

Hamilton Career Center
1481 Military St. South
Hamilton, AL 35570
205-921-7657

Huntsville Career Center
2535 Sparkman Drive

Huntsville, AL 35810
256-851-0537

Jackson Career Center
3090 Highway 43
Jackson, AL 36545
251-246-2453

Jefferson County Center for Workforce Development
3420 3rd Ave. South, Suite 200
Birmingham, AL 35222
205-323-7147

Luveme Career Center
886 Glenwood Rd.
Luveme, AL 36049
334-335-2300

Mobile Area Career Center
515 Springhill Plaza Court
Mobile, AL 36608
251-461-4146

Montgomery Career Center
1060 East South Blvd.
Montgomery, AL 36116
334-286-1746

Monroeville Career Center
33 Outlet Drive
Monroeville, AL 36460
251-575-7013

Opelika Career Center
2300 Frederick Rd.
Opelika, AL 36801
334-749-5065

Opp Career Center
1708 N. Main St.
LBW Community College/McArthur
  Campus
Opp, AL 36467
334-393-3782

Phil Campbell Career Center
2080 College Rd.
NW Shoals Community College
Phil Campbell, AL 35581
256-331-6285

Phoenix City Career Center
1104-C Highway 280 Bypass
Workforce Investment Building
Phoenix City, AL 36869
334-214-4828

Pell City Career Center
500 College Circle, Room 318
Pell City, AL 35125
205-338-5440

Roanoke Career Center
3862 Highway 431
Roanoke, AL 36274
334-863-8114

Scottsboro Career Center
706 East Laurel St.
Scottsboro, AL 35768
256-574-1720

Selma Career Center
1112 Water Ave.
Selma, AL 36703
334-872-0471

Shoals Career Center
500 South Montgomery Ave., Suite 102
Sheffield, AL 35600
256-383-5610

Talladega Career Center
235 Haynes St.
Suites A and B
Talladega, AL 35160
256-480-2109

Troy Career Center
1023 S. Brundidge St.
Troy, AL 36081
334-566-3920

Tuscaloosa Area Career Center
202 Skyland Drive
Tuscaloosa, AL 35405
205-758-7591

Walker County Career Center
2604 Viking Drive
Jasper, AL 35501
205-221-2576

ALASKA

Alaska Department of Labor and Workforce Development Centers

Anchorage Employment Security Tax
3301 Eagle St., Room 106
P.O. Box 241767
Anchorage, AK 99524-1767
907-269-4850
Fax: 907-269-4845

Fairbanks Employment Security Tax
675 7th Ave., Station L
Fairbanks, AK 99701-4596
907-451-2876
Fax: 907-451-2876

Juneau Employment Security Tax
1111 W. 8th St., Room 203

P.O. Box 115509
Juneau, AK 99811-5509
907-465-2787
Fax: 907-465-2374

Kenai Employment Security Tax
11312 Kenai Spur Hwy., Suite 2
Kenai, AK 99611-9106
907-283-2920
Fax: 907-283-5152

Wasilla Employment Security Tax
877 Commercial Drive
Wasilla, AK 99654-6937
907-352-2535
Fax: 907-373-2683

ARIZONA

Arizona Department of Economic Security
Re-Entry Program
P.O. Box 6123
Phoenix, AZ 85005
602-542-2271 or 602-542-6416
www.de.state.az.us/tp/portal.asp

Offers a range of services from information about job vacancies, career options, relevant employment trends to instruction on how to conduct a job search, write a resume, or interview with an employer.

Middle Ground Prison Reform, Inc.
139 East Encanto Dr.
Tempe, AZ 85281
480-966-8116
www.middlegroundprisonreform.org
middlegroundprisonreform@msn.com

Middle Ground Prison Reform offers coun-

seling, education, employment readiness training programs, and referrals to social service agencies.

Women Living Free
9220 Coolidge St.
Phoenix, AZ 85037
623-206-2823
Email: *tmb21762@aol.com*

This organization assists women in their transition by offering assistance in finding employment, offering counseling and support groups, with a focus on reunification of mother with their children. Participants must be high school graduates or be enrolled in G.E.D. classes or vocational training. Transitional housing is available upon release.

Workforce Centers by County

APACHE COUNTY

Apache County Workforce Partnership

74 North Main St., Suite 7
Eagar, AZ 85925
928-333-4454
Fax: 928-333-2903

COCHISE COUNTY

Arizona Department of Economic Security
1140 North F Ave.
Douglas, AZ 85607
520-364-4446

Arizona Department of Economic Security
7981 East Tacoma
Sierra Vista, AZ 85635
520-459-3206

Cochise College Career Action Center
901 Columbia
Sierra Vista, AZ 85635
520-515-5457

Cochise County Workforce Development
Douglas One-Stop
1706 East 10th St.
Douglas, AZ 85607
520-364-8904

Cochise County Workforce Development
Sierra Vista One-Stop
1843 Pasco San Luis
Sierra Vista, AZ 85635
520-458-9309
Fax: 520-417-9910
http://www.cpic-cas.org

COCONINO COUNTY

Arizona Department of Economic Security
397 Malpais Lane, #9
Flagstaff, AZ 86001
928-779-4557
http://coconino.az.gov/careercenter

Arizona Department of Economic Security
337 North Navajo
P.O. Box 4269
Page, AZ 86040
928-645-5201

Goodwill of Central Arizona
2225 North Steves Blvd.
Flagstaff, AZ 86004
928-526-9188

Sunnyside One-Stop Center
2403 North Izabel
Flagstaff, AZ
928-779-7011

Williams Library One-Stop Center
113 South First St.
Williams, AZ 86046
928-635-2263

GILA COUNTY

Arizona Department of Economic Security
605 South 7th St.
Globe, AZ 85501
928-425-3101

Arizona Department of Economic Security
112 East Highway 260
Payson, AZ 85541
928-472-9339

Gila County Division of Health and
Community Services
5515 South Apache Ave.
Globe, AZ 85501
928-425-7631
http://www.giolcountyaz.gov

GRAHAM COUNTY

Arizona Department of Economic Security
1938 West Thatcher Blvd.

Safford, AZ 85546
928-428-2911

Eastern Arizona College–
   Occupational Placement
615 North College Ave.
Thatcher, AZ 85552
928-428-8341

WIA Title I Service Center
826 West Main St.
Safford, AZ 85546
928-428-7386
Fax: 928-428-8074

GREENLEE COUNTY

Greenlee One-Stop Resource Center
Highway 191 and Ward Canyon Rd.
Clifon, AZ 85533
928-865-4151
Fax: 928-865-3566
http://www.arnex.net/-clifton_os

LA PAZ COUNTY

La Paz Career Center
113 Kofa Ave.
Parker, AZ 85344
928-669-9812
Fax: 928-669-6326
www.cola.paz.az.us/career.html

MARICOPA COUNTY

Arizona Department of Economic Security
163 North Dobson Rd.
Mesa, AZ 85201-6066
480-962-7678

Gilbert Career Center
735 North Gilbert Rd., Suite 134
Gilbert, AZ 85234-6066
480-497-0350

Vista Del Camino Center
7700 East Roosevelt
Scottsdale, AZ 85257
480-312-2323

West Valley Career Center
1840 North 95th Ave., Suite 160
Phoenix, AZ 85037
602-372-4200
Fax: 602-372-4290
http://www.hsd.maricopa.gov/mwc

MOHAVE COUNTY

Arizona Department of Economic Security
2601 Highway 95
Bullhead, AZ 86442
928-763-4154
Fax: 928-763-1526

Arizona Department of Economic Security
301 Pine St.
Kingman, AZ 86401
928-753-4333
Fax: 928-753-6746

Arizona Department of Economic Security
232 London Bridge Rd.
Lake Havasu, AZ 86403
928-854-0350
Fax: 928-680-7849

Mohave County Community and
   Economic Development Department
1355 Ramar Rd., Suite 3
Bullhead, AZ 86442
928-758-0702
Fax: 928-758-0737

Mohave County Community and
   Economic Development Department
700 West Beale St.
Kingman, AZ 86401
928-753-0723
Fax: 928-753-0776
TDD-928-753-0726
*www.mohave.az.us/webservices/cedd/wd
   d/onwstop/default.aspx*

Mohave County Community and Economic Development Department
2001 College Drive, Suite 122
Lake Havasu, AZ 86403
928-453-0710
Fax: 928-453-0728

NAVAJO COUNTY

Arizona Department of Economic Security
1500 East Cookey, Suite 410
Show Low, AZ 85901
928-532-4313
Fax: 928-532-4367

Arizona Department of Economic Security
319 East Third St.
Winslow, AZ 86047
928-289-4644 Ext. 101 and 103

PHOENIX CITY

Phoenix Workforce Connection Hope VI Community Training and Education
1150 South 7th Ave.
Phoenix, AZ 85007
602-534-2043

Phoenix Workforce Connection North
9801 North 7th St.
Phoenix, AZ 85020
602-861-0208

Phoenix Workforce Connection South
4732 South Central Ave.
Phoenix, AZ 85040
602-534-4732

Phoenix Workforce Connection West
Arizona Department of Economic Security
3406 North 51st Ave.
Phoenix, AZ 85031
623-247-3304
http://www.phoenix.gov/phxwc

PIMA COUNTY

Arizona Department of Economic Security
5441 East 22nd St., Suite 100
Tucson, AZ 85711
520-584-8226

Arizona Department of Economic Security
316 West Fort Lowell
Tucson, AZ 85705
520-293-1919

Arizona Department of Economic Security
195 West Irvington
Tucson, AZ 85713
520-741-7188

Jackson Employment Center
300 East 26th St.
Tucson, AZ 85713
520-882-5500

Kino Service Center
2797 East Ajo Way
Tucson, AZ 85713
520-243-6700
Fax: 520-243-6799
http://www.OimaWorks.com

Rio Nuevo One-Stop Career Center
340 North Commerce Park Loop
Tortolita Building
Tucson, AZ 85745
520-798-0500
Fax: 520-798-0599

PINAL COUNTY

Arizona Workforce Connection–Casa Grande
1015 East Florence Blvd.
Casa Grande, AZ 85222
520-374-3072

Central Arizona Association of Governments

414–B Marshall St.
Casa Grande, AZ 85222
520-836-1887
http://www.gilacounty.az.gov

Empowerment System, Inc. (Access
  Point)
2066 West Apache Trail, Suite 116
Apache Junction, AZ 85220
480-367-6937

SANTA CRUZ COUNTY

Santa Cruz County One-Stop Center
610 North Morley Ave.
Nogales, AZ 85621
520-375-7670
Fax: 520-281-1166
www.santacruzconnect.org

YAVAPAI COUNTY

Yavapai Workforce Affiliate Office
  Prescott Valley
8128 East Highway 69, Suite 211
Prescott Valley, AZ 86314
928-445-5100
Fax: 928-776-7630

Yavapai Workforce Connection–East
  County
1500 East Cherry St., Suite F
Cottonwood, AZ 86326
928-649-6867
Fax: 928-634-8258

Yavapai Workforce Connection–West
  County
221 North Marina, Suite 201
P.O.Box 2451
Prescott, AZ
928-778-1422
Fax: 928-778-1756

YUMA COUNTY

Career Resource Center
3826 West 16th St.

Yuma, AZ 85364
928-329-0990
Fax: 928-783-1825
*http://www.ypic.com/career_resource_
  center.html*

Somerton Career Center
201 Bingham Ave., #19
Somerton, AZ 85350
928-333-4454
Fax: 928-333-2903

TRIBAL NATIONS

Cocopah Indian Tribe
Sandy Johnson, Director
County 15 and Ave. G
Somerton, AZ 85350
928-627-8026
Fax: 928-627-2510
cococvt@cocopsh.com

Colorado River Indian Tribes
Doa Eddy, Director
13390 1st Ave. (location)
26600 Mohave Rd. (mailing address)
Mohave, AZ 85344
928-669-8555
Fax: 928-669-6085
edtde@npgcable.com

Fort Mojave Indian Tribes
Michel Medraso, Director
1599 Plantation Rd. (location)
P.O. Box 5896 (mailing address)
Mojave, AZ 86446
928-346-1787
Fax: 928-346-1788
michelmedrano@fortmojave.com

Gila River Indian Community
Lana Chanda, Director
192 South Skill Center Rd., Suite 208
Sacaton, AZ 85247
480-963-0902
Fax: 520-562-3590
Lana.chanda@gric.nsn.us

Hopi Tribe
Gail Pahona, WIA Program Adminis-
trator
Main St. off Highway 264 (location)
P.O. Box 123 (mailing address)
Kykotsmovi, AZ 86039
928-734-3541
Fax: 928-734-9575
gpahoma@hopi.nsn.us

Hualapai Tribe
Lucille Watahomigie,Director
460 Hualapai Way (location)
P.O. Box 179 (mailing address)
Kykotsmovi, AZ86039
928-734-3541
Fax: 928-734-9575
hualwia@yahoo.com

Pascua Yaqut Tribe
Greg Madril, Director
7474 South Camino de Oeste
Tucson, AZ 85757
520-879-2200
Fax: 928-879-5850
Greg.madril@pascuayaqui-nsn.gov

Quechan Indian Tribe
Earl Daniel, Director
628 Picacho Rd. (location)
P.O. Box 1899 (mailing address)
Yuma, AZ 85366
760-572-2314
Fax: 572-2735
e.daniel@quechantribe.com

Salt River Pima–Maricopa Indian
Community
James Smith, E and T Coordinator
10005 East Osborn Rd.

Scottsdale, AZ 85256
480-362-7966
Fax: 480-362-2562
James.smith@srpmic-nsn.gov

San Carlos Apache Tribe
Etta Key, Director
San Carlos Ave. (location)
P.O. Box 0 (mailing address)
San Carlos, AZ 85550
928-475-2305
Fax: 928-475-2707
ekey@cybertrails.com

Tohono O'odham Nation
Cody Juan, Director
SR 86 and Indian Route 19 (location)
P.O. Box 837 (mailing address)
Sells, AZ 85634
520-383-4251
Fax: 520-383-2533
Cody.juan@tonation-nsn.gov

White Mountain Apache Tribe
Marjorie Quade, Director
100 East Walnut St. (location)
P.O. Box 520 (mailing address)
Whiteriver, AZ 85941
928-338-4818
Fax: 928-338-4177
mquade@wmat.nsn.us

Yavapai-Apache Nation
Tanya Lewis–WIA Manager
2400 West Datsi
Camp Verde, AZ 86322
928-567-1062
Fax: 928-567-1064
Tlewis-moore@yan-tribe.org

ARKANSAS

Arkansas Enterprise Group
2304 W. 29th Ave
Pine Bluff, AR 71603

870-535-6233
aduran@southerngoodfaithfund.org
This program offers job training and place-

ment. Participants engage in a daily curriculum, which includes education, job readiness skills, personal development, and work experience.

Arkansas Voices for Children Left Behind
2715 Marshfield Ct.
Wrightsville, AR 72206
501-897-0809
www.arkansasvoices.com
lujo@aristotie.net

Center for Youth and Family Prison Project
5905 Forest Place, Suite 202
Little Rock, AR 72207
501-660-6886 ext. 3310

This program serves prisoners during and after incarceration, their children and the children's caretakers. Basic services offered, beginning during incarceration and continuing upon release of the prisoner, include: counseling (mental health as well as substance abuse), family crisis intervention, literacy programs, housing assistance, and employment services.

CURE
P.O. Box 56001
Little Rock, AR 72215
501-223-2620
501-519-0064
FAX:501-470-9039
Rehab4justice@yahoo.com

CURE is a grassroots organization from top to bottom. It does not hire professional leaders. Instead, its leaders come from the ranks of people formerly in prison and family members of friends of prisoners. This organization offers assistance to ex-offenders.

Arkansas State Unified Plan Workforce Investment Centers

Arkansas Department of Workforce Education:
3 Capitol Mall
Little Rock, AR 72201-1083
501-682-1500
Fax: 501-682-1509

Liaison: Mary Ellen Koettel
501-682-1528
501-682-1026

Arkansas Department of Human Services, County Operations:
P.O. Box 1437, Slot 1221
Little Rock, AR 72203
501-682-8375
Fax: 501-682-8367
Ruth.whitney@mail.state.ar.us
Liaison: Linda Greer
501-682-8257
Fax: 501-682-8281
Linda.greer@mail.state.-ar.us

Arkansas Department of Workforce Adult Education and Literacy Programs:
3 Capitol Mall
Little Rock, AR 72201
501-682-1970
Fax: 501-682-1982
Garland.hankins@mail.state.ar.us
Signatory Official: Steve Franks
501-682-1500
Fax:501-682-1509
Steve.franks@mail.state.ar.us

Arkansas Employment Security Department:
P.O. Box 2981
Little Rock, AR 72203-2981
501-682-2121
Fax: 501-682-2273
Aesd.mail@mail.state.ar.us
Director: Ed Rolle
Ed.rolle.aesd@mail.state.ar.us
Liaison: Carl Bayne
501-682-1491
Fax: 501-682-3223
Carl.bayne.aesd@mail.state.ar.us
Liaison: Sharon Robinette
501-682-5227
Fax: 501-682-3144
Sharon.robinette.aesd@mail.state.ar.us

Arkansas Rehabilitation Services:
P.O. Box 3781
Little Rock, AR 72203-3781
501-296-1600
Fax: 501-296-1655
JCWyvill@ars.state.ar.us
Assistant Commissioner: Roy Albert
501-296-1642
Fax: 501-296-1675
REAlbert@ars.state.ar.us
Commissioner: John C. Wyvill
501-296-1604

Arkansas Workforce Investment
    Board:
320 Executive Court, Suite 302
Little Rock, AR 72205
501-371-1020
Fax: 501-320-1030
Executive Director: Linda L Beene,
    Ed.D
llbeene@mail.state.ar.us
Deputy Director: Paul Murray
Paul.murray@mail.state.ar.us

CALIFORNIA

Abram Friedman Occupational Center
1646 South Olive St.
Los Angeles, CA 90015-6068
213-745-2013
afoc@earthlik.net
    This organization offers less than one year of training in 23 different vocations. You must be 18 years or older and functionally literate.

Academic Achievement Center
Educational Opportunity Program
6000 J. St.
Lassen Hall 2205
Sacramento, CA 95819
916-278-6183
www.csus.edu/eop
    This is a system wide program of the California State University campus that provides admission, counseling services, academic advising, financial assistance, and retention services to students with low-incomes. Participants must be California residents.

Allied Fellowship Services
1524 29th Ave
Oakland, CA 94601
510-535-1236
Slpysteph2@aol.com
    Employment services available to former prisoners include employment workshops,

health education, drug counseling, and job board. There is also a residential home for men with 30 beds.

Alternative Media Network
1827 Haight St.
P.O. Box 202
San Francisco, CA 94117
415-995-4692
    Publishes a "San Francisco Survival Manual" including a "Behind Bars" category. Send self-addressed stamped envelope and request to receive the catalog of other available publications.

Barrios Unidos
1817 Soquel Ave.
Santa Cruz, CA 95062
831-457-8208
831-457-0389
http://www.barriosunidos.net
    Post-release services. Performs Pow-wow/ Cinco De Mayo/Juneteenth ceremonies at Tracy and info packet related to cultural traditions.

Beil T'Shuvah
House of Return
8831 Venice Blvd.
Los Angeles, CA 90034
310-204-5200

www.beittshuvahia.org
info@beittshuvahia.org

This organization offers a residential re-entry facility for Jewish former prisoners. Services provided include drug counseling, education, and employment services.

Berkeley Oakland Support Services (BOSS)
P.O. Box 1996
Berkeley, CA 94701
510-649-1930
Email: *bossmail@self-sufficiency.org*

This agency offers pre-release and parole planning.

Bethesda Family Ministries International
3882 Stillman Park Cir. #19A
Sacramento, CA 95824
1-877-492-0115
http://www.bethesdafamily.org/
ed@bethesdafamily.org

This ministry ministers to offenders and ex-offenders, as well as their families, in the Sacramento area.

California Food Policy Advocates
116 New Montgomery St. Suite 633
San Francisco, CA 94105
415-777-4422
www.cfpa.net

Pre-release and parole planning services available only in the Bay area. Publishes How to Get Food and Money, The People's Guide to Welfare, Health and Other Services in California, and Como Obtener Dinero y Alimentos: La Guide Popular Para of Welfare, Services Medicos y Otros Services en California. Provides information on welfare, social security, food stamps, and agencies that provide emergency aid.

Casa Libre/Freedom House
845 S. Lake St.
Los Angeles, CA 90057
213-637-5614
www.casa-libre.org

This project offers a transitional living pro-gram for the homeless youth under the age of 18.

Centerforce, Division of Health Programs
2955 Kerner Blvd, 2nd Floor
San Rafael, CA 94901
415-458-9980
www.centerforce.org

In addition to coordinating HIV prevention programs in several California State Prisons, Centerforce provides case management, literacy, family support services, health education, parenting policy, research, training and consultation, and educational development.

Center for Children of Incarcerated Parents
P.O. Box 41-286
Eagle Rock, CA 90041
626-449-2470
http://www.e-ccip.org/index.htmlccip
@earthlink.net

CCIP's mission is the prevention of inter-generational crime and prevention. Its goals are the production of high quality documentation on the development of model services for children of criminal offenders and their families. CCIP provides research and resource information in four pivotal areas: education(parenting Classes, etc), family reunification, therapeutic services and information.

Central City Hospitality House
290 Turk St.
San Francisco, CA 94102
415-749-2119
www.hospitalityhouse.org
info@hospitalityhouse.org

This organization offers an emergency shelter/drop-in center, mail and message service, job referrals and placement, free clothing and counseling.

Community Construction Training Center
250 West 85th St.
Los Angeles, CA 90003
323-753-6211

This organization works with low-income individuals and former prisoners and provides job development and vocational training.

Community Information Center
P.O. Box 1834
Sacramento, CA 95812-1834
800-510-2020

This organization provides a public information and referral service to the Sacramento community. They also provide referrals to more than 1,400 community programs and services in the Sacramento area.

CRASH–Community Resources and
   Self Help
Information and Intake Office
927 24th St.
San Diego, CA 92102
619-233-8054
www.crashinc.org
intake@crashinc.org

This organization offers an outpatient daily treatment services and long-term(4–8 months or longer)residential programs. Services provided include individual and group counseling, vocational and educational services, socialism skills, recovery planning, and release prevention.

Critical Resistance: Beyond the Prison
   Industrial Complex
National Office; 1904 Franklin St.
   Suite 504
Oakland, CA 94612
510-444-0484
http://www.criticalresistance.org

Northeast Regional Office:
976 Longwood Ave.
Bronx, NY 10459
718-676-1672
crne@criticalresistance.org

Southern Regional Office:
930 N. Broad St.
New Orleans, LA 70119
504-304-3792
crsouth@criticalresistance.org

Critical Resistance provides information on the prison industrial complex and produces quarterly newspaper, "The Abolitionist." Please do not contact for legal help. CR has chapters in Baltimore, Chicago, Gainesville, Los Angeles, New Orleans, New York City, Tampa–St. Petersburg, and Washington D.C.

Delancy St. Foundation
600 Embarcadero
San Francisco, CA 94107
415-957-9800

During a two to four-year stay at Delancey St., residents learn social survival skills as well as academic and vocational skills.

East Los Angeles Skills Center
3921 Selig Place
Los Angeles, CA 90031
323-227-0018
elasc.adultinstruction.org
ram2103@lausd.k12ca.org

This organization offers a unique program for pre-release prisoners, incorporating both academic study and employment training.

Friends Outside
551 Stockton Ave
San Jose, CA 95126
408-295-6033
friend@friendsoutsideinscc.org

There are chapters nationwide that offer services to currently and formerly incarcerated people. They provide assistance in setting up people plans, job readiness, and connecting prisoners with drug treatment programs. They also contract with the California Department of Corrections to teach parenting classes in prisons, assist with child custody issues, and help with the reunification process.

Friends Outside
P.O. Box 4085
Stockton, CA 95204
209-955-0701
http://friendsoutside.org/gnewby@friends outside.org

Friends Outside is a nonprofit community based organization that has been providing programs and serves to families and individuals involved in the criminal justice system since 1955. They believe in respect for others; in the capacity of human beings to change; and in the importance of the family and the community in the development of resilient, responsible and capable people.

Haight Ashbury Free Medical Clinic
558 Clayton St.
San Francisco, CA 94117
415-487-5632
www.hafci.org
The HAFMC provides free health care to those in need, including substance abuse programs, HIV treatment, and care for the homeless.

Housing and Emergency Food Hotline Number
Los Angeles Area
310-551-2929 or dial 211
www.infoline-la.org
This organization attempts to connect former prisoners with shelter and food in their area.

Info Line Sacramento
828 I St., 5th Floor
Sacramento, CA 95814
918-498-1000
www.communitycouncil.org
infoline@communitycouncil.org
Info line provides information and referrals to the Sacramento community.

The Insight Prison Project
805 Fourth St. Suit 3
San Rafael, CA 94901
415-459-9800
http://www.insightprisonproject.org
Communication training in nonviolence in correctional facilities; expanding to include post-release training.

L.A. Mission
303 E 5th St
Los Angeles, CA 90013
213-629-1227
This organization provides emergency hous-

ing for 4 nights (every ten days), two meals, free clothing, shower and shave.

Loaves and Fishes
1321 North C St.
Sacramento, CA 95814
916-446-0874
www.sacramentoloavesandfishes.org
info@sacramentoloavesandfishes.org
This organization provides free noon meals, daytime hospitality shelter, health clinic, AIDS hospice, legal services, housing resources, emergency school for homeless children, and overnight shelter for women and children.

Los Angeles Free Clinic
8405 Beverly Blvd.
Los Angeles, CA 90048
323-653-1990 clinic
323-653-8622 counseling and social services
www.lafreeclinic.org
This organization offers medical, dental, legal, and counseling services.

Metropolitan Skills Center
2801 West 6th St.
Los Angeles, CA 90057
213-386-7269
This organization offers vocational training, English as a second language classes, high school diploma and GED classes.

Mexican American Opportunity Foundation
401 N Garfield Ave
Montebsello, CA 90640
323-890-9600
www.maof.org
This organization provides training and subsequent job placement, counseling, emergency shelter, legal assistance, food, clothing, and medical care, at a number of California locations.

Mothers Reclaiming Our Children
4167 Normandies Ave
Los Angeles, CA 90037
Working to create a nationwide program to

provide support to families, attend court hearings and trails, and work with attorneys. Provides advocacy work for prisoners and their families.

Northern California Service League
(NCSL)
28 Boardman Place
San Francisco, CA 94103
415-863-2323
www.norcalserviceleague.org
ncsl@norcalserviceleague.org
   NCSL provides support services to current and former prisoners in Northern California, including job training, life skills workshops, substance abuse counseling, parenting classes and legal referrals.

Pacific Youth Correctional Ministries
P.O. Box 8333
San Bernadino, CA 92412
562-596-5352
http://www.pycm.org/
   PYCM creates or facilitates model chaplaincy ministries with at risk and incarcerated youth through intervention.

Project Rebound
Associated Students, Inc.
Cesar Chavez Student Center
1650 Holloway Ave. T-138
San Francisco, CA 94132
415-405-0954
www.sfsu.edu/~rebound
rebound@sfsu.edu
   Project Rebound is a special admissions program for former prisoners wanting to enter San Francisco State University. They offer special guidelines concerning admissions and academic tutoring to new students.

Proteus, Inc.
1830 N Dinuba Blvd.
Visalia, CA 93291
559-733-5423
www.prpfeusinc.org
   Proteus, inc. participates in the statewide Jobs Plus program. They assist individuals in securing employment in Fresno. Tulare, Kings,

and Kern Counties and provide employment counseling, job skills, and job placement.

San Francisco Works
235 Montgomery St.
12th Floor
San Francisco, CA 94104-3103
415-217-5193
www.sfworks.org
   SFWorks offers life skills training, case management services, job training and placement.

Seventh Step Foundation–East Bay
Chapter
475 Medford Ave.
Hayward, CA 94541
510-278-0230
   This organization has a re-entry program called Freedom House that provides parolees with housing meals, clothing, and employment.

South Bay Regional Center (Episcopal
Community Services)
3954 Murphy Canyon Rd. Suite D-202
San Diego, CA 92123
888-505-8031
   Offers 3 and 6 month sessions for individuals referred by the court or probation office for misdemeanor, non-violent, or low-violence drug charges. AIDS Education classes are also required for those referred for convictions on possession of narcotics and prostitution.

State of California Department of Rehabilitation Communications
Office
P.O. Box 944222
Sacramento, CA 94244-2200
918-263-8952
www.rehab.cahwnet.gov
   This state agency provides assistance to prisoners and ex-prisoners with documented physical, emotional, or mental disability in finding employment.

Turing Point Central California
Visalia Reentry Center
1845 South Court St.

Visalia, CA 93277
559-732-5550

This is a work-furlough program operated in cooperation with the California Department of Corrections and Federal Prison System. It includes a 24-bed facility that is centrally located close to many potential places of employment for residents. Offers food, shelter, job placement, medical services, drug counseling, mental health services, legal assistance, and Christian counseling.

Welcome Home Ministries
Attn: Gloria
104 South Barnes St.
Oceanside, CA 92054
760-439-1136
www.welcomehomeministries.com
info@welcomehomeministries.com

This is a Christian organization that provides faith-based support for women in their transition from incarceration to society by providing toiletries, food, clothing, support groups, networking for jobs, housing, and rehabilitation.

The Workplace
3407 W. 6th Ste 705
Los Angeles, CA 90020
213-386-1994

The workplace provides job-placement services, pre-employment screening, and referrals for parolees and pre-release employment screening for prisoners. Some referrals for drug rehabilitation are available. Also works in Orange County.

California One-Stop Career Centers by County

ALAMEDA COUNTY

Alameda One-Stop Career Center
555 Appezzato Memorial Parkway,
    Room Portable P
Alameda, CA 94501
510-748-2208
www.eastbayworks.com

Eden Area Multiservice Center
24100 Amador St.
Hayward, CA 94544
510-670-5700
TTY: 510-265-8340
www.eastbayworks.com

The English Center, ECIW
66 Franklin St., Suite 300
Oakland, CA 94607
510-836-6700
www.eastbayworks.org

Lao Family Community Development
    Inc.
1551 23rd Ave.
Oakland, CA 94606
510-533-8850
www.eastbayworks.org

Merritt College One-Stop Shop
12500 Campus Drive, R105
Oakland, CA 94619
510-436-2449
www.eastbayworks.org

North Cities One-Stop Career Center
1918 Bonita Ave.
Berkeley, CA 94704
510-982-7128
TTY: 800-735-2929
www.rubiconprograms.org

Oakland Downtown One-Stop Career Center
1212 Broadway, Suite 100
Oakland, CA 94612
510-768-4473
TTY: 800-736-2922
www.eastbayworks.com

Oakland East One-Stop Career Centers
675 Hegenbeger Rd., 3rd Floor
Oakland, CA 94621
510-563-5200
www.eastbayworks.com

Tri-Cities One-Stop Career Center
39389 Cherry St.
Newark, CA 94560
510-742-2323
www.tricitiesonestop.com

Tri-Cities One-Stop Career Center
39155 Liberty St., Suite B200
Fremont, CA 94538
510-794-3669
www.eastbayworks.com

Tri-Valley One-Stop Career Center
5020 Franklin Drive
Pleasanton, CA 94588
925-485-5262
www.trivalleyonestop.com

Unity Council Multicultural One-
Stop Career Center
1900 Fruitvale Ave.
Oakland, CA 94601
510-535-6101
www.eastbayworks.org

AMADOR COUNTY

The Job Connection, Amador
245 New York Ranch Rd., Suite A
Jackson, CA 95642
209-223-4411

BUTTE COUNTY

Community Employment Center
2445 Carmichael Drive
Chico, CA 95928
530-895-4364
www.butteonestep.org

Community Employment Center
78 Table Mountain Blvd.
Oroville, CA 95965
530-538-7301
www.onestop.org

Oroville–North Valley Employment
Services
2348 Baldwin Ave.

Oroville, CA 95966
530-538-2228

CALAVERAS COUNTY

Job Connection Calaveras
700 Mt. Ranch Rd., Suite A
San Andreas, CA 95249
209-754-4242

COLUSA COUNTY

Colusa County One-Stop Partnership
146 Market St.
Colusa, CA 95932
530-458-0326
TTY: 800-735-2929
www.colusalstop.org

CONTRA COSTA COUNTY

EASTBAY Works One-Stop Business
and Career Center
4545 Delta Fair Blvd.
Antioch, CA 94509
925-706-4830
www.eastbayworks.com

EASTBAY Works One-Stop Business
and Career Center
261 Pine St.
Brentwood, CA 94513
928-634-2195
www.eastbayworks.com

EASTBAY Works One-Stop Business
and Career Center
4071 Port Chicago Highway Suite 250
Concord, CA 94520
925-671-4500
www.eastbayworks.com

EASTBAY Works One-Stop Career
Center
2300 El Portal Dr., Suite B
San Pablo, CA 94806
510-412-6740
www.eastbayworks.com

Richmond WORKS-Main
330 25th St.
Richmond, CA 94014
510-307-8014
www.richmondworks.org

DEL NORTE COUNTY

Del Norte Workforce Center
186 M. St., Suite B
Crescent City, CA 95531
707-464-8347
www.delnorteworkforcecenter.org

EL DORADO COUNTY

Job One-Stop Employment Resource
   Center
3047 Briw Rd.
Placerville, CA 95667
530-642-4850
www.goldensierra.com

FRESNO COUNTY

Fresno West Workforce Services
   Office
2555 South Elm St.
Fresno, CA 93706
559-445-5249

Mendota Workforce Services Office
655 Quince St., Suite C
Mendota, CA 93640
559-656-3081

Mobile Employment Center Hanford
Hanford, CA 93291
559-805-7265
www.proteusinc.org
   *This MEC serves multiple rural cities in
Fresno and Kings Counties every week.*

Workforce Connection Coalinga
311 Coalinga Plaza
Coalinga, CA 93210
559-230-3695
TTY: 559-935-9294
www.workforce-connection.corr

Workforce Connection Executive
   Plaza
1900 Mariposa Mall, Suite 280
Fresno, CA 93721
559-499-3709
www.workforce-connection.corr

Workforce Connection Manchester
   Center
3302 North Blackstone, Suite #155
Fresno, CA 93726
559-230-3600
TTY: 559-230-4063
www.workforce-connection.corr

Workforce Connection Mendota
720 Oiler St.
Mendota, CA 93640
559-655-2060
TTY: 559-655-6857
www.workforce-connection.corr

GLENN COUNTY

Glenn County Human Resource
   Agency
604 E. Walker St.
Orland, CA 95963
530-865-6102
http://hra.co.glenn.ca.us

HUMBOLDT COUNTY

Arcata City Hall
736 F St.
Arcata, CA 95621
707-825-2114

The Job Market
409 K St.
Eureka, CA 95501
707-445-6149
www.thejobmarket.org

The Job Market
729 Cedar St.
Garberville, CA 95542
707-923-2779

The Job Market
103 Willow St., Suite A
Hoopa, CA 95546
707-923-4953
www.thejobmarket.org

The Job Market
2755 McKinleyville Ave.
McKinleyville, CA 95519
707-839-6487
www.thejobmarket.org

Job Market Information Station
960 6th St.
Eureka, CA 95501
707-445-6000

IMPERIAL COUNTY

Brawley One-Stop Career Center
860 Main St.
Brawley, CA 92227
760-344-2131
TTY: 760-351-7141

Calexico One-Stop Career Center
301 Heber Ave.
Calexico, CA 92231
760-768-7171
TTY: 760-768-7164

El Centro East One-Stop Career Center
2695 S. 4th St.
El Centro, CA 92243
760-337-5000
TTY: 760-482-2930

El Centro West Satellite Office
1550 W. Main St.
El Centro, CA 92243
760-339-2722

Imperial Valley College Satellite Office
380 East Aten Rd., Bldg. 1700
El Centro, CA 92251

Winterhaven Satellite Office

676 Baseline Rd.
Winterhaven, CA 92283
760-572-0222

INYO COUNTY

Inyo County Health and Human Services
920 North Main St.
Bishop, CA 93514
760-872-1394
www.careerservicescenter.com

KERN COUNTY

Career Services Center
1600 E. Belle Terrace
Bakersfield, CA 93307
661-326-4473
TTY: 661-336-6839
www.careerservicescenter.com

Career Services Center
1816 Cecil Ave.
Delano, CA 93215
661-721-5800
TTY: 661-336-6839
www.careerservicescenter.com

Career Services Center
6401 Lake Isabella Blvd.
Lake Isabella, CA 93240
760-379-2074
TTY: 661-336-6839
www.careerservicescenter.com

Career Services Center
8300 Segrue Rd.
Lamont, CA 93241
661-635-4029
TTY: 601-336-6839
www.careerservicescenter.com

Career Services Center
2300 Highway 58
Mojave, CA 93505
661-824-7800
TTY: 661-336-6839
www.careerservicescenter.com

Career Services Center
1400 North Norma St., Suite 105
Ridgecrest, CA 92555
760-446-2595
TTY: 661-336-6839
www.careerservicescenter.com

Career Services Center
113 North Central Valley Highway
Shafter, CA 93263
661-746-8400
TTY: 661-336-6839
www.careerservicescenter.com

Career Services Center
119 North 10th St.
Taft, CA 93268
661-763-0200
TTY: 661-336-6839
www.careerservicescenter.com

KINGS COUNTY

Kings County One-Stop Job Center
124 N. Irwin St.
Hanford, CA 93230
559-585-3532
TTY: 800-735-2922
www.kingsworkforce.org/

LAKE COUNTY

Lake County One-Stop
55 1st St., Suite F
Lakeport, CA 95453
707-263-0630
www.northcentralcounties.org/1

LASSEN COUNTY

Alliance for Workforce Development,
   Inc.
Lassen County
1616 Chestnut St.
Susanville, CA 96130
530-257-5067
www.aworkforce.org

LOS ANGELES COUNTY

Ability First
201 S. Kinneloa Ave.
Pasadena, CA 91107
626-449-5661
*www.abilityfirst.org/center_pasa
   dena.htm*

Altadena Community Improvement
565 N. Rosemead Blvd.
Pasadena, CA 91107
626-798-3006
www.altadena.qpg.com

Arcadia Public Library
20 West Duarte Rd.
Arcadia, CA 91006
626-821-5567
www.library.ci.arcadia.ca.us

Build WorkSource Center
9207 Eton Ave.
Chatsworth, CA 91311
818-701-9800
TTY: 818-701-9850
www.buildworksource.com

Burbank Workforce Connection
301 East Olive Ave., #101
Burbank, CA 91502
818-238-5627
www.burbankworkforce.org

Career Transition Center
3447 Atlantic Ave.
Long Beach, CA 90807
562-570-3700
TTY: 562-570-4629
www.longbeachworkforce.org

Central San Gabriel Valley Work-
   Source Center
11635 E. Valley Blvd., Suite G
El Monte, CA 91731
626-258-0365
TTY: 626-442-1576
www.Goodwill.org

Cerritos Career Center
10900 E. 183rd St., Suite 350
Cerritos, CA 90703
562-402-9336
TTY: 562-860-7657
www.selaco.com

Chinatown WorkSource Center
787 North Hill St. #400
Los Angeles, CA 90012
213-808-1700
TTY: 213-808-1719
www.cscta.net

Citrus College
1000 West Foothill Blvd
Glendora, CA 91741
626-914-8700
www.citruscollege.edu

Compton Career Link One-Stop
    Center
700 N. Bullis Rd.
Compton, CA 90221
310-605-3050
TTY: 310-537-8073
www.comptocity.org

Downtown WorkSource Center
315 W. 9th St., #101
Los Angeles, CA 90015
213-629-5800
TTY: 213-430-0660
www.worksourcecalifornia.com

East Los Angeles Employment and
    Business Center
5301 Whittier Blvd., Second Floor
Los Angeles, CA 90022
323-867-7122
TTY: 323-832-1278
www.worksourcecalifornia.com

Foothill Employment and Training
    Connection
1207 E. Green St.
Pasadena, CA 91106
626-796-5627

626-584-8373
www.foothilletc.org

Harbor WorkSource Center
1851 N. Gaffey St. Suite F
San Pedro, CA 90731
310-732-5700
TTY: 310-732-5714
www.careerzone.torrnet.com

Hollywood North WorkSource
    Center
6464 Sunset Blvd., Suite 600
Los Angele, CA 90028
323-960-1300
TTY: 323-769-9187
www.mcsrehab.com

Hub Cities One-Step Career Center
2677 Zoe Ave., 1st Floor
Huntington Park, CA 90255
323-586-4700
TTY: 323-586-3597
www.hubcities.org

Jackie Robinson Center
1020 N. Fair Oaks Ave
Pasadena, CA 91101
626-744-7300
www.ci.pasadena.ca.us/human
    servcies/jackierobinsoncenter.asp

Jewish Vocational Service West Holly-
    wood WorkSource Center
5757 Wilshire Blvd. Promenade
    Three
Los Angeles, CA 90036
323-904-4900
TTY: 800-735-2929
www.jvsla.org

La Pintoresca Library
1356 North Raymond Ave.
Pasadena, CA 91103
626-744-4034
www.ci.pasadena.ca.us/library/Iapin
    toresca.asp

LA Urban League Pomona Work-
Source Center
264 E. Monterey Ave.
Pomona, CA 91767
909-623-9741
TTY: 909-469-2561
www.laul.org

LA Works One-Stop Career Center
5200 Irwindale Ave.
Irwindale, CA 91706
626-960-3964
TTY: 626-856-3735
www.laworks.org

Lafayette Park Satellite WorkSource
Center
520 S. Lafayette Park Place #400
Los Angeles, CA 90057
213-252-6100
TTY: 213-252-5483
www.worksourcecalifornia.com/

Lamanda Park Library
140 S. Altadena Blvd.
Pasadena, CA 91107
626-744-7266
*www.cipasadena.ca.us/library/liman
da.asp*

Los Angeles–Crenshaw Workforce
Services Office
5401 So. Crenshaw Blvd
Los Angeles, CA 90008
323-290-5100

Los Angeles Urban League Work-
Source Business and Career Center
12700 S. Avalon Blvd.
Los Angeles, CA 90061
323-600-1106
TTY: 323-242-2385
www.laul.org

Marina del Rey–West Los Angeles
WorkSource Center
13160 Mindanao Way, Suite 240

Marina del Rey, CA 90292
310-309-6000
TTY: 310-309-6018
www.worksourcecalifornia.com

Monrovia Adult School
920 S. Mountain Ave.
Monrovia, CA 91016
626-471-3035
www.monroviaschools.net/adult

Monrovia Public Library
321 S. Myrtle Ave.
Monrovia, CA 91016
626-256-8274
www.ci.monrovia.ca.us/city

Metro–North Los Angeles Work-
Source Center
342 San Fernando Rd.
Los Angeles, CA 90031
323-539-2000
Fax: 323-539-2093
www.goodwillsocial.org

Neighborhood Connections
1384 East Walnut St.
Pasadena, CA 91106
626-744-7290
*www.cipasadena.ca.us/humanservices/
neighborhoodconnections.asp*

Northeast San Fernando Valley Work-
Source Center
11623 Glenoaks Bl.
Pacoima, CA 91331
818-890-9400
TTY: 818-899-5530
www.wsca.cc

Partners for Progress/SASSFA One-
Stop Career Center
10400 Pioneer Blvd.
Santa Fe Springs, CA 90670
562-946-2237
TTY: 562-906-5807
www.pfpworksource.org

Pasadena Alumni Support
1395 E. Orange Grove
Pasadena, CA 91104
626-296-2641
www.pasconline.org

Pasadena Job Center
500 N. Lake Ave.
Pasadena, CA 91101
626-440-0112
www.foothilletc.org

Pasadena Main Library
285 East Walnut St.
Pasadena, CA 91101
626-744-4066
www.cipasdena.ca.us/library/central.asp

Pasadena Youth Center
88 S. Daisy Ave.
Pasadena, CA 91107
626-792-4070
www.foothilletc.org

Passageways
1020 South Arroyo Parkway
Pasadena, CA 91105
626-403-4888
*www.pacificclinics.org/homelespasadena.
htm*

PCC Community Education Center
3035 E. Foothill Blvd.
Pasadena, CA 91107
626-585-3000
*http://www.pasadena.edu/studentser
vices/careercenter/*

Renaissance Square Career Center
1900 Atlantic Ave.
Long Beach, CA 90806
562-570-3700
TTY: 562-570-4629
www.longbeachworkforce.org

Santa Catalina Library
999 E. Washington Blvd.
Pasadena, CA 91103

626-744-7272
*www.cipasadena.ca.us/library/santa
cat.asp*

Santa Clarita WorkSource Center
20655 Soledad Canyon Rd., Suite 25
Santa Clarita, CA 91351
661-424-1062
TTY: 661-250-8984
www.scworksource.com

South Bay One-Stop Business and
   Career Center
16801 S. Western Ave., Suite A
Gardena, CA 90247
310-217-9579
TTY: 310-327-3596

South Bay One-Stop Business and
   Career Center
110 South La Brea Ave., 5th Floor
Inglewood, CA 90301
310-680-3700
TTY: 310-674-6054

South Bay One-Stop Business and
   Career Center
320 Knob Hill Ave., Suite 8
Redondo Beach, CA 90277
310-318-0645
TTY: 310-316-9881

South LA WorkSource Center
7518-26 S. Vermont Ave.
Los Angeles, CA 90044
323-752-2115
TTY: 323-752-9215
www.cciworksource.org

South Valley WorkSource Center
1817 E. Ave. Q, A-12
Palmdale, CA 93550
661-265-7421
TTY: 661-265-9649
www.goodwillsocial.org

Southeast LA–Crenshaw WorkSource
   Center
3965 S. Vermont Ave.

Los Angele, CA 90037
323-730-7900
TTY: 323-730-7937
www.worksourcecalifornia.com

Southeast LA–Watts WorkSource
  Center
10950 South Central Ave.
Los Angeles, CA 90059
323-563-5682
TTY: 323-563-5684
www.wicac.org

Sun Valley WorkSource Center
9024 Laurel Canyon Blvd.
Sun Valley, CA 91352
818-504-0334
TTY: 818-504-1974
www.wscalnetwork.org

Torrance Workforce Services Office
1220 Engracia Ave.
Torrance, CA 90501
310-782-2101

Union Station
825 East Orange Grove Blvd
Pasadena, CA 91104
626-449-4550
www.unionstationfoundation.org

Van Nuys–North Sherman Oaks
  WorkSource Center
15400 Sherman Way, Suite 140
Van Nuys, CA 91406
818-781-2522
TTY: 818-374-7024

Verdugo Jobs Center
1255 South Central Ave.
Glendale, CA 91204
818-409-0476
TTY: 818-409-7236
VerdugoJobs.org

West Adams–Baldwin Hills Work-
  Source Center
5681 West Jefferson Blvd

Los Angeles, CA 90016
323-525-3740
TTY: 323-931-9076
www.laul.org

West Covina–Workforce Services
  Office
933 S. Glendora Ave.
West Covina, CA 91791
626-814-8234

Westlake WorkSource Center
1055 Wilshire Blvd, Suite 900A
Los Angeles, CA 90017
213-353-1677
TTY: 213-353-1685
www.westlake-worksource.org

Wilshire-Metro WorkSource
  Center
3550 Wilshire Blvd., Suite 500
Los Angeles, CA 90010
213-365-9829
TTY: 323-368-0047
www.communitycareer.org

Woman at Work
50 N. Hill Ave., Suite 300
Pasadena, CA 91106
626-796-6870
www.womenatwork1.org

Worksource California
Antelope Valley One-Stop Career
  Center
1420 West Ave. 1
Lancaster, CA 93534
661-726-4128
TTY: 661-951-2675
www.worksourcecalifornia.com

WorkSource California Career Partners
3505 North Hart Ave.
Rosemead, CA 91770
626-572-7272
TTY 626-569-0682
www.careerpartners.org

MADERA COUNTY

Madera County Workforce Assistance
  Center
209 East Seventh St.
Madera, CA 93638
559-662-4500
TTY: 559-674-7497
www.maderawac.org

Madera County Workforce Assistance
  Center
41969 Hwy 41
Oakhurst, CA 93644
559-683-6263

MARIN COUNTY

Marin Employment Connection Career Resource Center
120 N. Redwood Rd., East Wing, 2nd
  Floor
San Rafael, CA 94903
415-473-3300
TTY: 415-473-3344
www.marineemployment.org

MARIPOSA COUNTY

Job Connection Mariposa
5078 Bullion St. Suite A and C
Mariposa, CA 95338
209-966-3643
www.jobconnect.org

MENDOCINO COUNTY

Mendocino Works Employment Resource Center
76405 Covelo Rd.. #3
Covelo, CA 95428
707-983-0070
TTY: 800-735-2929
www.mendocinoworks.com

Mendocino Works Employment Resource Center
310 East Redwood Ave.
Fort Bragg, CA 95437

707-964-3218
TTY: 800-600-6950
www.mendocinoworks.com

Mendocino Works Employment Resource Center
631 South Orchard Ave.
Ukiah, CA 95482
707-467-5900
TTY: 800-735-2929
www.mendocinoworks.com

Mendocino Works Employment Resource Center
221 South Lenore Ave.
Willits, CA 95490
707-456-3760
TTY: 800-735-2929
www.mendocinoworks.com

MERCED COUNTY

Workforce Services Office
1075 H. St.
Los Banos, CA 93635
209-826-0420

Workforce Services Office
1205 West 18th St.
Merced, CA 95340
209-726-5407
www.edd.ca.gov

WorkNet Employment Resource Center
1200 W. 16th St.
Merced, CA 95340
209-724-2100
TTY: 209-726-3692
www.mercedworknet.com

WorkNet of Merced County Employment Resource Center
800 7th St.
Los Banos, CA 93635
209-826-7241
TTY: 209-826-3718
www.mercedworknet.com

MODOC COUNTY

Modoc Employment Center
221 North Main St.
Alturas, CA 96101
530-233-4161
www.aworkforce.org

MONO COUNTY

Career Services Center
107384 Highway 395
Walker, CA 96107
530-495-1262
www.CareerServicesCenter.com

Employers' Training Resources–Back-
to-Work Center
2001 28th St.
Bakersfield, CA 93301
661-336-6600
TTY: 661-336-6839
www.CareerServicesCenter.com

MONTEREY COUNTY

Monterey County Office for Employment and Training
248 Tenth St., Bldg. AA
Marina, CA 93933
831-384-0388
www.onestopmonterey.org

Monterey County One-Stop Career
Center
1760 Fremont Blvd., Suite D2
Seaside, CA 93955
831-889-8236
TTY: 831-393-0950
www.onestopmoneterey.org

One-Stop Career Centers of Monterey
County
King City Library
404 Broadway
King City, CA 93930

One-Stop Career Centers of Monterey
County

730 La Guardia St.
Salinas, CA 93905
800-870-4750
TTY: 831-755-4867
www.onestopmonterey.org

One-Stop Career Centers of Monterey
County
Department of Social Services
1322 Natividad Rd.
Salinas, CA 93906

NAPA COUNTY

Job Connection
650 Imperial Way, Suite 101
Nape, CA 94558
707-253-4291

NEVADA COUNTY

One-Stop Business and Career Center
715 Maltman Drive
Grass Valley, CA 95945
530-265-7088
http://www.nevadacountyonestop.org

Workforce Services Office
10775 Pioneer Trail 102
Truckee, CA 96161
530-582-7332

ORANGE COUNTY

Anaheim Workforce Center
50 South Anaheim Blvd. Suite 300
Anaheim, CA 92805
714-765-4350
TTY: 714-765-4376
www.anaheimwib.com

Orange County-One-Stop Center
125 Technology Drive West, Suite
200
Irvine, CA 92618
949-341-8000
TTY: 949-341-8000
www.oconestop.com

Orange County One-Stop Center
5405 Garden Grove Blvd. Suite 100
Westminister, CA 92683
714-241-4900
TTY: 714-241-4900
www.oconestop.com

Santa Ana Work Center
1000 East Santa Ana Blvd., Suite 200
Santa Ana, CA 92701
714-565-2600
TTY: 714-565-2669
www.santaanaworkcenter.org

Workforce Services Office
2450 E. Lincoln Ave. Suite 200
Anaheim, CA 92806
714-518-2315

PLACER COUNTY

One-Stop Career Center
11548 E. Ave.
Auburn, CA 95603
530-823-4831
www.goldensierra.com

One-Stop Career Center
1880 Sierra Garden Blvd.
Suite #100
Roseville, CA 95661
916-774-4074
www.goldensierra.com

PLUMAS COUNTY

Employment and Training Center
1953 E. Main St.
Quincy, CA 95971
530-283-1606
www.aworkforce.org

RIVERSIDE COUNTY

Empower Youth, Youth Opportunity
    Center
930 North State St.
Employer State Building

Hermet, CA 92543
909-765-6955
www.cfickids.org

Institute for Sales and Services Excel-
    lence
72-840 Highway 111, Suite C101
Palm Desert, CA 92260
760-776-7394
TTY: 760-863-2555
www.issexcellence.com

Mobile One-Stop
1151 Spruce St.
Riverside, CA 92507
951-955-3100
TTY: 951-955-8657
www.rivcojobs.com

The Oasis Youth Opportunities Center
351 Wilkerson Ave., Suite F
Perris, CA 92570
951-657-7105
www.rivcojobs.com

Planet Youth
400 West Graham
Lake Elsinore, CA 92530
909-471-8415
www.rivcojobs.com

The Win Center Youth Opportunity
    Center
45-570 Grace St., Suite 1
Indio, CA 92201
760-775-2887
www.rivcojobs.com

Workforce Development Center
1025 N. State St.
Hemet, CA 92543
951-791-3500
TTY: 951-765-1763
www.rivcojobs.com

Workforce Development Center
44-199 Monroe St., Suite B
Indio, CA 92201

760-863-2500
TTY: 760-863-2555
www.rivcojobs.com

Workforce Development Center
1151 Spruce St.
Riverside, CA 92507
951-955-3100
www.rivcojobs.com

Workforce Development Center
41002 County Center Drive, Suite
  205
Temecula, CA 92591
951-600-6000
TTY: 951-506-5837
www.rivcojobs.com

Workforce Services Office
1277 W. Hobson Way
Blythe, CA 92225
760-922-0103

Workforce Services Office
237 West River Rd.
Corona, CA 92880
951-340-4036

SACRAMENTO COUNTY

Sacramento Works One Career
  Center
7640 Greenback Ln.
7640 Greenback Ln.
Citrus Heights, CA 95610
916-676-2540
www.seta.net

Sacramento Works One Career
  Center
915 Broadway
Sacramento, CA 95818
916-324-6202
www.Asianresources.org

Sacramento Works One-Stop Career
  Center
1000 C St., Suite 100
Galt, CA 95632

209-744-7702
www.seta.net

Sacramento Works One-Stop Center
7000 Franklin Blvd., Suite 540
Sacramento, CA 95823
916-262-3200
www.seta.net

Sacramento Works One Career Center
5655 Hillsdale Blvd., Suite 8
Sacramento, CA 95842
916-263-4100
TTY: 916-263-2921
www.seta.delpaso.net

Sacramento Works One Career Center
5523 34th St.
Sacramento, CA 95820
916-452-3601
www.seta.net/www.lafcc.com

Sacramento Works One-Stop Career
  Center
5451 Lemon Hill Ave., Room 106
Sacramento, CA 95824
916-433-2620
www.seta.net

Sacramento Works One-Stop Career
  Center
2901 50th St.
Sacramento, CA 95817
916-227-0301
www.seta.net

Sacramento Works One-Stop Career
  Center
10638 Schirra Ave.
Mather, CA 95655
www.seta.net

Sacramento Works One-Stop Center
  Center
10381 Old Placeville Rd., Suite 150
Rancho Cordova, CA 95827
916-256-3255
www.seta.net

Sacramento Works One-Stop Career
Center
3725 Marysville Blvd.
Sacramento, CA 95838
916-266-8600
www.seta.net

Sacramento Works One Career Center
8401 A Gerber Rd.
Sacramento, CA 95828
916-689-3560
www.seta.net

SAN BENITO COUNTY

San Benito County One-Stop Career
Center
1111 San Felipe Rd., Suite 107
Hollister, CA 95023
831-637-5627
TTY: 831-637-3265
www.sbcjobs.org

SAN BERNARDINO COUNTY

City of San Bernardino One-Stop
Center
600 N. Arrowhead Ave, Suite 300
San Bernardino, CA 92401
909-888-7881
TTY: 800-735-2922
www.sbeta.com

High Desert Employment Resource
Center
15555 Main St., Suite G3/G4
Hesperia, CA 92345
760-949-8526
www.co.sanbernadion.ca.us/ecd/wdd

Rancho Cucamonga Employment Resource Center
9650 9th St., Suite A
Rancho Cucamonga, CA 91730
909-946-6606
www.co.sanbernardino.ca.us/ecd/wdd

Redlands Workforce Services Office

814 West Colton Ave.
Redlands, CA 92374
909-798-1796

San Bernardino Employment Resource Center
658 East Brier St.
San Bernardino, CA 92415
909-382-0440
TTY: 877-885-7654
www.co.sanbarnardino.ca.us/ecd/wdd

Victorville Workforce Services Office
15419 Cholame Rd.
Victorville, CA 92392
760-241-1682

SAN DIEGO COUNTY

Bonita Sunnyside Public Library
4375 Bonita Rd.
Bonita, CA 91902
619-472-6602
www.sandiegoatwork.com

East County Career Center
924 East Main St.
El Cajon, CA 92021
619-590-3900
http://eccc.guhsd.net

Mountain Empire Community
Center
Employment and Training Information Kiosk
976 Sheridan Rd.
Campo, CA 91906
619-478-5254
www.sandiegoatwork.com

North County Coastal Career Center
1949 Avenida del Oro, Suite 106
Oceanside, CA 92056
760-631-6150
760-758-3706
www.sandiegoatwork.com

North County Inland Career Center
463 N. Midway

Escondido, CA 92027
760-871-1962
www.sandiegoatwork.com

San Diego Metro Career Center
3910 University Ave.
San Diego, CA 92105
619-516-2200
www.sandiegoatwork.com

San Diego South Metro Career
  Center
4389 Imperial Ave.
San Diego, CA 92113
619-266-4200
619-266-4272
www.sandiegoatwork.com

Serra Mesa–Kearny Mesa
9005 Aero Drive
San Diego, CA 92123
888-884-7397
TTY: 858-694-4884
www.sandiegoatwork.com

South County Career Center
1111 Bay Blvd., Suite E
Chula Vista, CA 91911
619-628-0300
www.sandiegoatwork.com

South Metro–Grant Hill
3295 Market St.
San Diego, CA 92102
619-233-6829
www.sandiegoatwork.com

Spring Valley Library One-Stop Career Center
836 Kempton St.
Spring Valley, CA 91977
619-667-0133
www.sandiegoatwork.com

Vista Townsite Community Partnership
642 Vista Village Drive
Vista, CA 92084

760-806-3980
www.sandiegoatwork.com

SAN FRANCISCO COUNTY

Career Link Center
1800 Oakdale Ave.
San Francisco, CA 94124
415-970-7762
www.onestopsf.org

Chinatown Career Link Center
777 Stockton St.
San Francisco, CA 94108
415-421-2111
www.onestopsf.org

Civic Center Career Link Center
801 Turk St.
San Francisco, CA 94102
415-749-7503
www.onestopsf.org

Goodwill Career Link Center
1500 Main St.
San Francisco, CA 94103
415-575-2110
www.onestopsf.org

Mission Center Career Link Center
3120 Mission St.
San Francisco, CA 94110
415-401-4800
www.onestopsf.org

Western Addition Career Link Center
1449 Webster St.
San Francisco, CA 94103
415-655-2620
TTY: 415-515-2115
www.onestopsf.org

SAN JOAQUIN COUNTY

California Human Development Corporation
WorkNet Center
2607-A Wigwam Drive

Stockton, CA 95205
209-953-7350
www.sjcworknet.org

Delta WorkNet Center
5405 N. Pershing Ave., Suite A
Stockton, CA 95207
206-468-3500
www.sjcworknet.org

Manteca WorkNet Center
302 Northgate Drive
Manteca, CA 95336
209-825-1300
www.sjcworknet.org

Stockton WorkNet Center, Mobile
   Unit
56 S, Lincoln St.
Stockton, CA 95203
209-468-3515
www.sjcworknet.org

Stockton WorkNet Center
56 S. Lincoln St.
Stockton, CA 95203
209-468-3500
www.sjcworknet.org

Workforce Service Office
135 W. Fremont St.
Stockton, CA 95202
209-948-7856
www.sjcworknet.org

SAN JOAQUIN COUNTY

Tracy WorkNet Center
213 W. 11th St.
Tracy, CA 95376
209-833-1018
www.sjcworknet.org

SAN LUIS OBISPO COUNTY

Estrella Career Center
Cuesta College N. County Campus

2800 Buena Vista Drive, Bldg. 4000
Paso Robies, CA 93446
805-237-3014
805-237-4763
www.sloworkforce.com

SAN MATEO COUNTY

PeninsulaWorks
271 92nd St.
Daly City, CA 94015
650-301-8440
TTY: 650-301-8456
www.peninsulaworks.org

Peninsula Works, Job Training
1200 O'Brian Drive
Mento Park, CA 94025
650-330-6490
TTY: 650-330-6487
www.peninsulaworks.org

PeninsulaWorks
2500 Middlefield Rd.
Redwood City, CA 94063
650-367-0190
TTY: 800-735-2922
www.peninsulaworks.org

PeninsulaWorks
550 Quarry Rd.
San Carlos, CA 94070
650-596-1035
www.peninsulaworks.org

SANTA BARBARA COUNTY

Workforce Resource Center
130 E. Ortega
Santa Barbara, CA 93101
805-568-1296
www.workforceresource.com

Workforce Resource Center
1410 South Broadway, Suite A
Santa Maria, CA 93454
805-614-1550
www.workforceresource.com

SANTA CLARA COUNTY

CONNECT One-Stop Campus
420 S. Pastoria Ave.
Sunnyside, CA 94086
408-774-2365
TTY: 408-774-5448
www.connect.one-stop.org

Proven People Senior Employment
　Office
550 East Remington Drive
Sunnyside, CA 94087
408-730-7368
TTY: 408-730-7601
*www.novaworks.org/job_seeks:/proven_*
　people.html

Work 2 Future One-Stop
2450 S. Bascom Ave.
Campbell, CA 95008
408-369-3606
TTY: 408-369-3666
www.work2future.biz

Work 2 Future One-Stop
7800 Arroyo Circle, Suite A
Gilroy, CA 95020
408-846-1480
TTY: 408-846-7019
www.work2future.biz

Work 2 Future One-Stop
1290 Parkmoor Ave.
San Jose, CA 95126
408-277-2727
www.work2future.biz

SANTA CRUZ COUNTY

Career Center
2045 40th Ave., Suite B
Capitola, CA 95010
831-464-6286
TTY: 831-464-6280
www.workforcescc.com

Career Center
18 West Beach

Watsonville, CA 95076
831-763-8700
www.workforcescc.com

SHASTA COUNTY

Smart Business Resource Center
1201 Placer St.
Redding, CA 96001
530-246-7911
TTY: 530-245-1566
www.shastasmart.com

Workforce Services Office
1325 Pine St.
Redding, CA 96001
530-225-2185
www.shastasmart.com

SISKIYOU COUNTY

Workforce Connection
310 Boles St.
Weed, CA 96094
530-938-3231
www.siskiyouwc.org

Workforce Connection
818 S. Main St.
Yreka, CA 96097
530-842-7329
www.siskyouwc.org

SOLANO COUNTY

Solano Employment Connection
320 Campus Lane
Fairfield, CA 94534
707-864-3370
TTY: 800-735-2922
www.Solanoemployment.org

Solano Employment Connection
1440 Main St.
Vallejo, CA 94590
707-649-3604
TTY: 800-735-2922
www.SolanoEmployment.org

SONOMA COUNTY

Job Link Employer Resource Center
606 Healdburg Ave.
Santa Rosa, CA 95401
707-576-2850
www.socojoblink.org

Sonoma County Job Link
2245 Challenger Way
Santa Rosa, CA 95407
707-565-5550
TTY: 888-877-5379
www.socojoblink.org

STANISLAUS COUNTY

Alliance Worknet
629 12th St.
Modesto, CA 95364
209-558-9675
www.allianceworknet.com

Alliance Worknet (AW) Career Resource Center
251 E. Hackett Rd.
Lobby Area
Modesto, CA 95356
209-558-3977
www.stanalliance.com

Workforce Services Office
125 North Braodway
Turlock, CA 95380
209-669-2955

SUTTER COUNTY

Sutter County One-Stop
256 Wilbur Ave.
Yuba City, CA 95991
530-822-5120
TTY: 530-822-5104
www.sutteronestop.com

TEHAMA COUNTY

Job Training Center of Tehama
County

718 Main St.
Red Bluff, CA 96080
530-529-7000
530-527-2306

TRINITY COUNTY

Hayfork Job Link
Tule Creek Rd.
Hayfork, CA 96041
530-628-5172
www.trinityjoblink.org

JobLink, Weaverville
40 B Glen Rd.
Weaverville, CA 96093
530-623-5538
www.trinityjoblink.org

TULARE COUNTY

Community Services Employment
and Training, Orosi
12825 Ave. 413
Orosi, CA 93647
559-788-4140
http://www.cset.org/

Community Services Employment
and Training
1061 W. Henderson Ave.
Porterville, CA 93257
559-732-4194
www.cset.org

Community Services Employment
and Training
312 NW 3rd Ave.
Visalia, CA 93291
559-732-4194
http://www.cset.org

Mobile Employment Center
serving rural communities in Tulare
and Kern Counties
Porterville, CA 93258
559-805-7293
www.proteusinc.org

Proteus Inc., Porterville One-Stop
Service Center
54 N Main, Suite 10
Porterville, CA 93257
559-781-1852
http://www.proteusinc.org/

Tulare County Employment Connection
199 N L St. Dinuba, CA 93618
559-591-5065
TTY: 566-288-6612
www.tcwid.org

Tulare County Employment Connection Center
4025 W. Noble Ave., Suite B
Visalia, CA 93277
559-713-5000
TTY: 800-735-2929
www.tcwid.org

TUOLUMNE COUNTY

Job Connection Tuolumne
19890 Cedar Rd. North
Sonora, CA 95370
209-588-1150
TTY: 209-533-3396
www.jobconnect.org

VENTURA COUNTY

East Ventura County Job and Career
Center
980 Enchanted Way
Simi Valley, CA 93065
805-965-2211

Oxnard College Job and Career Center
4000 S. Rose Ave.
Oxnard, CA 93033
805-986-7300

Oxnard Job and Career Center
1400 Vanguard St., Suite C
Oxnard, CA 93033
805-385-9100

Santa Clara Valley Job and Career
Center
725 E. Main St., Suite 101
Santa Paula, CA 93060
805-933-8300

Thousand Oaks Job and Career Center
1423 Thousand Oaks Blvd, Suite 100
Thousand Oaks, CA 91360
805-374-9006

Ventura Job and Career Center
4651 Telephone Rd.
Ventura, CA 93001
805-654-3435

West Oxnard Job and Career Center
635 S. Ventura Rd.
Oxnard, CA 93030
805-382-6551

YOLO COUNTY

Yolo County Department of Employment and Social Services
500-A Jefferson Blvd., Suite 110
West Sacramento, CA 95605
916-375-6300
TTY: 800-735-2922
www.yolocounty.org/org/dess/ediv.htm

Yolo County One-Stop Career Center
26 North Cottonwood St.
Woodland, CA 95695
530-661-2750
TTY: 800-735-2922
www.yolocounty.org/org/dess/ediv.htm

YUBA COUNTY

Yuba County One-Stop Center for
Business and Workforce Development
1114 Yuba St.
Maryville, CA 95901
530-741-6213
www.yubalstop.org

These organizations provide training, education, and employment assistances to ex-offenders.

Casa Libre /Freedom House
845 S. Lake St.
Los Angeles, CA 90057
213-637-5614
www.casa-libre.org
   This project offers a transitional living program for the homeless youth under the age of 18.

Centerforce, Division of Health Programs
2955 Kerner Blvd, 2nd Floor
San Rafael, CA 94901
415-458-9980
www.centerforce.org
   In addition to coordinating HIV prevention programs in several California State Prisons, Centerforce provides case management, literacy, family support services, health education, parenting policy, research, training and consultation, and educational development.

Central City Hospitality House
290 Turk Street
San Francisco, CA 94102
415-749-2119
www.hospitalityhouse.org
info@hospitalityhouse.org
   This organization offers an emergency shelter/drop-in center, mail and message service, job referrals and placement, free clothing and counseling.

Center for Children of Incarcerated Parents
P.O. Box 41-286
Eagle Rock, CA 90041
626-449-2470
http://www.e-ccip.org/index.htmlccip@earthlink.net
   *CCIP's mission is the prevention of intergenerational crime and prevention. Its goals are the production of high quality documentation on the development of model services for children of criminal offenders and their fam-*ilies. *CCIP provides research and resource information in four pivotal areas: education(parenting Classes,etc), family reunification, therapeutic services and information.*

Community Construction Training Center
250 West 85th St.
Los Angeles, CA 90003
323-753-6211
This organization works with low-income individuals and former prisoners and provides job development and vocational training.

Community Information Center
P.O. Box 1834
Sacramento, CA 95812-1834
800-510-2020
   This organization provides a public information and referral service to the Sacramento community. They also provide referrals to more than 1,400 community programs and services in the Sacramento area.

CRASH-Community Resources and Self Help
Information and Intake Office
927 24th St.
San Diego, CA 92102
619-233-8054
www.crashinc.org
intake@crashinc.org
   This organization offers an outpatient daily treatment services and long-term(4-8 months or longer)residential programs. Services provided include individual and group counseling, vocational and educational services, socialism skills, recovery planning, and release prevention.

Critical Resistance: Beyond the Prison Industrial Complex
National Office:
1904 Franklin St. Ste. 504
Oakland, CA 94612
510-444-0484
http://www.criticalresistance.org
Northeast Regional Office:

976 Longwood Ave.
Bronx, NY 10459
718-676-1672
crne@criticalresistance.org
Southern Regional Office:
930 N.Broad St.
New Orleans, LA 70119
504-304-3792
crsouth@criticalresistance.org

    Critical Resistance provides information on the prison industrial complex and produces quarterly newspaper, "The Abolitionist." Please do not contact for legal help. CR has chapters in Baltimore, Chicago, Gainesville, Los Angeles, New Orleans, New York City, Tampa-St. Petersburg, and Washington DC.

Delancy Street Foundation
600 Embarcadero
San Francisco, CA 94107
415-957-9800

    During a two to four-year stay at Delancey Street, residents learn social survival skills as well as academic and vocational skills.

East Los Angeles Skills Center
3921 Selig Place
Los Angeles, CA 90031
323-227-0018
elasc.adultinstruction.org
ram2103@lausd.k12ca.org

    This organization offers a unique program for pre–release prisoners, incorporating both academic study and employment training.

Friends Outside
551 Stockton Ave
San Jose, CA 95126
408-295-6033
friend@friendsoutsideinscc.org

    There are chapters nationwide that offer services to currently and formerly incarcerated people. They provide assistance in setting up people plans, job readiness, and connecting prisoners with drug treatment programs. They also contract with the California Department of Corrections to teach parenting classes in prisons, assist with child custody issues, and help with the reunification process.

Friends Outside
P.O. Box 4085
Stockton, CA 95204
209-955-0701
http://friendsoutside.org/gnewby@friend soutside.org

    Friends Outside is a nonprofit community based organization that has been providing programs and serves to families and individuals involved in the criminal justice system since 1955. They believe in respect for others; in the capacity of human beings to change; and in the importance of the family and the community in the development of resilient, responsible and capable people.

Haight Ashbury Free Medical Clinic
558 Clayton St.
San Francisco, CA 94117
415-487-5632
www.hafci.org

    The HAFMC provides free health care to those in need, including substance abuse programs, HIV treatment, and care for the homeless.

Housing & Emergency Food Hotline
  Number
Los Angeles Area
310-551-2929 or dial 211
www.infoline-la.org

    This organization attempts to connect former prisoners with shelter and food in their area.

Info Line Sacramento
828 I Street, 5th Floor
Sacramento, CA 95814
918-498-1000
www.communitycouncil.org
infoline@communitycouncil.org

    Info line provides information and referrals to the Sacramento community.

L.A. Mission
303 E 5th St
Los Angeles, CA 90013
213-629-1227
This organization provides emergency housing for 4 nights(every ten days),

two meals, *free clothing, shower and shave.*

Loaves & Fishes
1321 North C Street
Sacramento, CA 95814
916-446-0874
www.sacramentoloavesandfishes.org
info@sacramentoloavesandfishes.org
   This organization provides free noon meals, daytime hospitality shelter, health clinic, AIDS hospice, legal services, housing resources, emergency school for homeless children, and overnight shelter fo women and children.

Los Angles Free Clinic
8405 Beverly Blvd.
Los Angeles, CA 90048
323-653-1990-clinic
323-653-8622-counseling and social
   services
www.lafreeclinic.org
   This organization offers, medical, dental, legal, and counseling services.

Metropolitan Skills Center
2801 West 6th St.
Los Angeles, CA 90057
213-386-7269
   This organization offers vocational training, English as a second language classes, high school diploma and GED classes.

Mexican American Opportunity
   Foundation
401 N Garfield Ave
Montebsello, CA 90640
323-890-9600
www.maof.org
   This organization provides training and subsequent job placement, counseling, emergency shelter, legal assistance, food, clothing, and medical care, at a number of California locations.

Mothers Reclaiming Our Children
4167 Normandies Ave
Los Angeles, CA 90037

Working to create a nationwide program to provide support to families, attend court hearings and trails, and work with attorneys. Provides advocacy work for prisoners and their families.

Northern California Service League
   (NCSL)
28 Boardman Place
San Francisco, CA 94103
415-863-2323
www.norcalserviceleague.org
ncsl@norcalserviceleague.org
   NCSL provides support services to current and former prisoners in Northern California, including job training, life skills workshops, substance abuse counseling, parenting classes and legal referrals.

Project Rebound
Associated Students, Inc
Cesar Chavez Student Center
1650 Holloway Ave. T-138
San Francisco, CA 94132
415-405-0954
www.sfsu.edu/-rebound
rebound@sfsu.edu
   Project Rebound is a special admissions program for former prisoners wanting to enter San Francisco State University. They offer special guidelines concerning admissions and academic tutoring to new students.

Pacific Youth Correctional Ministries
P.O. Box 8333
San Bernadino, CA 92412
562-596-5352
http://www.pycm.org/
   PYCM creates or facilitates model chaplaincy ministries with at risk and incarcerated youth through intervention.

Proteus, Inc
1830 N Dinuba Blvd.
Visalia, CA 93291
559-733-5423
www.prpfeusinc.org
   Proteus, inc. participates in the statewide

Jobs Plus program. They assist individuals in securing employment in Fresno. Tulare, Kings, and Kern Counties and provide employment counseling, job skills, and job placement.

San Francisco Works
235 Montgomery Street
12th Floor
San Francisco, CA 94104-3103
415-217-5193
www.sfworks.org
    SFWorks offers life skills training, case management services, job training and placement.

Seventh Step Foundation-East Bay
    Chapter
475 Medford Ave.
Hayward, CA 94541
510-278-0230
    This organization has a re-entry program called Freedom House that provides parolees with housing meals, clothing, and employment.

South Bay Regional Center(Episcopal
    Community Services)
3954 Murphy Canyon Rd. Ste. D-
    202
San Diego, CA 92123
888-505-8031
    Offers 3 and 6 month sessions for individuals referred by the court or probation office for misdemeanor, non-violent, or low-violence drug charges. AIDS Education classes are also required for those referred for convictions on possession of narcotics and prostitution.

State of California Department of Rehabilitation Communications
    Office
P.O. Box 944222
Sacramento, CA 94244-2200
918-263-8952
www.rehab.cahwnet.gov
    This state agency provides assistance to prisoners and ex-prisoners with documented physical, emotional, or mental disability in finding employment.

The Insight Prison Project
805 Fourth Street Suit 3
San Rafael, CA 94901
415-459-9800
http://www.insightprisonproject.org
    Communication training in nonviolence in correctional facilities; expanding to include post-release training.

The Workplace
3407 W. 6th Ste 705
Los Angeles, CA 90020
213-386-1994
    The workplace provides job-placement services, pre-employment screening, and referrals for parolees and pre-release employment screening for prisoners. Some referrals for drug rehabilitation are available. Also works in Orange County.

Turing Point Central California
Visalia Reentry Center
1845 South Court Street
Visalia, CA 93277
559-732-5550
    This is a work-furlough program operated in cooperation with the California Department of Corrections and Federal Prison System. It includes a 24-bed facility that is centrally located close to many potential places of employment for residents. Offers food, shelter, job placement, medical services, drug counseling, mental health services, legal assistance, and Christian counseling.

Welcome Home Ministries
Attn: Gloria
104 South Barnes St.
Oceanside, CA 92054
760-439-1136
www.welcomehomeministries.com
info@welcomehomeministries.com
    This is a Christain organization that provides faith-based supports for women in their transition from incarceration to society by provided toiletries, food, clothing, support groups, networking for jobs, housing, and rehabilitation.

COLORADO

Colorado Criminal Justice Reform
  Coalition
1212 Mariposa St. #6
Denver, CO 80204
303-825-0122
303-825-0304
http://www.ccjrc.org
  *A network of organizations, faith commu-
nities, and individuals working to reverse the
trend of mass incarceration in Colorado.
Quarterly newsletter:"Colorado Justice Report."
Re-entry guide for parolees, referrals and community resource list.*

Colorado Ex-Offender Employment
Colorado Division of Employment
  and Training
639 E. 18th Ave.
Denver, CO 80203
303-830-3000
  *This organization provides job referrals and
development for former prisoners.*

Colorado Prison Association-Volun-
  teers of America
2660 Larimer St.
Denver, CO 80205
303-297-0408
  *Emergency loans referrals to recently released
inmates.*

CURE
3470 S. Poplar St. #406
Denver, CO 80224
303-758-3390
FAX: 303-758-7627
www.coloradocure.org
Dianne@coloradocure.org
  *CURE is a grassroots organization-from top
to bottom. It does not hire professional leaders.
Instead, its leaders come from the ranks of people formerly in prison and family members of
friends of prisoners. This organization offers
assistance to ex-offenders.*

Empowerment Programs, Inc.
1600 York St. Suite 201
Denver, CO 80206
303-320-1989
www.empowermentprogram.org
empower-info@empowermenprogram.org
  *Services include job training, placement
and referrals, support services, housing and
rental assistance for women who are former
prisoners, on parole, and prostitutes.*

Impact of Life
1107 Garden of the Gods Rd
Colorado, Spring, CO 80907
719-632-0644
http://www.impactlife.org/
  *Impact of Life is a combination of 3 min-
istries-Kid's Crossing, Daughters of destiny,
and Library of Hope. Library of Hope is one
of the largest distribution ministries, reaching
one-quarter of all prisons in the United States.
Daughters of Destint reaches out to incarcerated women and teen girls and help them address their specific needs. Finally, Kid's Crossing
provides family-friendly camps hosted in prisons all across country, allowing children to
have the opportunity to spend an entire day in
a Christian atmosphere with their incarcerated
mother or father.*

United Way of Colorado
303-561-2111 or just dial 211
www.unitedwaydenver.org
  *Referrals to recently released inmates for jobs,
shelter, and rent assistance.*

Workforce Centers

Adams County Department of
  Human Services
7190 Colorado Blvd.
Commerce City, CO 80022
303-227-2677
Fax: 303-227-2655

Alamosa
305 Murphy Drive, Unit B
Alamosa, CO 81101
719-589-5158
TTY: 719-589-5150
Fax: 719-589-4474

Aurora
12510 E. Iliff Ave., Suite 303
Aurora, CO 80014
303-337-4610 or 303-337-4612
Fax: 303-755-5514

Boulder
4875 Pearl East Circle Suite 301
Boulder, CO 80301
303-444-9140
TTY: 303-444-8136
Fax: 303-444-9140

Business Enterprise Program (BEP)
2211 West Evans Ave., Building B
Denver, CO 80223
303-866-3484
TTY: 303-866-3484
Fax: 303-866-3933

Canon City Rehabilitation
172 Justice Center Rd.
Canon City, CO 81212
719-275-2318 ext. 3076
Fax: 719-546-0968

Colorado Springs
110 Parkside Drive
Colorado, CO 80910-3198
719-635-3585
Fax: 719-635-3177
TTY: 719-635-0529

Craig
480 Barclay
Craig, CO 81625
970-824-3246 ext. 20
Fax: 970-824-7108

Delta Workforce Center
206 Ute St.

Montrose, CO 81416
970-874-5781 ext. 12
Fax: 970-249-2602

Denver Metro
2211 West Evans Ave.
Denver, CO 80223
Bldg.A
303-866-2500
Fax: 303-866-3418
Fax: 303-866-3419
Bldg.B
303-866-3100
TTY: 303-866-3984 or 303-866-
3980
Fax: 303-866-3491
Fax: 303-866-3496

Developmental Disabilities Resource
Center
11177 W. 8th Ave., Suite 300
Lakewood, CO 80215
303-462-6688
Fax: 303-462-6689

Division of Vocational Rehabilitation,
Administration
1575 Sherman St., 4th Floor
Denver, CO 80203
303-866-870-4150
Tool Free-866-870-4595
TTY: 303-866-4150
Fax: 303-866-4905 or 303-866-
4908
www.cdhs.state.co.us/dvr/

Durango
425 West Building
835 Second Ave.
Durango, CO 81301
970-247-3161
TTY: 970-247-7940
Fax: 970-247-8324

Edwards
69 Edwards Access Rd., Suite 9
Edwards, CO 81632

970-926-1515
Fax: 970-926-7287

Fort Collins
2850 McClelland Drive, #2000
Fort Collins, CO 80525
970-223-9823
TTY: 970-223-4265
Fax: 970-223-0718

Foot Hills Gateway
301 Skyway Drive
Fort Collins, CO 80525
970-266-5436
Fax: 970-266-2623

Frisco
602 Galina
Frisco, CO 80443
970-668-0234
Fax: 970-668-3216

Glenwood Springs
Glenwood Springs Mall
51027 Highway 6 and 24, #173
Glenwood Springs, CO 81601
970-945-9174
TTY: 970-945-9174
Toll Free 888-681-9152
Fax: 970-928-0885

Golden
3500 Illinois St.
Golden, CO 80401
303-866-4121
TTY: 303-866-4125
Fax: 303-866-4122

Grand Junction
222 South 6th St., Room #215
Grand Junction, CO 81501
970-248-7103
TTY: 970-248-7103
Fax: 970-248-7118

Grand Junction Career Center
2955 North Ave.
Grand Junction, CO 81501

970-248-7103
Fax: 970-248-7118

Greeley
822 7th St., Suite 350
Greenley, CO 80631
970-353-5409
Fax: 970-353-3367

Greenwood Village
6000 Greenwood Plaza Blvd, Suite
  105
Greenwood Village, CO 80111
303-221-2089
Fax: 303-221-3099

Lamar
1006 South Main St.
Lamar, CO 81052
719-336-7712
TTY: 719=336-7712
Fax: 719-336-7713

Limon
P.O. Box 99
825 Second St.
Limon, CO 80828
719-775-8819
TTY: 719-775-8819
Fax: 719-775-9517

Longmont
825 Delaware Ave., #306
Longmont, CO 80501
303-776-6878
TTY: 303-485-6438
Fax: 303-776-7783

Montrose
1010 South Cascade Ave., Suite C
Montrose, CO 81401
970-249-4468
TTY: 970-249-4468
Fax: 970-249-2602

Northglenn
11990 Grant St., #201
Northglenn, CO 80223

303-866-2110
TTY: 303-866-2130
Fax: 303-866-2111

Pikes Peak Workforce Center
2306 E. Pike Ave.
Colorado Springs, CO
719-667-3796
Fax:719-635-3177

Pueblo
720 North Main #320
Pueblo, CO 81003
719-544-1406
TTY: 719-546-0968
Fax: 719-544-1634

The Resource Exchange
418 South Weber
Colorado Springs, CO 80903
719-380-1100
Fax: 719-635-3177

Rocky Ford Workforce Center
801 Chestnut Ave.
Rocky Ford, CO 81067
719-254-3358
Fax: 719-254-3350

Salida
7990 W. U.S. Highway 50, Unit E
Saida, CO 81201
719-539-9670

TTY: 719-539-9670
Fax: 719-539-9675

Starpoint
700 S. 8th St.
Canon City, CO 81212
719-544-1634
Fax: 719-544-1406

Steamboat Springs
Sundance at Fishcreek
345 Anglers Drive-Suite C-Building
  E
P.O. Box 883284
Steamboat Springs, CO 80477
970-871-4853
Fax: 970-871-4987

Sterling
Northeastern Junior College
Walker Hall, Room 1
100 College Ave.
Sterling, CO 80751
970-522-3737
TTY: 970-522-3737
Fax: 970-522-8571
Trinidad Workforce Center
140 North Commercial
Trinidad, CO 81082
888-734-2211
Fax: 719-846-7594

CONNECTICUT

Community Partners in Action
110 Bartholomew Ave. Suite
  3010
Hartford, CT 06106
860-566-2030
dhayden@cpa-ct.org
www.cpa-ct.org
   This organization offers a variety of post-release services to former prisoners in Connecticut.

Community Renewal Team, Inc.
555 Windsor St.
Hartford, CT 06120
860-560-5471
   Offers a number of re-entry programs.

Families in Crisis, Inc.
30 Arbor St. North Wing
Hartford CT 06106
860-236-3593

Families in Crisis provides a range of counseling and support services to inmates and their families individual and family counseling, crisis intervention, case management, court management, court outreach, transportation, childcare, parent education groups,, support groups, training programs, after school program for children of incarcerated parents. No collect calls at office.

Families in Crisis, Inc., New Haven
48 Howe St.
New Haven, CT 06511
203-498-7790

Families in Crisis, Inc., Waterbury
232 N Elm St.
Waterbury, CT 06702
203-573-8656

Family Re-entry
9 Mott Ave. Suite 104
Norwalk, CT 06850
203-838-0496

Provides counseling and therapy services, parent education, information, referrals, mentoring and gifts for children, offenders and their families across a variety of sites (e.g., adult probation, day incarceration centers, alternative to incarceration centers, residential substance abuse treatment facilities, pre-release prison programs).

People Empowering People
UConn Cooperative Extension Service
Box 70
Haddam, CT 06438

Provides life skills and leadership training, mentoring, and support to families and friends of offenders.

Perception Programs, Inc.
P.O. Box 407, 54 North St.
Willimantic, CT 06226
860-450-7122 No collect calls

Perception Programs serves substance abusers, offenders, and people living with HIV in northeastern Connecticut. Programs include residential work release and treatment programs for men and women, short-term residential

substance abuse treatment for male prisoners in transition back to community life(including men with dual substance abuse and mental health diagnoses), outpatient substance treatment, and residential treatment and education programs that act as alternatives to incarceration for adults and adolescents. Program fees may apply.

STRIVE/New Haven
904 Howard Ave. 2nd Floor
New Haven, CT 06511
203-777-1720
www.strivenewhaven.com

The STRIVE program provide job training and job retention skills, and assist participants in their job search.

STRIVE/South Arsenal Neighborhood Development (SAND)
1500 Main St.
Hartford, CT 06120
860-278-8460
info@sandcorporation.com

The STRIVE programs provide job training and job retention skills, and assist participants in their job search.

Connecticut Works Workforce Centers

Enfield
620 Enfield St.
Enfield, CT 06082
860-741-4081
TTY/TDD: 860-741-4299
Fax: 860-741-4290

Hartford
3580 Main St. 1st Floor
Hartford, CT 06120
860-256-3800
TTY/TDD: 860-566-3311
Fax: 860-256-3580

Manchester
Next to Bank of America
893 Main St.

Manchester, CT 06040
860-643-2222
Fax: 860-643-0006
New Britain
260 LaFayettee St.

New Britain, CT 06053
860-827-6200
860-827-6220
TTY/TDD: 860-827-6246
Fax: 860-827-6210

DELAWARE

Prison to Work Program
Delaware Department of Labor
4425 N Market St.
Wilmington, DE 19802
302-761-8039
Sherese.brewington-c@state.de.us

   The website provides particularly useful information for job seekers. Resource rooms at local Career Centers offer privacy and are equipped with computers/internet access, resume preparation software, and many other resources. Two different video series are available and cover topics relevant for offenders.

Human Resource Management Offices

Barratt Building
Kent County
821 Silver Lake Rd., Suite 201
Dover, DE 19904
302-739-1990
Fax: 302-739-2543

Carvel State Office Building
New Castle County
820 N. French St.
Wilmington, DE 19801
302-577-8977
Fax: 302-577-3996

Haslet Armory
Kent County
122 William Penn St.
Dover, DE 19901
302-739-4195
Fax: 302-739-3000

One-Stop Centers Work Force Development

Chenango, Delaware, Otsego
Administrative Office
12 Dietz St.
Oneonta, NY 13820
607-432-4800

Delhi, New York
Delaware County
One-Stop Center
One Gallant Ave.
Delhi, NY 13753
607-746-7477

Norwich, New York
Chenango County
One-Stop Center
1 O'Hara Drive
Norwich, NY 13815
607-334-2201

Oneonta, New York
Otsego Center
One-Stop
12 Dietz St.
Oneonta, NY 13020
607-432-4800

Sidney New York
Delaware County
One-Stop Center
21 Liberty St.
Sidney, NY 13838
607-561-7550

FLORIDA

CURE
P.O. Box 320732
Tampa, FL 33679
http://www.flcure.org
   CURE is a grassroots organization-from top to bottom. It does not hire professional leaders. Instead, its leaders come from the ranks of people formerly in prison and family members of friends of prisoners. This organization offers assistance to ex-offenders.

Florida Department of Corrections
2601 Blair Stone Rd.
Tallahassee,
FL 32399-2500
850-488-5021
http://www.dc.state.fl.us

Florida Department of Education
Capitol Building, Room PL 08
Tallahassee, FL 32399-0400
850-487-1785
850-413-0378
www.firn.edu/doe/index.html

Florida Department of Labor, Employment, and Training
Liaison: Larry McIntyre
1320 Executive Center Drive, Atkins Building #200
Tallahassee, FL 32339-0667
850-488-9250
850-488-0249(fax)
larrymcintyre@jb.fdles.state.fl.us

Florida Workforce Investment Board
Director: Thomas D. McGurk
Agency for Workforce Innovation
1320 Executive Center Drive
300 Atkins Building
   Tallahassee, FL 32399-0667
850-921-5421
805-487-1753(fax)
thomasmcgurk@jb.fdles.state.fl.us

Governor's Liaison: Mary B. Hooks
Labor and Employment Security Department
2021 Capitol Circle SE, Hartman Building #303
Tallahassee, FL 32339-2152
850-488-8930(fax)
marybhooks@fdles.state.fl.us

Free Inside Ministries
11225 U.S. Hwy 19 North
Clearwater, FL 33764
727-467-4333
*http://www.freeinside.org/
infor@freeinside.org*
   Free Inside Ministries collaborates with Christian and community-oriented organizations to evangelize, disciple, and assist in the complete recovery of individuals impacted by substance abuse and incarceration.

Workforce Development Board Centers by Region

ALACHUA/BRADFORD REGION 9

Alachua and Bradford Counties
BCN Associates, Inc.
Liaison: Rachel Bishop-Cook
408 West University Ave., Suite 604
Gainesville, FL 32601
352-334-4088
352-377-5242(fax)
Rachel@bcnassociates.com

BIG BEND REGION 5

Gadsden, Leon, Wakulla Counties
Big Bend Jobs and Education Council, Inc.
Liaison: J. Wyatt Pope
565 East Tennessee St.
Tallahassee, FL 32208
850-414-6085

850-410-2595(fax)
Wyatt.pope@bigbend-workforce.org

BREVARD COUNTY REGION 13

Brevard Workforce Development
  Board
Liaison: Linda South
597 Haverty Court, Suite 40
Rockledge, FL 32955
321-504-2060
321-504-2065(fax)
lsouth@job-link.net

BROWARD COUNTY

Workforce One
Liaison: Mason Jackson
3800 Inverarry Blvd., Suite 400
Lauderhill, FL 33319
954-535-2345
954-535-2346 (fax)
masonjacks@broward-workforce.org

CENTRAL FLORIDA REGION 12

Lake Orange, Osceola, Seminole,
  Sumter Counties
Workforce Central Florida
Liaison: Gary Earl
1801 Lee Rd., Suite 270
Winter Park, FL 32789-2165
407-741-4365
407-741-4376(fax)
gearl@msn.com

CHIPOLA REGION 3

Calhoun, Holmes, Jackson, Liberty,
  Washington Counties
Chipola Regional Workforce Planning
  Board, Inc.
Liaison: Freida Sheffield
P.O. Box 947
Chipey, FL 32428
850-638-6081
850-638-3093 (fax)

freidas@jep3.state.fl.us
Citrus/Levy/Marion Region 10:

CITRUS, LEVY, MARION COUNTIES

CLMWorks Workforce Development
  Board
Liaison: Thomas "Rusty" Skinner
2300 SE 17th St., Suite 1000
Ocala, FL 34471
352-732-1355
352-732-1718 (fax)
tskinner@clmworkforce.com

DADE AND MONROE COUNTIES REGION 23

Dade, Monroe Counties
Jobs and Education Partnership Regional Board for Dade and Monroe
  Counties
Liaison: Harriet Spivak
3403 NW. 82nd Ave., Suite 300
Miami, FL 33122-1029
305-594-7615
305-477-0113(fax)
harriet@jep-tec.org

ESCAROSA REGION 1

Escambia and Santa Rosa Counties
Escarosa Regional Workforce Development Board, Inc.
9111 Sturdevant Drive
Pensacola, FL 32514
850-473-0939
850-473-0935(fax)
escarosa@bellsouth.net

FIRST COAST REGION 8

Clay, Duval, Nassau, Putman, St.
  Johns Counties
First Coast Workforce Development,
  Inc.
Liaison: Lynn Grafel
2141 Loch Rane Blvd., Suite 107
Orange Park, FL 32073-4239

904-213-3050
904-272-8977 (fax)
worksource@worksourcefl.com

FLAGLER/VOLUSIA COUNTIES;
WDB 11

Flagler and Volusia Counties
Workforce Development Board of
  Flagler and Vohisia Counties
Liaison: Lawrence Tomasetti
1901 Mason Ave., Suite 110
Daytona Beach, FL 32117
386-274-3850
386-274-3864 (fax)
larryt@wdb-fve.org

FLORIDA CROWN REGION 7

Baker, Columbia, Dixie, Gilchrist,
  Union Counties
Florida Crown Workforce Development Board
Liaison: James E. Carr
1430 South 1st St., Suite 2
Lake City, FL 32025-5750
386-752-5713
386-752-6461 (fax)
jecarr@flcrown.org

GULF COAST REGION 4

Bay, Franklin, Gulf Counties
Gulf Coast Workforce Board
Liaison: Kimberly L. Shoemaker
Gulf Coast Community College
5230 West U.S. Highway 98
Panama City, FL 32401-1058
850-913-3285
850-913-3269 (fax)
kshoemaker@mail.ge.ee.fl.us

HEARTLAND REGION 19

De Soto, Hardee, Highlands Counties
Heartland Workforce Investment Board
Liaison: James L. Gose
600 West College Drive

Avon Park, FL 33825
863-453-6661
863-784-7209 (fax)
gosej@sfcc.fl.us

HILLSBOROUGH COUNTY; WDB 15

Hillsborough County Workforce Development Board
Liaison: Max Selko
9250 Bay Plaza Blvd., Suite 320
Tampa, FL 33619
813-744-5547
813-744-5764 (fax)
seikom@workforcetampa.com

NORTH FLORIDA REGION 6

Hamilton, Jefferson, Lafayette, Madison, Suwannee, Taylor Counties
North Florida Workforce Development Board/WAGES Coalition
Liaison: William M. Deming
P.O. Box 267
400 West Base St., 2nd Floor
Madison, FL 32341
850-973-2672
850-973-6497 (fax)
demingm@nfwdb.org

OKALOOSA/WALTON COUNTIES
REGION 2

Okaloosa and Walton Counties
Workforce Development Board of
  Okaloosa and Walton Counties
Liaison: Mary Lou Reed
109 8th Ave.
Shalimar, FL 32579
850-651-2315
850-651-3165 (fax)
mired@seii.net

PALM BEACH COUNTY; WDB 21

Palm Beach County Workforce Development Board, Inc./WAGES
  Coalition

Liaison: Ken Montgomery 2051 Martin Luther King Jr. Blvd. #302
Rivera Beach, FL 33404
561-841-0207
561-841-0280 (fax)
kmontgomery@pbcwdb.com

PASCO/HERMANDO COUNTIES REGION 16

Hernando, Pasco Counties
Pasco-Hernando Jobs and Education Partnership Regional Board
Liaison: Lee Elizey
P.O. Box 15790
Brookville, FL 34609
352-797-5781
352-797-5785 (fax)
ice@pasco–hermando.com

PINELLAS COUNTY REGION 14

Worknet Pinellas
Liaison: Bonnie Moore
4525 140th Ave. North, Suite 906
Clearwater, FL 33760
727-524-4334
727-524-4350 (fax)
bamoore@co.pinelias.fl.us

POLK COUNTY REGION 17

Polk County Workforce Development Board
Liaison: Nancy Thompson
205 East Main St., Suite 107
Bartow, FL 33830
863-519-0100

863-534-8501 (fax)
Nancy_thompson@polkworks.org

SOUTHWEST FLORIDA REGION 24

Dade, Monroe Counties
Southwest Florida Workforce Development Board
Liaison: Joseph Paterno
24311 Walden Center Drive #200
Bonita Springs, FL 34134
941-992-8000
941-948-3359 (fax)
Paterno_joe@hotmail.com

SUNCOAST; WDB 18

Manatee, Sarasota Counties
Suncoast Workforce Development Board
Liaison: Mary Helen Kress
1750 17th St., Building J-2
Sarasota, FL 34234
941-361-6090
941-361-6141 (fax)
mnkress@swdb.org

TREASURE COAST; WDB 20

Indian River, Martin, Okeechobee, St. Lucie Counties
Workforce development Board of the Treasure Coast
Liaison: Nan Rose Griggs
9350 South Federal Highway
Port St. Lucie, FL 34952
561-335-3030
561-335-0677 (fax)
ngriggs@tcjobs.org

GEORGIA

Active Parenting Publishing
1955 Vaughn Rd, NW

Suite 108
Kennesaw, GA 30144-7808

800-825-0060
http://www.activeparenting.com/prison-programs.htm
cservice@activeparenting.com

This curriculum publisher has a variety of books and resources specifically designed for the children and families of inmates. Mamma Loves Me From Away and A Visit With Daddy are two of their large selection.

Crison Ministries with Women
465 Blvd., SE
Suite 205
Atlanta, GA 30312
404-622-4314

This organization provides transitional housing, counseling, job-training, and support services.

CURE
759 Willow Gate Circle, Apt C
Liburn, GA 30047

CURE is a grassroots organization from top to bottom. It does not hire professional leaders. Instead, its leaders come from the ranks of people formerly in prison and family members of friends of prisoners. This organization offers assistance to ex-offenders.

Epiphany Ministry
P.O. Box 192
Danville, GA 31017
478-962-0794
http://www.epiphanyministry.org/

Epiphany Ministry provides small group and one-on-one follow up in juvenile prisons and promotes the involvement of volunteers in on-going juvenile prison ministry. It offers juveniles an opportunity to change their lives and value sytems through a three-day short course in Christianity and ongoing follow up.

The Open Door Community
910 Ponce de Leon Ave NE
Atlanta, GA 30306-4212
404-974-9652
www.opendoorcommunity.org

Serves meals, provides showers and change of clothes, and a free medical clinic.

Project Welcome Home
P.O. Box 61660
Savannah, GA 31420
Or
8400 A Abercorn St
Savannah, GA 31406
914-351-1661 or 912-920-9411
Mamasky07@aol.com

Provides women and youth with services, such as literacy motivation, referral service, housing and a mentoring service.

Workforce Development Centers by County

APPLING COUNTY

Heart of Georgia Altamaha Area-Job Training Unlimited
7 South Duval St.
Claxton, GA 30417
912-739-6097
Fax: 932-739-7126

ATKINSON COUNTY

Southeast Georgia Area Regional Development Center
1725 South Georgia Parkway, West
Waycross, GA 31503
912-285-6097
Fax: 912-285-6126

BACON COUNTY

Southeast Georgia Area Regional Development Center
1725 South Georgia Parkway, West
Waycross, GA 31503
912-285-6097
Fax: 912-285-6126

BAKER COUNTY

Southwest Georgia Area Regional Development Center
30 E. Broad St.

Camilla, GA 31739
229-522-3594

BALDWIN COUNTY

Middle Georgia Area Consortium
124 Osigian Blvd, Suite A
Warner Robins, GA 31088
479-953-4771
Toll Free: 800-537-1933
Fax: 479-953-2509

BANKS COUNTY

Georgia Mountains Area Workforce
  Investment Board
2481 Hilton Blvd, Suite B
Gainesville, GA 30501
770-538-2727
Fax: 770-538-2730

BARROW COUNTY

NE Georgia Area Regional Development Center
305 Research Drive
Athens, GA 30161-2795
706-369-5703
Toll Free 800-533-5872
Fax: 706-369-5792

BARTOW COUNTY

NW Georgia Area Coosa Valley Regional Development Center
1 Jackson Hill Drive
Rome, GA 30161
706-295-6485
Toll Free: 800-332-1965
Fax: 706-802-5567

BEN HILL COUNTY

South Georgia Area Workforce Investment Board
327 W. Savannah Ave.
Valdosta, GA 31601
229-333-5277

BERRIEN COUNTY

SE Georgia Area Regional Development Center
1725 South Georgia Parkway
West Waycross, GA 31503
912-285-6097

BIBB COUNTY

Macon/Bibb Area Office of Workforce
  Development
200 Cherry St., Suite 400-B
Macon, GA 31201
478-751-7333

BLECKLEY COUNTY

Heart of Georgia Altamaha Area Job
  Training Unlimited
7 South Duval St.
Claxton, GA 30417
912-739-7158

BRANTLEY COUNTY

Southeast Georgia Area Regional Development Center
1725 South Georgia Parkway, West
Waycross, GA 31503
912-285-6097

BROOKS COUNTY

South Georgia Area Workforce Investment Board
327 W. Savannah Ave.
Valdosta, GA 31601
229-333-5277

BRYAN COUNTY AND BULLOCH COUNTY

Coastal Georgia Area Workforce Services
5618 White Bluff Rd.
Savannah, GA 31405
912-351-6379

BURKE COUNTY

Richmond/Burke Area Job Training
 Authority
209 7th St., 5th Floor
Augusta, GA 30903
706-721-1858
Toll Free 877-633-9799
Fax: 706-721-7395

BUTTS COUNTY

West Central Georgia Area Workforce
 Development Corporation
1710 Highway 16 West
Griffin, GA 30223
770-229-9799
Toll Free 800-633-9799
Fax: 770-229-9924

CALHOUN COUNTY

Southwest Georgia Area Workforce
 Investment Board
30 E. Broad St.
Camilla, GA 31730
229-522-3594

CAMDEN COUNTY

Coastal Georgia Area Workforce Services
5618 White Bluff Rd.
Savannah, GA 31405
912-351-6379

CANDLER COUNTY

Heart of Georgia Altamaha Area-Job
 Training Unlimited
7 South Duval St.
Claxton, GA 30417
912-739-7158
Fax: 912-739-7126

CARROLL COUNTY

West Central Georgia Area Workforce
 Development Corporation

1710 Highway 16 West
Griffin, GA 30223
770-229-9799
Toll Free 877-633-9799
Fax: 770-229-9924

CATOOSA COUNTY

NW Georgia Area Coosa Valley Regional Development Center
1 Jackson Hill Drive
Rome, GA 30161
706-295-6485
Toll Free 800-332-1965
Fax: 706-802-5567

CHARLTON COUNTY

Southeast Georgia Area Regional Development Center
1725 South Georgia Parkway, West
Waycross, GA 31503
912-285-6097
Fax: 912-285-6126

CHATHAM COUNTY

Coastal Georgia Area Workforce Services
5618 White Bluff Rd.
Savannah, GA 31405
912-351-6379

CHATTAHOOCHEE COUNTY

Lower Chattahoochee Area Columbus
 Consolidated Government Job
 Training Division
420 10th St.
Columbus, GA 30161
706-295-6485

CHATTOOGA COUNTY

NW Georgia Area Coosa Valley Regional Development Center
1 Jackson Hill Drive
Rome, GA 30161

706-295-6485
Toll Free 800-332-1965
Fax: 706-802-5567

CHEROKEE COUNTY

Atlanta Regional Area ARC-Workforce Development Division
40 Courtland St, NE
Atlanta, GA 30303-2538
404-463-3100
Toll Free 800-516-5872
Fax: 404-463-3105

CLARKE COUNTY

NE Georgia Area Regional Development Center
305 Research Drive
Athens, GA 30605-2795
706-369-5703
Toll Free 800-533-5872
Fax: 706-369-5792

CLAY COUNTY

Lower Chattahoochee Area Columbus Consolidated Government Job Training Division
420 10th St.
Columbus, GA 31901
706-653-4529

CLAYTON COUNTY

Atlanta Regional Area ARC-Workforce Development Division
40 Courtland, NE
Atlanta, GA 30303-2538
404-463-3100
Toll Free 800-516-5872
Fax: 404-463-3105

CLINCH COUNTY

Southeast Georgia Area Regional Development Center
1725 South Georgia Parkway, West
Waycross, GA 31503

912-285-6097
Fax: 912-285-6126

COBB COUNTY

Cobb County Area CobbWorks
463 Commerce Park Drive, Suite 100
Marietta, GA 30060
770-528-4300

COFFEE COUNTY

Southeast Georgia Area Regional Development Center
1725 South Georgia Parkway, West
Waycross, GA 31503
912-285-6097
Fax: 912-285-6126

COLQUITT COUNTY

Southwest Georgia Area Workforce Investment Board
30 E. Board St.
Camilla, Georgia 31730
229-522-3594

COLUMBUS COUNTY

East Central Georgia Area Consortium, Inc.
674 Washington Rd., Suite A
Thompson, GA 30824
706-595-8941
Toll Free 800-251-3882
Fax: 706-597-9713

COOK COUNTY

South Georgia Area Workforce Investment Board
327 W. Savannah Ave.
Valdosta, GA 31601
229-333-5277

COWETA COUNTY

West Central Georgia Area Workforce Development Corporation

1710 Highway 16 West
Griffin, GA 30223
270-229-9799
Toll Free 877-633-9799
Fax: 770-229-9924

CRAWFORD COUNTY

Middle Georgia Area Consortium,
Inc.
124 Osigian Blvd, Suite A
Warner Robins, GA 31088
478-953-4771
Toll Free 800-537-1933
Fax: 770-229-9924

CRISP COUNTY

Middle Flint Area Regional Development Center
228 West Lamer St.
Americus, GA 31709
229-931-2909

DADE COUNTY

NW Georgia Area Coosa Valley Regional Development Center
1 Jackson Hill Drive
Rome, GA 30161
706-295-6485
Toll Free 800-332-1965
Fax: 706-802-5567

DAWSON COUNTY

NW Georgia Mountains Area Workforce Investment Board
2481 Hilton Drive, Suite B
Gainesville, GA 30501
770-538-2727
Fax: 770-538-2730

DECATUR COUNTY

Southwest Georgia Area Workforce
Investment Board
30 E. Board St.

Camilla, GA 31730
229-522-3594

DEKALB COUNTY

DeKalb County Area Workforce Development
320 Church St.
Decatur, GA 30030
404-687-3400

DODGE COUNTY

Heart of Georgia Altamaha Area Job
Training Unlimited
7 South Duval St.
Claxton, GA 30417
912-739-7158
Fax: 912-739-7126

DOOLY COUNTY

Middle Flint Area Regional Development Center
228 West Lamar St.
Americus, GA 31709
229-931-2909

DOUGHERTY COUNTY

Southwest Georgia Area Workforce
Investment Board
30 E. Board St.
Camilla, GA 31730
229-522-3594

DOUGLAS COUNTY

Atlanta Regional Area ARC Workforce Development Division
40 Courtland St, NE
Atlanta, GA 30303-2538
404-463-3100
Toll Free 800-516-5872
Fax: 404-463-3105

EARLY COUNTY

Southwest Georgia Area Workforce
Investment Board

30 E. Broad St.
Camilla, GA 31730
229-522-3594

ECHOLS COUNTY

South Georgia Area Workforce Investment Board
327 W. Savannah Ave.
Valdosta, GA 31601
229-333-5277

EFFINGHAM COUNTY

Coastal Georgia Area Workforce Services
5618 White Bluff Rd.
Savannah, GA 31405
912-351-6379

ELBERT COUNTY

NE Georgia Area Regional Development Center
305 Research Drive
Athens, GA 30605-2795
706-369-5703
Too Free-800-533-5872
Fax: 706-369-5792

EMANUEL COUNTY

Heart of Georgia Altamaha Area Job Training Unlimited
7 South Duval St.
Claxton, GA 30417
912-739-7158

EVANS COUNTY

Heart of Georgia Altamaha Area Job Training Unlimited
7 South Duval St.
Claxton, GA 30417
912-739-7158

FANNIN COUNTY

NW Georgia Area Coosa Valley Regional Development Center

1 Jackson Hill Drive
Rome, GA 30161
706-295-6485
Toll Free 800-332-1965
Fax: 706-802-5567

FAYETTE COUNTY

Atlanta Regional Area ARC Workforce Development Division
40 Courtland St, NE
Atlanta, GA 30303-2538
404-463-3100
Toll Free: 800-516-5872
Fax: 404-463-3105

FLOYD COUNTY

NW Georgia Area Coosa Valley Regional Development Center
1 Jackson Hill Drive
Rome, GA 30161
770-295-6485
Toll Free 800-332-1965
Fax: 706-802-5567

FORSYTH COUNTY

Georgia Mountains Area Workforce Investment Board
2481 Hilton Drive, Suite B
Gainesville, GA 30501
770-538-2727
770-538-2730

FRANKLIN COUNTY

Georgia Mountains Area Workforce Investment Board
2481 Hilton Drive Suite B
Gainesville, GA 30501
770-538-2727
770-538-2730

FULTON COUNTY

City of Atlanta Area Atlanta Workforce Development Agency

818 Pollard Blvd, SW
Atlanta, GA 30315
404-658-WORK(9675)

Fulton County Outside of the City
  of Atlanta Workforce Development
115 Martin Luther King, Jr. Drive,
  SW, Suitge 300
Atlanta, GA 30303
404-730-4751

GILMER COUNTY

NW Georgia Area Coosa Valley Regional Development Center
1 Jackson Hill Drive
Rome, GA 30161
706-295-6485
Toll Free 800-332-1965
Fax: 706-802-5567

GLASCOCK COUNTY

East Central Georgia Area Consortium, Inc.
674 Washington Rd., Suite A
Thomson, GA 30874
706-595-8941
Toll Free 800-251-3682
Fax: 706-597-9713

GLYNN COUNTY

Coastal Georgia Area Workforce Services
5618 White Bluff Rd.
Savannah, GA 31405
912-351-6379

GORDON COUNTY

NW Georgia Area Coosa Valley Regional Development Center
1 Jackson Hill Drive
Rome, GA 30161
706-295-6485
Toll Free: 800-332-1965
Fax: 706-802-5567

GRADY COUNTY

Southwest Georgia Area Workforce
  Investment Board
30 E. Board St.
Camilla, GA 31730
229-522-3594

GREENE COUNTY

NE Georgia Area Regional Development Center
305 Research Drive
Athens, GA 30605-2795
706-369-5703
Toll Free: 800-533-5872
Fax: 706-369-5792

GWINNETT COUNTY

Atlanta Regional Area ARC Workforce Development Division
40 Courtland St., NE
Atlanta, GA 30303-2538
404-463-3100
Toll Free 800-516-5877
Fax: 404-463-3105

HABERSHAM COUNTY

Georgia Mountains Area Workforce
  Investment Board
2481 Hilton Drive Suite B
Gainesville, GA 30501
770-538-2727
770-538-2730

HALL COUNTY

Georgia Mountains Area Workforce
  Investment Board
2461 Hilton Drive Suite B
Gainesville, GA 30501
770-538-2727
770-538-2730

HANCOCK COUNTY

East Central Georgia Area Consortium, Inc.

674 Washington Rd., Suite A
Thomson, GA 30501
706-595-8941
Toll Free 800-251-3882
Fax: 706-597-9713

HARALSON COUNTY

NW Georgia Area Coosa Valley Regional Development Center
1 Jackson Hill Drive
Rome, GA 30161
706-295-6485
Toll Free 800-332-1965
Fax: 706-807-5567

HARRIS COUNTY

Lower Chattahoochee Area Columbus Consolidated Government Job Training Division
429 10th St.
Columbus, GA 31901
706-653-4529

HART COUNTY

Georgia Mountain Area Workforce Investment Board
2481 Hilton Drive, Suite B
Gainesville, GA 30501
770-536-2727
770-536-2730

HEARD COUNTY

West Central Georgia Workforce Development Corporation
1710 Highway 16 West
Griffin, GA 30223
770-229-9799
Toll Free 877-633-9799
Fax: 770-229-9924

HENRY COUNTY

Atlanta Regional Area ARC Workforce development Division

40 Courtland St., NE
Atlanta, GA 30303-2538
404-463-3100
Toll Free 800-516-5872
Fax: 404-463-3105

HOUSTON COUNTY

Middle Georgia Area Consortium, Inc.
124 Osigian Blvd, Suite A
Warner Robins, GA 31088
479-953-4771
Toll Free 800-537-1933
Fax: 478-953-2509

IRWIN COUNTY

South Georgia Area Workforce Investment Board
327 W Savannah Ave.
Valdosta, GA 31601
229-333-5277

JACKSON COUNTY

NE Georgia Area Regional Development Center
305 Research Drive
Athens, GA 30605-2795
706-369-5703
Toll Free 800-533-5872
Fax: 706-369-5792

JASPER COUNTY

NE Georgia Area Regional Development Center
305 Research Drive
Athens, GA 30605-2795
706-369-5703
Toll Free 800-533-5872
Fax: 706-369-5792

JEFF DAVIS COUNTY

Heart of Georgia Altamaha Area Job Training Unlimited

7 South Duval St.
Claxton, GA 30417
912-739-7158

JEFFERSON COUNTY

East Central Georgia Area Connection, Inc.
674 Washington Rd., Suite A
Thomson, GA 30824
706-595-8941
Toll Free 800-251-3882
Fax: 706-597-9713

JENKINS COUNTY

East Central Georgia Area Consortium, Inc.
674 Washington Rd.. Suite A
Thomson, GA 30824
706-595-8941
Toll Free 800-251-3882
Fax: 706-597-9713

JOHNSON COUNTY

Heart of Georgia Altamaha Area Job
Training Unlimited
7 South Duval St.
Claxton, GA 30417
912-739-7158

JONES COUNTY

Middle Georgia Area Consortium, Inc.
124 Osigian Blvd, Suite A
Warner Robins, GA 31088
478-953-4771
Toll Free 800-537-1933
Fax: 478-953-2509

LAMAR COUNTY

West Central Georgia Area Workforce
Development Corporation
1710 Highway 16 west
Griffin, GA 30223
770-239-9799
Toll free-877-633-9799
Fax: 770-229-9924

LANIER COUNTY

South Georgia Area Workforce Investment Board
327 W. Savannah Ave.
Valdosta, GA 31601
229-333-5277

LAURENS COUNTY

Heart of Georgia Altamaha Area Job
Training Unlimited
7 South Duval St.
Claxton, GA 30417
912-739-7158

LEE COUNTY

Southwest Georgia Area Workforce
Investment Board
30 E. Board St.
Camille, GA 31730
229-522-3594

LIBERTY COUNTY

Coastal Georgia Area Workforce Services
5618 White Bluff Rd.
Savannah, GA 31405
912-351-6379

LINCOLN COUNTY

East Central Georgia Area Consortium, Inc.
674 Washington Rd., Suite A
Thomson, GA 30824
706-595-8541
Toll Free 800-251-3882
Fax: 706-597-9713

LONG COUNTY

Coastal Georgia Area Workforce Services
5618 White Bluff Rd.
Savannah, GA 31405
912-351-6379

LOWNDES COUNTY

South Georgia Area Workforce Investment Board
327 W. Savannah Ave.
Valdosta, GA 31601
229-333-5277

LUMPKIN COUNTY

Georgia Mountains Area Workforce Investment Board
2481 Hilton Drive, Suite B
Gainesville, GA 30501
770-538-2727
770-538-2730

MACON COUNTY

Middle Flint Area Regional Development Center
228 West Lamar St.
Americus, GA 31709
229-931-2909

MADISON COUNTY

NE Georgia Area Regional Development Center
305 Research Drive
Athens, GA 30605-2795
706-369-5703
Toll Free 800-533-5872
Free: 706-369-5792

MARION COUNTY

Middle Flint Area Regional Development Center
228 West Lamar St.
Americus, GA 31709
229-595-8941

MCDUFFIE COUNTY

East Central Georgia Area Consortium, Inc.
674 Washington Rd., Suite A
Thomson, GA 30824
706-595-8941
Toll Free 800-251-3882
Fax: 706-597-9713

MCINTOSH COUNTY

Coastal Georgia Area Workforce Services
5618 White Bluff Rd.
Savannah, GA 31404
912-351-6379

MERIWETHER COUNTY

West Central Georgia Area Workforce Development Corporation
1710 Highway 16 West
Griffin, GA 30223
770-229-9799
Toll Free 977-633-9799
Fax: 770-229-9924

MILLER COUNTY

Southwest Georgia Area Workforce Investment Board
30 E. Broad St.
Camilla, GA 31730
229-522-3594
   Fax: 229-522-3597

MITCHELL COUNTY

Southwest Georgia Area Workforce Investment Board
30 E. Board St.
Camilla, GA 31730
229-522-3594

MONROE COUNTY

Middle Georgia Area Consortium, Inc
124 Osigian Blvd, Suite A
Warner Robins, GA 31088
478-953-4771
Toll Free 800-537-1933
Fax: 478-953-2509

MONTGOMERY COUNTY

Heart of Georgia Altamaha Area Job
 Training Unlimited
7 South Dural St.
Claxton, GA 30417
912-739-7158

MORGAN COUNTY

NE Georgia Area Regional Development Center
305 Research Drive
Athens, GA 30605-2795
706-369-5703
Toll Free 800-533-5872
Fax: 706-399-5792

MURRAY COUNTY

NW Georgia Area Coosa Valley Regional Development Center
1 Jackson Hill Drive
Rome, GA 30161
706-295-6485
Toll Free 800-332-1965
Fax: 706-802-5567

MUSCOGEE COUNTY

Lower Chattahoochee Area Columbus
 Consolidated Government Job
 Training Division
420 10th St.
Columbus, GA 31901
706-653-4529

NEWTON COUNTY

NE Georgia Area Regional Development Center
305 Research Drive
Athens, GA 30605-2795
706-369-5703
Toll Free 800-533-5872
Fax: 706-369-5792

OCONEE COUNTY

NE Georgia Area Regional Development Center

305 Research Drive
Athens, GA 30605-2795
706-369-5703
Toll Free 800-533-5872
Fax: 706-369-5792

OGLETHORPE COUNTY

NE Georgia Area Regional development Center
305 Research Drive
Athens, GA 30605-2795
706-369-5703
Toll Free 800-533-5872
Fax: 706-369-5792

PAULDING COUNTY

NW Georgia Area Coosa Valley Regional Development Center
1 Jackson Hill Drive
Rome, Georgia 30161
706-295-6489
Toll Free 800-332-1965
Fax: 706-802-5567

PEACH COUNTY

Middle Georgia Area Consortium,
 Inc.
124 Osigian Blvd. Suite A
Warner Robins, GA 31088
478-953-4771
Toll Free 800-537-1933
Fax: 478-953-2509

PICKENS COUNTY

NW Georgia Area Coosa Valley Regional Development Center
1 Jackson Hill Drive
Rome, GA 30161
706-295-6485
Toll Free 800-332-1965
Fax: 706-802-5567

PIERCE COUNTY

Southeast Georgia Area Regional Development Center

1725 South Georgia Parkway West
Waycross, GA 31503
912-285-6097

PIKE COUNTY

West Central Georgia Area Workforce
    Development Corporation
1710 Highway 16 West
Griffin, GA 30223
770-229-9799
Toll Free 877-633-9799
Fax: 770-229-9924

POLK COUNTY

NW Georgia Area Coosa Valley Regional Development Center
1 Jackson Hill Drive
Rome, GA 30161
706-295-6485
Toll Free 800-332-1965
Fax: 706-802-5567

PULASKI COUNTY

Middle Georgia Area Consortium, Inc.
124 Osigian Blvd. Suite A
Warner Robins, GA 31088
478-953-4771
Toll Free 800-537-1933
Fax: 478-953-2509

PUTMAN COUNTY

Middle Georgia Area Consortium,
    Inc.
124 Osigian Blvd. Suite A
Warner Robins, GA 31088
478-953-4771
Toll Free 800-537-1933
Fax: 478-953-2509

QUITMAN COUNTY

Lower Chattahoochee Area Columbus
    Consolidated Government Job
    Training Division

420 10th St.
Columbus, GA 31901
706-653-4529

RABUN COUNTY

Georgia Mountains Area Workforce
    Investment Board
2481 Hilton Drive Suite B
Gainesville, GA 30501
770-538-2727
770-538-2730

RANDOLPH COUNTY

Lower Chattahoochee Area Columbus
    Consolidated Government Job
    Training Division
420 10th St.
Columbus, GA 31501
706-653-4529

RICHMOND COUNTY

Richmond/Burke Area Job Training
    Authority
209 7th St., 5th Floor
Augusta, GA 30903
706-721-1858
Toll Free 800-735-0205
Fax: 706-721-7395

ROCKDALE COUNTY

Atlanta Regional Area ARC-Workforce Development Division
40 Courtland St., NE
Atlanta, GA 30303-2538
404-463-3100
Toll free-800-516-5872
Fax: 404-463-3105

SCHLEY COUNTY

Middle Flint Area Regional Develop-
    ment Center
228 West Lamer St.
Americus, GA 31709
229-931-2909

SCREVEN COUNTY

East Central Georgia Area Consortium, Inc.
674 Washington Rd., Suite A
Thomson, GA 30824
706-595-8941
Toll Free 800-251-3882
Fax: 706-597-9713

SEMINOLE COUNTY

Southwest Georgia Area Workforce
Investment Board
30 E. Board St.
Camilla, GA 31730
229-522-3594

SPALDING COUNTY

West Central Georgia Area Workforce
Development Corporation
1710 Highway 16 West
Griffin, GA 30223
770-229-9799
Toll Free 877-633-9799
Fax: 770-229-9924

STEPHENS COUNTY

Georgia Mountains Area Workforce
Investment Board
2481 Hilton Drive, Suite B
Gainesville, GA 30501
770-538-2727
770-538-2730

STEWART COUNTY

Lower Chattahoochee Area Columbus
Consolidated Government Job
Training Division
420 10th St.
Columbus, GA 31901
706-653-4529

SUMTER COUNTY

Middle Flint Area Regional Development Center

228 West Lamar St.
Americus, GA 31709
229-931-2909

TALBOT COUNTY

Lower Chattahoochee Area Columbus
Consolidated Government Job
Training Division
420 10th St.
Columbus, GA 31901
706-653-4529

TALIAFERRO COUNTY

East Central Georgia Area Consortium, Inc.
674 Washington Rd., Suite A
Thomson, GA 30824
706-595-9941
Toll Free 800-251-3882
Fax: 706-597-9713

TATTNALL COUNTY

Heart of Georgia Altamaha Area Job
Training Unlimited
7 South Duval St.
Claxton, GA 30417
912-739-7158

TAYLOR COUNTY

Middle Flint Area Regional Development Center
228 West Lamar St.
Americus, GA 31709
229-931-2909

TELFAIR COUNTY

Heart of Georgia Altamaha Area Job
Training unlimited
7 South Duval St.
Claxton, GA 30417
912-739-7158

TERRELL COUNTY

Southwest Georgia Area Workforce
Investment Board

30 E. Board St.
Camilla, GA 31730
229-522-3594

THOMAS COUNTY

Southwest Georgia Area Workforce
 Investment Board
30 E. Board St.
Camilla, GA 31730
229-522-3594

TIFT COUNTY

South Georgia Area Workforce Investment Board
327 W. Savannah Ave.
Valdosta, GA 31601
229-333-5277

TOOMBS COUNTY

Heart of Georgia Altamaha Area Job
 Training Unlimited
7 South Duval St.
Claxton, GA 30417
912-739-7158

TOWNS COUNTY

Georgia Mountains Area Workforce
 Investment Board
2481 Hilton Drive, Suite B
Gainesville, GA 30501
770-538-2727
770-538-2730

TREUTIEN COUNTY

Heart of Georgia Altamaha Area Job
 Training Unlimited
7 South Duval St.
Claxton, GA 30417
912-739-7158

TROUP COUNTY

West Central Georgia Area Workforce
 Development Corporation

1710 Highway 16 West
Griffin, GA 30223
770-229-9799
Toll Free 877-633-9799
Fax: 770-229-9924

TURNER COUNTY

South Georgia Area Workforce Investment Board
327 W. Savannah Ave.
Valdosta, GA 31601
229-333-5277

TWIGGS COUNTY

Middle Georgia Area Consortium,
 Inc.
124 Osigian Blvd. Suite A
Warner Robins, GA 31088
478-953-4771
Toll Free 800-537-1933
Fax: 478-953-2509

UNION COUNTY

Georgia Mountains Area Workforce
 Investment Board
2481 Hilton Drive, Suite B
Gainesville, GA 30501
770-538-2727
770-538-2730

UPSON COUNTY

West Central Georgia Area Workforce
 Development Corporation
1710 Highway 16 West
Griffin, GA 30223
770-229-9799
Toll Free 877-633-9799
Fax: 770-229-9924

WALKER COUNTY

NW Georgia Area Coosa Valley Regional Development Center
1 Jackson Hill Drive

Rome, GA 30223
770-229-9799
Toll Free 800-312-1965
Fax: 706-802-5567

WALTON COUNTY

NE Georgia Area Regional Development Center
305 Research Drive
Athens, GA 30605-2795
706-369-5703
Toll Free 800-533-5872

WARE COUNTY

Southeast Georgia Area Regional Development Center
1725 South Georgia Parkway West
Waycross, GA 31503
912-285-6097

WARREN COUNTY

East Central Georgia Area Consortium, Inc.
674 Washington Rd., Suite A
Thomson, GA 30824
706-595-8941
Toll Free 800-251-3882
Fax: 706-597-9713

WASHINGTON COUNTY

East Central Georgia Area Consortium, Inc.
674 Washington Rd., Suite A
Thomson, GA 30824
706-595-8941
Toll Free 800-251-3882
Fax: 706-597-9713

WAYNE COUNTY

Heart of Georgia Altamaha Area Job Training Unlimited
7 South Duval St.
Claxton, GA 30417
912-739-7158

WEBSTER COUNTY

Middle Flint Area Regional Development Center
228 West Lamar St.
Americus, GA 31709
229-931-2909

WHEELER COUNTY

Heart of Georgia Altamaha Area Job Training Unlimited
7 Duval St.
Claxton, GA 30417
912-739-7158

WHITE COUNTY

Georgia Mountains Area Workforce Investment Board
2481 Hilton Drive, Suite B
Gainesville, GA 30501
770-538-2727
770-538-2730

WHITFIELD COUNTY

Georgia Area Coosa Valley Regional Development Center
1 Jackson Hill Drive
Rome, GA 30161
706-295-6485
Toll Free 800-332-1965
Fax: 706-802-5567

WILCOX COUNTY

Heart of Georgia Altamaha Area Job Training Unlimited
7 Duval St.
Claxton, GA 30417
912-739-7158

WILKES COUNTY

East Central Georgia Area Consortium, Inc.
674 Washington Rd., Suite A
Thomson, GA 30824
706-595-8941

Toll Free 800-251-3882
Fax: 706-597-97133

WILKINSON COUNTY

Middle Georgia Area Consortium,
  Inc.
124 Osigian Blvd, Suite A
Warner Robins, GA 31088
478-953-4771

Toll Free 800-537-1933
Fax: 478-953-2509

WORTH COUNTY

Southwest Georgia Area Workforce
  Investment, Inc.
30 E. Board St.
Camilla, GA 31730
229-522-3594

HAWAII

Goodwill Industries of Hawaii, Inc.
2610 Kilihau St.
Honolulu, HI 96819-2020
808-836-0313
www.higoodwill.org
info@higoodwill.org

    Goodwill industries of Hawaii, Inc., provides occupational skills training, job placement, and support services to people with various barriers to employment.

John Howard Association
200 N. Vineyard Blvd. Suite 330
Honolulu, HI 96817
808-537-2917
jha@hula.net

    Provides counseling and related services for individuals involved in the criminal justice system, individuals with criminal records, delinquents, at-risk youth, and adjudicated youthful offenders and their families, halfway houses for female offenders, transitional residence for adjudicated youth, anger management programs for juvenile offenders, and public education on corrections, crime prevention and alternatives to incarceration.

YMCA of Oahu
1040 Richards St.
Honolulu, HI 96813
808-538-7061
www.ymcaoahu.org

    The YMCA provides programs in the areas

of social development, job development and skills training, childcare, and transitional housing.

Department of Labor and Industrial Relations

Big Island-Hawaii
Employer Services
1990 Kinoole St., Room 101
Hilo, HI 96720-5203
808-974-4095
Fax: 808-974-4085
E-mail: DLIR Employer Services Hilo

Kauai Island
Employer Services
3-3100 Kuhio Hwy Suite 12
Lihue, HI 96766-1153
808-274-3025
Fax: 808-274-3046
E-mail: DLIR Employer Tax

Maui Island
Employer Services
54 S. High St., Room 201
Wailuku, HI 96793
808-984-8410
Fax: 808-984-8444
Fax: 808-675-0025
E-mail: DLIR Employer Services
  Maui

Oahu-Island
Employer Services
830 Punchbowl St., Room 437
Honolulu, HI 96813
808-586-8915
Fax: 808-586-8929
E-mail: DLUR UI Employer Tax
E-mail: QWRS software/wage reports
This organization provides employment assistance to ex-offenders.

One-Step Centers

www.hawaii.gov/abor/wdd/

HILO
1990 Kinoole St.
Hilo, HI 96720
808-981-2860

HONOLULU
830 Punchbowl St. #112
Honolulu, HI 96813
808-586-8700

KANOHE
45-1141 Kamehameha Hwy.
Kaneohe, HI 96744
806-233-3700

KAUAI
3100 Kuhio Hwy. C-9
Lihue, HI 96766
808-274-3060

KONA
74-5665 Luhia St. #C-4
Kailua-Kona, HI 96740
808-327-4770
They offer workshops in resume writing, job search, dress for workplace and interviewing techniques.

MAUI
2064 Wells St. #108
Wailuku, HI 96763
808-984-2091

MOLOKAI
55 Makaena Place
Room 4
Kaunakakai, HI 96748
808-563-1755

WAIPAHU
Waipahu Civic Center
94-275 Mokuota St. #300
Waipahu, HI 96797
808-575-0010

IDAHO

CURE
Lewiston, ID
208-798-3041
cureidaho@qmail.com
   CURE is a grassroots organization from top to bottom. It does not hire professional leaders. Instead, its leaders came from the ranks of people formerly in prison and family members of friends of prisoners. This organization provides services to ex-offenders.

Department of Commerce and Labor
317 W. Main St.

Boise, ID 83735
208-332-3575
www.idahoworks.org
   This center offers more than 17 programs: a variety of self-service options, a comprehensive resource center, and staff are available at each career center.

Idaho Works Career Center
317 W. Main St.
Boise, ID 83735
208-334-6112
RMADSEN@jobservice.us

www.idahoworks.org/IW_career.shtml
This center offers more than 17 programs: a variety of self-service options, a comprehensive resource center, and staff are available at each career center.

Idaho Department of Labor Workforce Offices

Blackfoot County Office
155 North Maple
Blackfoot, ID 83221-0009
208-236-6713
Fax: 208-785-5036

Blaine County Office
513 Main St., Suite 1
Halley, ID 83333-8417
208-788-3526
Fax: 208-788-3041

Bonners Ferry County Office
6541 Main St.
Bonners Ferry, ID 83805-8521
208-267-5581
Fax: 208-267-3797

Canyon County Office
4514 Thomas Jefferson St.
Caldwell, ID 83605-5100
208-364-7781
Fax: 208-454-7720

Coeur d'Alene County Office
1221 W. Ironwood Drive, Suite 200
Coeur d'Alene, ID 83814-1402
208-769-1558
Fax: 208-769-1574

Emmett County Office
2030 South Washington
Emmett, ID 83617-9450
208-364-7780
Fax: 208-365-6599

Grangeville County Office
305 North State St.
P.O. Box 550

Grangesville, ID 83530-0550
208-983-0440
Fax: 208-983-0302

Idaho Falls County Office
1515 E. Lincoln Rd.
Idaho, ID 83401-3653
208-557-2500
Fax: 208-525-7268

Magic Valley County Office
420 Falls Ave.
Twin, ID 83301-3320
208-735-2500
Fax: 208-736-3007

McCall County Office
299 S. 3rd St.
McCall, ID 83638-0966
208-634-7102
Fax: 208-634-2965

Meridian County Office
205 E. Watertower Lane
Meridian, ID 83642-6282
208-364-7785
Fax: 208-895-8441

Moscow County Office
1350 Troy Rd., Suite 1
Moscow, ID 83843-3995
208-882-7571
Fax: 208-882-8324

Mountain County Office
1993 East 8th North
Mountain Home, ID 83647-2333
Fax: 208-587-2964

Orofino County Office
410 Johnson Ave.
P.O. Box 391
Orofino, ID 83544-0391
208-476-5506
Fax: 208-476-3471

Pocatello County Office
430 North 5th Ave.
Pocatello, ID 83205-4087

208-236-6710
Fax: 208-232-0865

Rexburg County Office
1133 Sticks Ave.
Rexburg, ID 83440-0158
208-557-2501
Fax: 208-356-0042

Salmon County Office
1301 Main St., Suite 1
Salmon, ID 83467
208-756-2234
Fax: 208-756-4672

Sandpoint County Office
2101 West Pine St.

Sandpoint, ID 83864-9327
208-263-7544
Fax: 208-265-0193

Silver County Office
35 Wildcat, Suite A
Kellogg, ID 83837-2253
208-783-1202
Fax: 208-783-5561

Soda Springs County Office
95 E. Hooper Ave. #20
P.O. Box 576
Soda Springs, ID 83276
208-236-6711
Fax: 208-547-4763

ILLINOIS

Chicago Jobs Council
29 E. Madison St.
Chicago, IL 60602
312-252-0460
www.cjc.net
   An organization of 100 community based, organizations, civic groups, and businesses that give direct assistance as well as advocate for better public policy surrounding jobs and public education.

Chicago Legal Advocacy for Incarcerated Mothers
70 East Lake St.
Suite 1120
Chicago, Il 60601-5959
312-675-0912
http://claim-il.org/thirdcoast/claim-il.org/index.html
   Chicago Legal Advocacy for Incarcerated Mothers (CLAIM) provides legal and educational services to maintain the bond between imprisoned mothers and their children. CLAIM advocates for policies and programs that benefit families of imprisoned mothers and reduce incarceration of women and girls. Will accept

collect calls from correctional facilities at: 312-675-0911.

Community Re-entry Project
661 E. 79th St.
Chicago, Il 60619
773-874-7390
www.members.tripod.com/TheFreedom Train/CRPabout.html
   This program is designed to approach to transitional problems experienced by the ex-offender, in a holistic systematic fashion. This involves connecting community resources with the specific problems returned offenders will encounter.

CURE
4904 S Drexel Blvd
Chicago, Il 60615
madeoday@qmail.com
www.incure.org
   CURE is a grassroots organization from top to bottom. It does not hire professional leaders. Instead, its leaders come from the ranks of people formerly in prison and family members of friends of prisoners. This organization offers assistance to ex-offenders.

Prison Mail
P.O. Box 1244
Wheaton, IL 60189
http://www.prisonmail.org/

Prison Mail believes that maintaining relationships with family and friends is vital both to inmate as well as to those on the outside. Their service (for a monthly fee) makes communications a bit easier.

Rita's Ministry
P.O. Box 248
Aurora, Il 60507
630-966-0252
http://www.ritasministry.org/

Restoring Inmates to America's Society provides transitional assistance to ex-offenders and their families.

Safer Foundation
571 West Jackson Blvd
Chicago, IL 60861
312-922-2200
www.saferfoundation.org

This organization offers a variety of post-release services to former prisoners in Illinois. Write for more details.

St. Leonard's Ministries
2100 W. Warren Blvd.
Chicago, IL 60612
312-738-1414

Residential care and case management for recently released individuals, mental health referrals, programs to strengthen families and employment services.

Women's Self-Employment Project
S. Lasalle St. Suite 1850
Chicago, IL 60603
312-606-8255
www.wsep.net

Entrepreneurial training to low-income women on how to start your own business.

Local Area Workforce Centers

WORKFORCE INVESTMENT AREA 1

Lake County Workforce Development Department

Chris Stevens Director
1 N Genesee St. First Floor
Waukengan, IL 60085
847-377-2225
Fax: 847-949-6538
cstevens@lakecountyil.gov
www.lakecountyjobcenter.com

Lake County Workforce Investment Board
Manager: Vicky Gordon
1 N. Genesee St. First Floor
Waukengan, IL 60085
847-377-2225
Fax: 847:949-6538
Vgordon@lakecountyil.gov
http://lakecountyjobcenter.com/work_force_board/index.htm

LOCAL AREA WORKFORCE AREA 2

McHenry County Workforce Investment Department
Assistant Director: Mary Wolff
815-338-7100. Ext 228
WIB Director: Carl Martens
815-338-7100 Ext. 214
cwmarten@co.mchenry.il.us

McHenry County Workforce Network
Director: Julie Courtney
500 Russell Court
Woodstock, IL 60098
815-338-7100. Ext. 218
Fax: 815-338-7125
jacourtn@co.mchenry.Il.us
www.Mchenrycountyworkforce.org

WORKFORCE INVESTMENT AREA 3

Boone and Winnebago Counties Workforce Investment Board, Inc.
Executive Director: Darcy Buchoiz
3134 Eleventh St.
Rockford, Il 61109
815-395-6609

Fax: 815-229-2796
dbuchoiz@theworkforceconnection.org
www.theworkforceconnection.org

Rock River Training Corporation
Executive Director: Michael Williams
303 N. Main St.
Rockford, IL 61101
815-395-8012
mwilliams@rockrivertraining.org

WORKFORCE INVESTMENT AREA 4

Northwest Illinois Workforce Investment Board
Manager: Kate Ramsey
500 Gusty Trail
Pearl City, Il 61062
815-443-2535
Fax: 815-443-2535 (call first)
Katewib4@aeroinc.net

Partners for Employment
Executive Director Kathy Day
315 B First Ave.
Sterling, IL 61081
815-625-3623. Ext. 103
815-625-3664
Kathy.Day@highland.edu
Program Coordinator: Sharel Wolber
Sharel.Wolber@highland.edu

WORKFORCE INVESTMENT AREA 5

River Valley Workforce Investment Board
150 S. Lincolnway, Suite 200
North Aurora, IL 60542
630-859-9923
Fax 630-859-9928
www.rivervalleywib.org

WORKFORCE INVESTMENT AREA 6

DuPage County Workforce Development Division
Director: Sue Clark
2525 Cabot Drive, Suite 302
Lisle, IL 60532

630-955-2044
Fax 630-955-2046
Kane County
Executive Director: Sheila McCraven
719 South Batavia, Building A
Geneva, IL 60134
630-232-5932
Fax: 630-208-0116
mccravensheila@co.kane.il.us
www.worknetdupage.org

WORKFORCE INVESTMENT AREA 7

Cook County President's Office of Employment Training
Director: Karen Crawford
69 W. Washington St., Suite 2860
Chicago, IL 60602
312-603-0208
Fax: 312-603-9991
kscrawf@cookcountygov.com

Cook County Workforce Investment Board
Lead Staff: George M. Ward
202 S. Halsted, ATOC Building, Prairie State College
Chicago Heights, IL 60411
708-709-7895
Fax: 708-709-7832
GWARD@cookcountygov.com

WORKFORCE INVESTMENT AREA 8

Illinois WorkNet Center Arlington Heights and Evanston Business and Career Services, Inc.
Center Manager: Al Saulys
723 W. Algonquin Rd.
Arlington Heights, IL 60005
847-437-9395
Fax: 847-981-7493
asaulys@worknetncc.com

The Workforce Board of Northern Cook County
Executive Director: Jennifer Serino-Stasch

2604 E. Dempster, Suite 502
Park Ridge, Il 60068
847-699-0105
Fax: 847-699-9155
istasch@workforceboard.org

The Workforce Boards of Metropolitan Chicago
Regional Coordinator: Jan Etzkorn
214 N. Ottawa St.
Joliet, IL 60432
217-553-2560
Fax: 815-727-5669
Jetz66@aol.com

WORKFORCE INVESTMENT AREA 9

Chicago Department of Family and Support Services
Office of Police and Advocacy: Christian Denes
312-743-1527
Fax: 312-743-0400
Christian_denes@cityofchicago.org

Chicago Workforce Board
Acting Executive Director: Joanna Greene
60 W. Randolph, Suite 200
Chicago, IL 60601
312-644-3739
Fax: 312-644-6399
jgreene@chicagoworkforceboard.com

City of Chicago Department of Community Development
Director of Policy: Jeffery C. Marcella
1615 W. Chicago Ave.
Chicago, Il 60622
312-746-7464
Fax: 312-746-7878
jmarcella@cityofchicago.org
www.cityofchicago.org/mowd

WORKFORCE INVESTMENT AREA 10

City of Chicago Department of Community Development

Project Coordinator of Policy: Carole Ko
312-746-7116
Fax: 312-746-7878
caroleko@cityofchicago.org

Workforce Investment Board of Will County
Manager: Pat Fera
214 N. Ottawa St.
Joliet, IL 60432
815-727-5670
Fax: 815-727-5669
pfera@willcountyillinois.com
www.willcountyworkforceboard.com

Workforce Services Division of Will County
Sue Flessner, Administrative Manager
815-727-444 Ext. 124
Fax: 815-727-5669
sflessner@willcountyillinois.com
www.jobs4people.org

WORKFORCE INVESTMENT AREA 11

Grundy Livingston Kankakee Workforce Board
Executive Director: Elisabeth Dunbar
187 S. Schuyler Ave., Suite 560
Kankakee, IL 60901
815-935-0074
Fax: 815-936-3766
edunbar@glkwb.com
Program Director: Ladonna Russell
lrussell@glkwb.com

Grundy Workforce Services
Director of Workforce Development: Sandy Mol
1715 N. Division St.
Morris, IL 60450
815-942-0566
Fax: 815-942-1547
smol@jjc.edu

Kankakee Workforce Services
Director: Margaret Cooper

202 N Schuyler Ave., Suite 201
Kankakee, IL 60901
815-802-8962
Fax: 815-933-0370
mcooper@kcc.edu
Assistant Director: Mary Jo Martyn
815-802-8964
mmartyn@kcc.edu

WORKFORCE INVESTMENT AREA 12

Business Employment Skills Team, Inc.
Executive Director: Pam Furlan
3691 Cougar Drive, Unit B
Peru, IL 61354
Pmfurlan@aol.com
www.best-inc.org

NCI Works, Inc.
Chief Financial Officer: Becky Lambert
3691 Cougar Drive Unit B
Peru, IL 61354
815-224-7930
Fax: 815-224-7933
Beck_lambert@best-inc.org
www.nciworks.org

WORKFORCE INVESTMENT AREA 13

Partners in Job Training and Placement
Assistant Division Manager: Jeanette
  Dawson
4703 16th St. Suite H
Moline, IL 61265
309-736-9621. Ext. 107
Fax: 309-764-0156
idawson@pitp.org

Workforce Development Board of
  Rock Island, Henry, and Mercer
  Counties
Director: Chuck Stewart
1504 Third Ave.
Rock Island, IL 61201
209-793-5206
Fax: 309-793-5204
cstewart@pitp.org

WORKFORCE INVESTMENT AREA 14

LWA 14 Western Illinois
Director, Blanche Shoup
49 North Prairie, Suite B. P.O. Box
  231
Galesburg, IL 61402
309-344-1575
Fax: 309-344-2446
lwa14@grics.net

WORKFORCE INVESTMENT AREA 15

City of Peoria Workforce Development Department
Director: Ali Bashir
211 Fulton, Suite 300
Peoria, IL 61602
309-495-8920
Fax: 309-495-8999
bali@workforcenetwork.com

WORKFORCE INVESTMENT AREA 16

United Workforce Development
  Board
Executive Director: Gary Cicciu
207 E. Hamilton Rd.
Bloomington, IL 61704
309-826-0040
Fax: 309-828-2967
gcicci@careerlink16.com
www.careerlink16.com
Division Manager: Paula Nachtrieb
309-495-8926
pnachtrie@workforcenetwork.com
www.workforcenetwork.com
Division Manager: Bruce Marston
309-495-8924
Brnaston@workforcenetwork.com

WORKFORCE INVESTMENT AREA 17

Champaign Consortium
Executive Director: Al Anderson
1307 N. Mattis Ave.
Champaign, IL 61821

217-278-5700. Ext. 230
Fax: 217-398-9641
Alanders_55@yahoo.com
Assistant Director: Joanne Freeman
217-278-5700. Ext 222
chamcons@aol.com
Customer Service Unit Chief: Rick
Krandel
217-278-5700. Ext. 205
www.cuatwork.org

WORKFORCE INVESTMENT AREA 18

Vermillion County Job Training Partnership
Executive Director: Brian Hensgen
407 N. Franklin St.
Danville, IL 61832
217-442-3044. Ext. 235
Fax: 217-442-0305
bhensgen@dacc.edu
www.vermillioncountyietc.com
Coordinator of Adult and Dislocated
Workers Services: Jonathan Jett
217-442-3044. Ext. 239
jjett@dacc.edu

WORKFORCE INVESTMENT AREA 19

Workforce Investment Solutions
Program Manager: Karen Alien
757 W. Pershing Rd.
Decatur, Il 62526
217-875-8750. Ext. 231
Fax: 217-872-5883
kallen@mdwis.org
Executive Director: Robyn McCoy
217-872-5870
Fax: 217-872-2275
Mccoy5889@aol.com
www.worknet119.org

WORKFORCE INVESTMENT AREA 20

Land Of Lincoln Workforce Alliance
Executive Director: Anna Schneider
1300 S. Ninth St.

Springfield, IL 62703
Fax: 217-524-6096
aschneider@worknet20.org
Program Services Director: Sharmin
Doering
217-535-3288
Fax: 217-535-3119
shard@co.sangamon.il.us
www.worknet20.org

LOCAL WORKFORCE INVESTMENT AREA 21

West Central Development Council
Executive Director: Mik Arnett
116 S. Plum St. P.O. Box 260
Carlinville, IL 62626-0260
217-854-9642
Fax: 217-854-4765
mik@west-central.org

WORKFORCE INVESTMENT AREA 22

Madison County Employment and
Training Department
Executive Director: Dave Stoecklin
101 E. Edwardsville Rd.
Wood River, Il 62095
618-296-4310
Fax: 618-656-6945
dstoecklin@mceld.org
Assistant Executive Director: Matt
Jones
618-296-4315
mjones@MCETD.org
www.madisonbondwib.org

WORKFORCE INVESTMENT AREA 23

CrossRd.s Workforce Board
Executive Director: James Mc Shane 111
80 Broadway, Suite 101
Mattoon, IL 61938-9650
217-235-2942, Ext. 8225
Fax: 217-235-2943
jmcshane@cwib.net
www.cwib.net

WORKFORCE INVESTMENT AREA 24

CEFS Economic Opportunity Corp.
Director, Workforce Development:
  Kevin Bushur
1805 Banker St.
Effingham, IL 62454
217-342-2193. Ext. 117
Fax: 217-342-4701
kbushur@cefseoc.org
Workforce Training Supervisor:
  Elaine Nuding
217-342-2023
enuding@cefseoc.org

Mid America Workforce Investment
  Board
Manager: Scott L. Rhoden
19 Public Square, Suite 200
Belleville, IL 62220
618-277-6790. Ext. 3254
Fax: 618-277-1877
scott@jgd.org
Andrea Applegate
217-235-2942. Ext. 8224
AApplegate@cwib.net
Robert Stephenson
216 E. Main St.
Olney, IL 62450
618-392-7777
Fax: 618-392-7015
bstephenson@cwib.net
www.mawib.com

WORKFORCE INVESTMENT AREA 25

Intergovernmental Grants Department
Division Manager: Melinda Nicholson
618-277-6790. Ext. 3257
Fax: 618-355-4279
mnicholson@jgd.org

Program Development Supervisor:
  Narilyn Stringfellow
618-277-6790. Ext. 3266
mstringfellow@jdg.org
Chris Johnson
618-277-6790. Ext. 3259
Chris@igd.org

Man-TraCon Corporation
Chief Executive Officer: Kathy
  Lively
3000 W. DeYoung St., Suite 800-B
Marion, IL 62959
618-998-0970. Ext. 237
Fax: 618-996-1291
kathylively@mantracon.org
Adult Program Director: Michelle
  Cerutti
618-998-0970. Ext. 229
michellecerutti@mantracon.org
Business Services Administrator:
  Rosie Robinson
618-998-0970. Ext. 224
rosierobinson@mantracon.org
Roxanne Brewer-Coffey
618-998-0970. Ext. 271
Roxannebrewer-coffey@mantracon.org

WORKFORCE INVESTMENT AREA 26

Gateway Workforce Solutions
Consultant: Bill Hanke
618-972-2903
Fax:618-692-1912
bhanke@charter.net
Southern 14-Workforce Investment
  Board, Inc.
Executive Coordinator: James Murphy
P.O. Box 186
Carmi, IL 62821
618-382-5024
Fax:618-382-7038
jmurphy@shawneelink.net

INDIANA

The Adult Center for Education, a
Fletcher Place Ministry
1831 E. Prosepct Ave.
Indianapolis, IN 46203
317-916-1427

The first program, Survival Skills, is a ten-week series of seminars that teach basic day-to-day life skills. Upon graduation from Survival Skills, computer training, writing workshops and job placement assistance are available.

CURE
P.O. Box 62
Camby, IN 46113
317-831-0765
novaalpha@aol.com
www.incure.org

CURE is a grassroots organization from top to bottom. It does not hire professional leaders. Instead, its leaders come from the ranks of people formerly in prison and family members of friends of prisoners. This organization offers assistance to ex-offenders.

Dismas House of Michiana
521 S. St. Joseph St.
PO Box 4571
South Bend, IN 46634
574-233-8522
www.dismas.org

Dismas House is a supportive community shared by recently released inmates, college students, and local volunteers. Typical length of stay is four to six months. Residents are expected to find employment and leave the community with a stable income, sense of self-worth and hope for a sober and productive future.

OAR-Offender Aid and Restoration
1426 W. 29th Suite 101
Indianapolis, IN 46208
317-612-6804

Assists those recently released from the Mar-

ion County jail, providing substance abuse therapy information and referral to needed services, and placement in job training programs.

PACE-Public Action in Correctional
Effort-Case Management
1426 W. 29th St. Suite 204
Indianapolis, IN 46208
317-612-6800

Serves as counselors to ex-offenders seeking assistance with employment, housing, food clothing, and personal problems. Job seeking skills are taught and job referrals are maintained for client use.

Prison Ministries of Indiana
PO Box 199242
Indianapolis, IN 46219
317-927-0007
www.prisonministries.info
danberlinpmi@aol.com

Provides assistance to recently released inmates in the form of information and referral to needed services, placement in job training programs, as well as providing assistance in obtaining housing, food and clothing.

Salvation Army Adult Rehabilitation
Center
711 Washington St.
Indianapolis, IN 46202
317-638-6585

Provides counseling and work therapy as part of a residential rehabilitation program for ex-offenders, alcoholics, and drug abusers. Program length is usually six months. Services adult males 21 and older only.

WorkOne Region 1

JASPER COUNTY

Rensselaer Express
116 N. Van Rensselaer St.
Rensselaer, IN 47978

219-866-4330
Fax: 219-866-2748

LAKE COUNTY

Crown Point Center Express
1166 N Main St.
Crown Point, IN 46307
219-661-8985
Fax: 219-661-8916

East Chicago Center Express
4818 Indianapolis, IN 46312
219-398-2601
Fax: 219-392-8637

Gary WorkOne
3522 Village Circle (Old Shopping
   Village Shopping Center)
Gary, IN 46409
219-981-1520
219-981-4100
Fax: 219-884-5148

Hammond WorkOne Columbia Plaza
   Center
5243 Hohman Ave.
Hammond, IN 46320
219-933-8332
Fax: 219-933-8370

LAPORTE COUNTY

Michigan City Express
344 Dunes Plaza
Michigan City, IN 46360
219-872-5575
Fax: 219-873-3226

WorkOne LaPorte Sagamore Center
300 Legacy Plaza W.
LaPorte, IN 46350
219-362-2175
219-362-1198

NEWTON COUNTY

Morocco Express
4117 S. 240 W. Suite 400

Morocco, IN 47963
800-661-2258
Fax: 219-285-2213

PORTER COUNTY

WorkOne Portage Center
Ameriplex Commercial Park
1575 Adler Circle, Suite A
Portage, IN 46368
219-762-6592
Fax: 219-762-1052

WorkOne Valparaiso
3100 Ivy Tech Drive
Valparaiso, IN 46383
219-476-4764
Fax: 219-476-4760

PULASKI COUNTY

WorkOne Express Winamac
123 N. Market St., Suite A
Winamac, IN 46996
574-946-6300
Fax: 574-946-3628

STARKE COUNTY

Knox Express
53 W. Lake St.
Knox, IN 46534
574-772-6882
Fax: 574-772-6899

WorkOne Region 2

ELKHART COUNTY

WorkOne Elkhart
430 Waterfall Drive
Elkhart, IN 46516
574-295-0105
Fax: 574-228-3282

FULTON COUNTY

Rochester Express
909 Main St., Suite 101

Rochester, IN 46975
574-223-8542
Fax: 574-223-6172

KOSCITIUSKO COUNTY

Warsaw Express
715 S Buffalo St.
Warsaw, IN 46580
574-269-3050
Fax: 574-268-2391

MARSHALL COUNTY

Marshall County WorkOne Express
  Center
316 Kingston Rd.
Plymouth, IN 46563
574-936-8919
Fax: 574-936-5112

ST. JOSEPH COUNTY

WorkOne St. Joseph County
851 S. Maretta St.
South Board, IN 46618
574-237-9675
Fax: 574-239-2672

WorkOne Region 3

ADAMS COUNTY
126 S 1st St.
Decatar, IN 46733
260-724-2037
Fax:260-724-7513

ALLEN COUNTY
201 E. Rudsill Blvd., Suite 102
Ft. Wayne, IN 46606
260-745-3555
Fax: 260-745-7757

DEKALB COUNTY
936 W. 15th St.
Auburn, IN 46706

260-925-0124
Fax: 260-925-5118

GRANT COUNTY
Grant County Center
850 N. Miller Ave.
Marion, IN 46952
765-668-8911
Fax: 765-662-7499

HUNTINGTON COUNTY
Huntington County Express
1314 Flaxmill Rd.
Huntington, IN 46750
260-356-7109
Fax: 260-366-7114

LAGRANGE COUNTY
LaGrange County Express
848 N. Detroit St.
LaGrange, IN 46761
260-499-4835
Fax: 260-499-4836

NOBLE COUNTY
524 Professional Way
Kandallville, IN 46755
260-599-1000
Fax: 260-599-1001

STEUBEN COUNTY
Steuben County Express
317 S. Wayne St., Suite 1D
Angola, IN 46703
260-665-7541
Fax: 260-655-7160

WABASH COUNTY
Wabash County Express
1143 N. Cass St.
Wabash, IN 46703
260-563-8421
Fax: 260-563-8424

WELLS COUNTY

Wells County Express
3156 E. State Rd.
Bluffton, IN 46714
260-824-0865
Fax: 260-824-0859

WHITLEY COUNTY

Whitley County Express
119 Hoosier Drive
Columbia, IN 46725
260-246-8611
Fax: 260-248-8318

WorkOne Region 4

BENTON COUNTY

Benton County residents may seek services from any WorkOne location in Indiana

CARROLL COUNTY

Carroll County residents may seek services from any WorkOne location in Indiana.

CASS COUNTY

Logansport Express
P.O. Box 7014
1 Ivy Tech Way
Logansport, IN 46947
574-722-6652
Fax: 574-753-8653

CLINTON COUNTY

Frankfort Express
1111 S Jackson St.
Frankfort, IN 46041
765-654-5400
Fax: 765-654-6382

FOUNTAIN COUNTY

Covington Express
P.O. Box 188
418 Washington St.
Covington, IN 47932
765-793-4861
Fax: 765-793-4884

HOWARD COUNTY

WorkOne Kokomo
P.O. Box 1371
709 S. Reed Rd.
Kokomo, IN 46903
765-459-0571
Fax: 765-457-3144

MIAMI COUNTY

Peru WorkOne Express
425 W. Main St.
Peru, IN 46970
765-472-3562
Fax: 765-473-8654

MONTGOMERY COUNTY

Crawfordsville Express
201 E. Jefferson St.
Crawfordville, IN 47933
765-362-4096
Fax: 765-362-4471

TIPPECANOE COUNTY

Workone Lafayette
620 Park East Blvd.
Lafayette, IN 46905
765-474-5411
Fax: 474-7036

TIPTON COUNTY

Tipton Express
1202 S. Main St, Suite A
Tipton, IN 46072
765-675-2545
Fax: 765-675-2853

WARREN COUNTY

Warren County residents mat seek services from any WorkOne location in the state of Indiana.

WHITE COUNTY

1500 E. North Main St.
Monticello, IN 47960

574-583-4128
Fax: 574-583-4128

WorkOne Region 5

BOONE COUNTY

Lebanon Express
125 Lakeshore Drive
Lebanon, IN 46052
765-482-0160
Fax: 765-482-0178

HAMILTON COUNTY

Fishers Express
10204 Lantern Rd.
Fishers, IN 46037
317-841-8194
Fax: 317-841-8275

HANCOCK COUNTY

Greenfield Express
836 S. State St.
Greenfield, IN 46140
317-462-7711
Fax: 317-462-6340

HENDRICKS COUNTY

Hendricks County residents may seek services at any WorkOne location in Indiana.

JOHNSON COUNTY

Franklin Express
600 Banta St.
Franklin, IN 46131
317-736-5531
Fax: 317-736-8402

MADISON COUNTY

222 E. 10th St., Suite B
Anderson, IN 46016
765-642-4981
Fax: 765-641-6557

MORGAN COUNTY

WorkOne Mooresville Express
490 St. Clair St.

Mooresville, IN 46158
317-834-3907
Fax: 317-834-4937

SHELBY COUNTY

WorkOne Shelbyville
2325 Intelliplex Dr. Suite 204
Shelbyville, IN 46176
317-392-3251
Fax: 317-392-3419

WorkOne Region 6

BLACKFORD COUNTY

Blackford County WorkOne Center
1301 N. High St., Suite B
Hartford City, IN 47348
765-348-4928
Fax: 765-348-9930

DELAWARE COUNTY

Delaware County WorkOne Center
P.O. Box 1407
201 E. Charles St., Suite 100
Muncie, IN 47305
765-741-1861 Ext. 1232

FAYETTE COUNTY

Fayette County WorkOne Center
710 Eastern Ave.
Connersville, IN 47331
765-825-3191 Ext. 232
Fax: 765-825-9659

HENRY COUNTY

Henry County WorkOne Center
3011 S. 14th St.
New Castle, IN 47362
765-529-3010 Ext. 221
Fax: 765-521-2779

JAY COUNTY

Jay County WorkOne Center
107 S. Meridian St.

Portland, IN 47371
260-726-8315 Ext. 221
Fax: 260-726-8431

RANDOLPH COUNTY

Randolph County WorkOne Center
Winchester, IN 47394
765-584-5627 Ext. 10
Fax: 260-584-2536

RUSH COUNTY

Rush County WorkOne Center
103 N. Morgan St.
Rushville, IN 45173
765-932-5921 Ext. 21
Fax: 260-938-4127

WAYNE COUNTY

Wayne County WorkOne Center
3771 South W.
Richmond, IN 47374
765-962-8591 Ext. 257
Fax: 260-966-3431

WorkOne Region 7

CLAY COUNTY

Clay County Express
17 W. National St.
Brazil, IN 47834
812-448-2636
Fax: 812-448-2638

PARKE COUNTY

Parke County Express
110 S. Market St.
Rockville, IN 47872
765-569-2021
Fax: 765-569-2023

PUTNAM COUNTY

Putnam County Express
620 Tennessee St., Suite 8
Greencastle, IN 46135

765-653-2421
Fax: 765-653-2423

SULLIVAN COUNTY

Sullivan County Express
35 W. Jackson St.
Sullivan, IN 47882
812-268-3358
Fax: 812-268-3359

VERMILLION COUNTY

Vermillion County Express
1302 N. 9th St.
Clinton, IN 47842
765-832-3523
Fax: 765-838-3625

VIGO COUNTY

WorkOne Terre Haute
30 N. 9th St.
Terre Haute, IN 47808
812-234-6602
Fax: 812-234-7644

WorkOne Region 8

BROWN COUNTY

Nashville Express
P.O. Box 699
240 East Main St.
Nashville, IN 47448
812-988-6968
Fax: 812-988-5780

DAVIESS COUNTY

Washington Express
8 NE 21 St.
Washington, IN 47501
812-254-7734
Fax: 812-264-7736

GREENE COUNTY

WorkOne Linton
P.O. Box 69

1600 N.E. A St.
Linton, IN 47441
812-547-4479
Fax: 812-547-2025

LAWRENCE COUNTY
WorkOne Bedford
P.O. Box 40
918 10th St., Suite 200
Bedford, IN 47421
812-279-4400
Fax: 812-279-9207

MARTIN COUNTY
WorkOne Loogootee Express
123 Cooper St.
Loogootee, IN 47553
812-295-2722
Fax: 812-295-5424

MONROE COUNTY
WorkOne Bloomington
P.O. Box 3000
4501 Landmark Ave.
Bloomington, IN 47402
812-331-6000
Fax: 812-331-6010

ORANGE COUNTY
Paoli Express
1075 N Sandy Hook Rd.
Paoli, IN 47454
812-723-2369
Fax: 812-723-2379

OWEN COUNTY
Spencer Express
205 E. Morgan St., Suite B
Spencer, IN 47460
812-829-6511
Fax: 812-829-1631

WorkOne Region 9
BARTHOLOMEW COUNTY
WorkOne Columbus

4555 Central Ave., Suite 1300
Columbus, IN 47203
812-376-3351
Fax: 812-372-7626

DEARBORN COUNTY
WorkOne Lawrenceburg
230 Mary Ave., Suite100
Lawrenceburg, IN 47025
812-537-1117
Fax: 812-537-4046

DECATUR COUNTY
Greenburg Express
1820 N. Broadway St.
Greenburg, IN 47240
812-663-8597
Fax: 812-662-6205

JACKSON COUNTY
Seymour Express
212 W. 2nd St.
Seymour, IN 47274
812-522-9074
Fax: 812-523-6109

JEFFERSON COUNTY
WorkOne Madison
P.O. Box 1078
620 Green Rd.
Madison, IN 47250
812-346-6030
Fax: 812-265-1805

JENNINGS COUNTY
North Vernon Express
P.O.Box 963
1200 W.OandM Ave.
North Vernon, IN 47625
812-346-6030
Fax: 812-346-6036

OHIO COUNTY
Ohio County residents may seek services from any WorkOne location in the state of Indiana.

RIPLEY COUNTY

Ripley County residents may seek services from any WorkOne location in the state of Indiana.

SWITZERLAND COUNTY

Switzerland County residents may seek services from any WorkOne location in the state of Indiana.

WorkOne Region 10

CLARK COUNTY

Jeffersonville Express
1613 E. 8th St.
Jeffersonville, IN 47130
812-283-6595
Fax: 812-283-6835

CRAWFORD COUNTY

English Express
304 Indiana Ave.
English, IN 47118
812-338-4980
812-408-4980
Fax: 812-338-4985

FLOYD COUNTY

WorkOne New Albany
P.O. Box 1287
3310 Grant Line Rd.
New Albany, IN 47151
812-948-6102
Fax: 812-948-6118

HARRISON COUNTY

Corydon Express
101 W. Hwy 62
Corydon, IN 47112
812-738-8911
Fax:
812-738-9973

SCOTT COUNTY

Scottsburg Express
P.O. Box 462
1092 W. Community Way
Scottsburg, IN 47170
812-752-0369
Fax: 812-752-5197

WASHINGTON COUNTY

Salem Express
1707 N. Shelby St.
Salon, IN 47167
812-883-2283
Fax: 812-883-1544

WorkOne Region 11

DUBOIS COUNTY

WorkOne Southwest
P.O. Box 664
850 College Ave.
Jasper, IN 47546
812-482-3007
Fax: 812-634-1597

GIBSON COUNTY

WorkOne Southeast
P.O. Box 578
112 N. Prince St.
Priceton, IN 47670
812-386-7963
Fax: 812-385-0431

KNOX COUNTY

WorkOne Southwest
1500 N. Chestnut
Vincennes, In 47591
812-882-8770
Fax: 812-882-4535

PERRY COUNTY

WorkOne
700 Main St.
Tell City, IN 47586
812-548-4076
Fax: 812-547-5111

PIKE COUNTY

WorkOne Southwest
816 Main St.

Petersburg, In 47567
812-354-6800

POSEY COUNTY

Workone Southwest
306 Kimball
Mt. Vernon, IN 47620
812-838-3663
Fax: 812-838-3578

SPENCER COUNTY

WorkOne Southwest
319 S. 5th, Suite 5

Rockport, IN 47635
812-649-4077
Fax: 812-649-9049

VANDERBURGH COUNTY

Vanderburgh Southwest
700 E. Walnut St.
Evansville, IN 47713
812-424-4473
Fax: 812-421-3189

IOWA

CURE
P.O. Box 41005
Des Moines, IA 50311
515-277-6296
JabWab@msn.com

CURE is a grassroots organization from top to bottom. It does not hire professional leaders. Instead, its leaders come from the ranks of people formerly in prison and family members of friends of prisoners. This organization offers assistance to ex-offenders.

Iowa Workforce Development Offices

Algona Office
117 East Call St.
Algona, IA 50511-2451
515-295-7219
Fax: 515-295-6916

Ames Office
52406-0729
Ames, IA 50010-0410
515-232-6572
Fax: 515-232-0209

Atlantic Office
508 Poplar

Atlantic, IA 50022-1252
712-243-2351
Fax: 712-243-5584

Boone Office
718 Eighth St.
Boone, IA 50036-2705
515-432-5806
Fax: 515-432-5403

Burlington Office
1000 N. Roosevelt Ave.
P.O. Box 609
Burlington, IA 52601-0609
319-763-1671
Fax: 319-753-5881

Carroll Office
619 N. Carroll St.
Carroll, IA 51401-2332
712-792-2685
Fax: 712-792-6605

Cedar Rapids Office
800 7th St., SE
P.O. Box 729
Cedar Rapids, IA 52406-0729
319-365-9474
Fax: 319-365-9270

Centerville Office
1015 N. 18th St., Suite B
Centerville, IA 52544
641-856-6371
Fax: 641-437-4498

Charles City Office
NIACC Charles City Center
200 Harwood Drive
Charles City, IA 50616-2211
541-228-5136
Fax: 641-228-5526

Cherokee Office
923 South Second St.
Cherokee, IA 51012-1599
712-225-2274
Fax: 712-225-2274

Clarinda Office
121 South 15th St., Office A
Clarinda, IA 51632-2245
712-542-6563
Fax: 712-542-5986

Clinton Office
2740 S. 17th St.
Clinton, IA 52732-7040
563-242-1703
Fax: 563-242-1304

Council Bluffs Office
300 West Broadway, SUITE 13
Council Bluff, IA 51503-9030
712-242-2100
Fax: 712=242-2155

Creston Office
215 North Elm
Creston, IA 50801-2305
641-782-2119
Fax: 641-782-7060

Dakota City/Humboldt Office
203 Main St.-Courthouse
P.O. Box 100
Dakota City, IA 50529-0100
515-332-2145
Fax: 515-332-2146

Davenport Office
902 W. Kimberly Rd., Suite 51
Davenport, IA 52806-5783
563-445-3200
Fax: 563-445-3240

Davenport Office
326 West 3rd St., Suite 910
Davenport, IA 52801
563-336-3499
Fax: 563-336-3494

Decorah Office
1111 Paine St., Suite G
Decorah, IA 52101-2411
563-382-0457
Fax: 563-387-0905

Denison Office
1231 Broadway, Suite 201
Denison, IA 52101-2411
563-382-0457
Fax: 563-382-0905

Des Moines Office
430 East Grand Ave.
Des Moines, IA 50309-1920
515-281-9619
Fax: 515-281-9640

Dubuque Office
680 Main St., 2nd Floor
Dubuque, IA 52001
563-556-5800
Fax: 563-556-0154

Emmetsburg Office
2008 10th St.
P.O. Box 323
Emmetsburg, IA 50636-2444
712-852-3412
Fax: 712-852-3175

Estherville Office
620 1st Ave. South
Estherville, IA 51334
712-362-7327
Fax: 712-362-7742

Fairfield Office
112 South Court, Suite B
Fairfield, IA 52556-3327
641-472-5466
Fax: 641-472-5056

Fort Dodge Office
Three Triton Circle
Fort Dodge, IA 50501-5729
515-576-3131
Fax: 515-955-1420

Fort Madison Office
610 Eighth St.
Fort Madison, IA 52627-2866
319-372-4412
Fax: 319-372-5008

Glenwood Office
101 Central St., Suite 105
P.O. Box 269
Glenwood, IA 51534-0269
712-527-5214
Fax: 712-527-5214

Harlan Office
1210 7th St., Suite D
Harlan, IA 51537-1755
712-755-3777
Fax: 712-755-7343

Iowa City Office
1700 S. 1st Ave., Suite 11B
Iowa City, IA 52240
319-351-1035
Fax: 319-351-4433

Keokuk Office
106 Washington
Keokuk, IA 52632-2313
319-524-1862
Fax: 319-524-8362

Manchester Office
223 West Main
Manchester, IA 52057-1533
563-927-4447
Fax: 563-927-6534

Maquoketa Office
501 West Washington St.
P.O. Box 777
Maquoketa, IA 52060
563-652-5000
Fax: 563-244-7198

Marshalltown Office
3405 South Center St.
P.O. Box 497
Marshalltown, IA 50401-0497
641-754-1400
Fax: 641-754-1443

Mason City Office
600 South Pierce
Mason City, IA 50401-4836
641-422-1524
Fax: 641-422-1543

Mason City (NIACC)
North Iowa Area Community College
    Activity Center, Room 209
Mason City, IA 50401
641-422-4292
Fax: 641-422-4430

Mount Pleasant Office
217 East Monroe
Mount Pleasant, IA 52641-1918
319-385-4241
Fax: 319-385-4358

Muscatine Office
2213 Grand Ave.
Muscatine, IA 52761-5650
563-263-3521
Fax: 563-263-5037

New Hampton Office
951 North Linn Ave., Suite 4
New Hampton, IA 50659-1203
641-394-4649
Fax: 641-394-6909

Newton Office
600 N. 2nd Ave. W, Suite S
Newton, IA 50208-3049

641-792-5131
Fax: 641-702-9908

Oelwein Office
400 S. Frederick Ave.
Oelwein, IA 50662-2505
319-283-2751
Fax: 319-283-2436

Orange City Office
400 Central Ave., NW, Suite 1000
Orange City, IA 51041
712-707-9870
Fax: 712-707-9872

Osceola Office
2520 W. McLane
P.O. Box 321
Osceola, IA 50213-0321
641-342-4955
Fax: 641-342-6168

Oskaloosa Office
408 South 11th St.
Oskaloosa, IA 52577-3402
641-673-9494
Fax: 641-672-1224

Ottumwa Office
310 West Main
P.O. Box 717
Ottumwa, IA 52501-0717
641-684-5401
Fax: 641-684-4351

Ottumwa Office
Indian Hills Community College
    Campus 651 Indian Hills Drive,
    Suite 1
Ottumwa, IA 641-682-8577
Fax: 641-682-0102

Pella Office
612 Franklin St., Suite 101
Pella, IA 50219-1685
641-628-4511
Fax: 641-626-8353

Perry Office
607 1st St.

Perry, IA 50220-1804
515-465-3537
Fax: 515-465-5669

Pocahontas Office
400 NW 7th St.
Pocahontas, IA 50574-1626
712-335-4244
Fax: 712-335-4244Ext. 11

Red Oak Office
1000 North Broadway
Red Oak, IA 51566-1408
712-623-2569
Fax: 712-623-3227

Shenandoah Office
500 North Broad St.
Shenandoah, IA 51601-1316
712-246-4470
Fax: 712-246-5112

Sioux City Office
2508 4th St.
Sioux City, IA 51101-2298
712-233-9030
Fax: 712-277-8438

Spencer Office
217 W. 5th St.
P.O. Box 1087
Spencer, IA 51301
712-262-1971
Fax: 712-262-1963

Storm Lake Office
824 Flindt Drive, Suite 106
Storm Lake, IA 50588-3206
712-732-1576
Fax: 712-732-2536

Washington Office
1201 Industrial Park Drive
P.O.Box 344
Washington, IA 52353
319-653-4787
Fax: 319-398-1043

Waterloo Office
3420 University Ave., Suite G

Waterloo, IA 50701
319-235-2123
Fax: 319-235-1066

Waverly Office
1221 4th St. SW
Waverly, IA 60677
319-352-3844
Fax: 319-352-3142

Webster City Office
403 Elm St.
Webster, IA 50595
515-832-3562
Fax: 515-832-3562

KANSAS

CURE
2137 North Battin
Wichita, KS 67208
316-612-8654
Carterhopeinc316@aol.com

CURE is a grassroots organization from top to bottom. It does not hire professional leaders. Instead, its leaders come from the ranks of people formerly in prison and family members of friends of prisoners. This organization offers assistance to ex-offenders.

Forever Crowned Ministry
2046 E. 9th St. North
Wichita, KS 67214
316-267-1244
www.forevercrowned.org
fcmin@2046@msn.com

This is a faith-based organization that offers job search assistance, job mediation, job readiness training, resume assistance and basic computer skills, as well as mentoring counseling and life skills training to individuals with criminal histories.

Kansas Workforce Centers

Atchison Workforce Center
818 Kansas Ave.
Atchison, KS 66002-2396
913-367-4311
Fax: 913-367-4265

Butler Workforce Center

2318 W. Central Ave.
El Dorado, KS 67042-3207
316-321-2350
TTY: 711
Fax: 316-321-7653

Cowley Workforce Center
Strother Field
22215 Tupper St.
Winfield, KS 67156-7326
620-221-7790
TTY: 711
Fax: 620-229-8133

Junction City Workforce Center
1012 W. 6th St., Suite A
Junction City, KS 66441-3998
785-762-8870
TTY: 711
Fax: 785-762-3078

KANSASWORKS
Neosho Community College
801 W. 10th St.
Chanute, KS 66720-2704
620-431-2820 Ext. 634/635
620-431-1554
Fax: 620-431-2375

KANSASWORKS
1135 S. Country Club Drive, Suite 2
Colby, KS 67701-3666
785-462-6862

TTY: 711
Fax: 785-462-8371

KANSASWORKS
2308 First Ave.
Dodge City, KS 67801-2560
620-227-2149
TTY: 711
Fax: 620-227-9667

KANSASWORKS
512 Market St.
Emporia, KS 66801-3934
620-342-3355
TTY: 620-343-1025
Fax: 620-342-2806

KANSASWORKS
107 E. Spruce St.
Garden City, KS 67846-5446
620-276-2339
TTY: 711
Fax: 620-276-7306

KANSASWORKS
1025 Main St.
Great Bend, KS 67530-4429
620-793-5445
TTY: 711
Fax: 620-793-5445
Fax: 620-793-3188

KANSASWORKS
332 E. 8th St.
Hays, KS 67601-4145
785-625-5674
TTY: 711
Fax: 785-625-0092
KANSAS WORKS Mobile Workforce
  Center
332 E. 8th St.
Hays, KS 67601-4145
785-625-5654
Cell: 820-255-3705
Fax: 785-625-0092

KANSASWORKS
Hutchinson Community College

609 E. 14th
Hutchinson, KS 67501-5836
620-665-3559
TTY: 711
Fax: 620-728-8161

KANSASWORKS
200 ARCO Place, Suite 101
Independence, KS 67301-5304
620-332-5904
TTY: 620-332-5926
Fax: 620-331-0856

KANSASWORKS
1801 N. Kansas Ave., Room T-154
Liberal, KS 67901-2054
620-417-1958
TTY: 711

KANSASWORKS
122 W, Main, 2nd Floor
Bank of America Building
McPherson, KS 67460
620-245-0202

KANSASWORKS
Hutchinson Community College-
  Newton
203 Broadway
Newton, KS 67114-2223
316-283-7000
TTY: 711
Fax: 316-283-2016

KANSASWORKS
Fort Scott Community College
Miami County Campus
501 S. Hospital Drive, Suite 300
Paola, KS 66071-2111
913-294-4178, Ext 18
TTY: 620-332-1661
Fax: 913-294-5186

KANSASWORKS
105 W. Euclid
Pittsburg, KS 66762-5101
620-231-4250

TTY: 620-232-9815
Fax: 913-294-5186

KANSASWORKS
203 10th St.
Salina, KS 67401-2115
785-827-0385
TTY: 711
Fax: 785-827-0385
Fax: 785-827-2307

Lawrence Workforce Center
2540 Iowa St., Suite R
Lawrence, KS 66046-5754
785-840-9675
Fax:785-865-5465

Leavenworth (Vet Outreach)
ACAP (Army Career and Alumni
  Program) Office
428 McPherson Ave.
Ft. Leavenworth, KS 66027-1310
913-684-2227
TTY: 711
Fax: 913-684-2598

Leavenworth Workforce Center
515 Limit St., Suite 200
Leavenworth, KS 66048-4490
913-651-1800
TTY: 913-682-6717
Fax: 913-682-1804

Manhattan Vets Center
205 S. 4th St., Suite 1B
Manhattan, KS 66502-6111
785-587-8257
TTY: 711
Fax: 785-539-4982

Manhattan Workforce Center
205 S. 4th St., Suite K
Manhattan, KS 66502-6166
785-539-5691
Fax: 785-539-5697

Johnson County Workforce Center
9221 Quivira Rd.
Overland Park, KS 66215-3905
913-577-5900
TTY: 913-341-1507
Fax: 913-642-7260

Topeka Workforce Center
1430 S.W. Topeka Blvd.
Topeka, KS 66612-1819
785-235-5627
Fax: 785-233-5899

Wichita Workforce Center
150 N. Main, Suite 100
Wichita, KS 67202-1321
316-771-6800
TTY: 316-771-6844
Fax: 316-771-6890

Wichita Workforce Center (Vets Center)
Wichita Vets Center
251 N. Water
Wichita, KS 67202-1292
316-685-2221 ext 41080

Wyandotte County Workforce Center
552 State Ave.
Kansas City, KS 66101-2403
913-279-2600
TTY: 913-281-1942
Fax: 913-342-9676

KENTUCKY

CURE
P.O. Box 221-481
Louisville, KY 40252-1481

CURE is a grassroots organization from top
to bottom. It does not hire professional leaders.
Instead, its leaders come from the ranks of peo-
ple formerly in prison and family members of
friends of prisoners. This organization offers
assistance to ex-offenders.

Kentucky Workforce Office Locations

Services offered include orientation to services, initial assessment of skills, aptitudes and support service needs, career counseling, job search and placement assistance.

ADAIR COUNTY REGION 1

Adair Co. Local Office
969 Campbellsville Rd.
Columbia, KY 42728
270-384-6335
Fax: 270-384-0415

ALLEN COUNTY REGION 1

Bowling Green Career Center
803 Chestnut St.
P.O. Box 90003
Bowling Green, KY 42102
270-746-7425
Fax: 270-746-7825
DCI Fax: 746-7171

ANDERSON COUNTY REGION 3

Office of Employment and Training
1121 Louisville Rd., Suite 6
Frankfort, KY 40601
502-564-7046
502-564-3512
Fax: 502-564-7794

BALLARD COUNTY REGION 1

Paducah Career Center
416 South 6th St.
270-575-7000
Fax: 270-575-7008

BARREN COUNTY REGION 3

Glasgow Area Career Center
445 North Green St.
Glasgow, KY 42141
270-651-2121
270-651-2111
Fax: 270-651-8916

BATH COUNTY REGION 4

Gateway Career Center
126 Bradley Ave.
Morehead, KY 40351
606-783-8525
Fax: 606-783-8429
Fax: 606-783-8522

BELL COUNTY REGION 4

Middlesboro Local Office
725 North 19th St.
P.O. Box Drawer 578
Middlesboro, KY 40965-0578
606-248-2792
Fax: 606-248-6483

BOONE COUNTY REGION 3

One-Stop Northern Kentucky
8020 Veterans Memorial Drive
Florence, KY 41042-1895
659-371-0808
Fax: 859-371-1539

BOURBON COUNTY REGION 3

Central Kentucky Job Center
1000 W. Main St., Suite 5
Georgetown, KY 40324
502-863-2402
Fax: 502-563-1966

BOYD COUNTY REGION 4

Ashland One-Stop
1844 Carter Ave.
Ashland, KY 41101
606-920-2024
Fax: 606-920-2026

BOYLE COUNTY REGION 3

Central Kentucky Job Center
121 East Braodway
Danville, KY 40422
859-239-7411
Fax: 859-239-7541

BRACKEN COUNTY REGION 4

Marysville One-Stop Career Center
201 Government St., Suite 101
Marysville, KY 41056
606-564-3347
Fax: 606-564-3829

BREATHITT COUNTY REGION 4

Breathitt County Local Office
355 Broadway
Jackson, KY 41339
606-436-3161 Ext. 205
Breckinridge County see Hardin
County

BULLITT COUNTY REGION 3

Kentuckiana Works One-Stop
505 Buffalo Run Rd., Suite 100
Shepherdsville, KY 40165
502-955-9131
Fax: 957-0436

BUTLER COUNTY REGION 1

Bowling Green Career Center
803 Chestnut St.
Bowling Green, KY 42102
270-746-7425
Fax: 270-746-7825
DCI Fax: 270-746-7171

CALDWELL COUNTY REGION 1

Breathitt Career Center
110 Riverfront Drive
P.O. Box 1128
Hopkinsville, KY 42241-1128
270-889-6509
Fax: 270-889-6599

CALLOWAY COUNTY REGION 1

Murray Discovery Center
208 South 5th St.
Murray, KY 42071

270-761-3903
Fax: 270-761-3907

CAMPBELL COUNTY REGION 3

320 Garrard St.
Covington, KY 41011-1790
859-292-6666
UI Direct Line: 859-292-6670
Fax: 859-292-6675

CARLISLE COUNTY REGION 1

Paducah Career Center
416 South 6th St.
Paducah, KY 42003
270-575-7000
Fax: 270-575-7008

CARROLL COUNTY REGION 3

One-Stop Northern Kentucky
400 A 4th St.
Carrollton, KY 41008
502-732-4602
Fax: 502-732-5825

CARTER COUNTY REGION 4

Ashland Career Center
1844 Carter Ave.
Ashland, KY 41101
606-920-2024
Fax: 606-920-2026

CASEY COUNTY REGION 1

Casey County Career Center
3609 North U.S. 127
Liberty, KY 42539
606-787-1405

CHRISTIAN COUNTY REGION 1

Breathitt Career Center
110 Riverfront Drive
P.O. Box 1128
Hopkinsville, KY 42241-1128
270-889-6509

270-889-6516
Fax: 270-889-6599

Lee Soldier and Family Support Center
Fort Campbell Community Activities
  Business Center
5661 Screaming Eagle Blvd
Fort Campbell, KY 42223
270-798-4293
Fax: 931-431-9402

CLARK COUNTY REGION 3

Office and Employment and Training
15 West Lexington Ave.
Winchester, KY 40391
859-737-7793
Fax: 859-737-7310

CLAY COUNTY REGION 1

Clay County Job Sight
1535 Shamrock Rd.
Manchester, KY 40962
606-598-5127
Fax: 606-598-4380

CLINTON COUNTY REGION 1

Clinton County Career Center
100 South Cross St.
Albany, KY 42602
606-387-0620
606-387-0654
Fax: 606-677-0352

CRITTENDEN COUNTY REGION 1

Madisonville
56 Federal St.
Madisonville, KY 42431
270-824-7562
270-824-7516
Fax: 270-824-7589

CUMBERLAND COUNTY REGION 1

Somerset Career Center
410 East Mt. Vernon

P.O. Box 29
Somerset, KY 42502
606-677-4124
606-677-4125
Fax: 606-677-4119

DAVIESS COUNTY REGION 1

Owensboro Area Career Center
121 E. Second St., Suite 10
Owensboro, KY 42303
270-687-7297
Fax: 270-687-7268
DCI Fax: 270-687-7080

EDMONSON COUNTY REGION 1

Bowling Green Career Center
803 Chestnut St.
P.O. Box 90003
Bowling Green, KY 42102
270-746-7425
Fax: 270-746-7825
DCI Fax: 270-746-7171

ELLIOT COUNTY REGION 4

Ashland Career Center
1844 Carter Ave.
Ashland, KY 41101
606-920-2024
Fax: 606-920-2026

ESTILL COUNTY REGION 4

Central Kentucky Job Center
595 South Keeneland Drive
Richmond, KY 40475
859-624-2564
Fax: 859-624-1075

FAYETTE COUNTY REGION 3

Central Kentucky Job Center
1055 Industry Rd. 2nd Floor
Lexington, KY 40505-3823
859-425-2180
Fax: 859-225-5106

FLEMING COUNTY REGION 4

Maryville One-Stop Career Center
201 Government St., Suite 101
Maryville, KY 41056
606-564-3347
Fax: 606-564-3829

FLOYD COUNTY REGION 4

Office of Employment and Training
686 North Lake Drive
Prestonsburg, KY 41653
606-889-1772/1773
606-889-1776/1777
606-889-1778/1782
Fax: 606-889-1775

FRANKLIN COUNTY REGION 3

Office of Employment and Training
1121 Louisville Rd., Suite 6
Frankfort, KY 40601
502-564-7046
502-564-3512
Fax: 502-564-7794

FULTON COUNTY REGION 1

319 Soth 7th St.
Mayfield, KY 42066
270-247-3857
270-247-8125
Fax: 270-247-8902

GALLATIN COUNTY REGION 1

One-Stop Northern Kentucky
8020 Veterans Memorial Drive
Florence, KY 41042-1895
859-371-0808
Fax: 859-371-5103

GARRARD COUNTY REGION 3

121 East Broadway
Danville, KY 40422
859-239-7411
Fax: 859-239-7541

GRANT COUNTY

One-Stop Northern Kentucky
320 Garrard St.
Covington, KY 41011-1790
859-292-6666
859-292-6670
Fax: 859-292-6675

One-Stop Northern Kentucky
8020 Veterans Memorial Drive
Florence, KY 41042-1895
859-371-0808
Fax: 859-371-5103

GRAVES COUNTY REGION 1

Mayfield One-Stop Career Center
319 South 7th St.
Mayfield, KY 42066
270-247-3857
270-247-8125
Fax: 270-247-8902

Workforce Transition Center
Mayfield Plaza
Mayfield, KY 42066
270-247-2300

GRAYSON COUNTY REGION 1

Lincoln Trail Career Center
125 East Market St., Suite 21
Leitchfield, KY 42754
270-259-4912
1-866-662-0006
Fax: 270-259-8502

GREEN COUNTY REGION 1

Campbellsville Career Center
1311 East Broadway, Suite C
Campbellsville, KY 42718
270-789-1352
270-465-2335 WIA
Fax: 270-789-4082

GREENUP COUNTY REGION 4

Ashland Career Center
1844 Carter Ave.

Ashland, KY 41101
606-920-2024
606-920-2026

HANCOCK COUNTY SEE DAVIESS COUNTY

HARDIN COUNTY REGION 1

Fort Knox
P.O. Box 215
Fort Knox, KY 40121-0215
606-624-5337
Fax: 502-624-2407

Lincoln Trail Career Center
916 North Mulberry St.
P.O. Box 1386
Elizabethtown, KY 42702-1386
270-766-5115
270-766-5110
1-800-455-5587
Fax: 270-766-5112
DCI Fax: 270-766-5183

HARLAN COUNTY REGION 4

Harlan Office
124 South Cumberland
Harlan, KY 40831
606-573-3160
Fax: 606-573-5903

HARRISON COUNTY REGION 3

Central Kentucky Job Center
1000 West Main St., Suite 5
Georgetown, KY 40324
502-863-2402
Fax: 502-863-1966
Hart County see Barren County

HENDERSON COUNTY REGION 1

Henderson Office
212 North Water St.
P.O. Box 1269
Henderson, KY 42419

270-826-2746
Fax: 270-831-2717

HENRY COUNTY REGION 3

Kentuckiana Works One-Stop
600 West Cedar
Louisville, KY 40202
502-595-4003
502-595-3164
502-595-4636/4617
WIA: 502-595-0099
Fax: 502-595-4623
DCI: 502-595-4701
DCI Fax: 502-595-4859

HICKMAN COUNTY REGION 1

Mayfield One-Stop Career Center
319 South 7th St.
Mayfield, KY 42066
270-247-3857
270-247-8125
Fax: 270-247-8902

HOPKINS COUNTY REGION 1

Job Net Career Center
755 Industrial Park Rd.
Madisonville, KY 42431
270-821-9966

Madisonville Office
56 Federal St.
Madisonville, KY 42431
270-824-7582
Fax: 270-824-7589

JACKSON COUNTY REGION 1

Jackson County Career Center
1100 Educational Mountain Drive
P.O. Box 1390
McKee, KY 40447
606-287-3573
Fax: 606-287-3574

JEFFERSON COUNTY REGION 3

Kentuckiana Works One-Stop
600 West Cedar

Louisville, KY 40202
502-595-4003
502-595-3164
502-595-4636/4617
WIA: 502-595-0099
Fax: 502-595-4623
DCI: 502-595-4701/4705
DCI Fax: 502-595-4859

Nia Center
2900 West Broadway
Louisville, KY 40211
502-574-4100
Fax: 502-574-1197

Preston Highway
6201 Gene Preston Highway
Louisville, KY 40219
Vets: 502-595-4187
502-595-4188
502-595-4150/3098
Fax: 502-595-4349

Shepherdsville Work One-Stop Office
505 Buffalo Rub Rd., Suite 100
Shepherdsville, KY 40165
502-955-9131
Fax: 502-957-0436

Shelby Office
31 Mt. Rushmore Ct.
Shelbyville, KY 40065
502-633-5045
Fax: 502-633-1453

VA DuPont Clinic
Professional Towers–Mental Health
   Clinic DuPont Circle
Louisville, KY 40211
502-287-6986

Veterans Administration Medical
   Center
800 Zorn Ave.
Louisville, KY 40206
502-287-4000

Veterans Center
1347 South Third St.

Louisville, KY 40208
502-634-1916
Fax: 502-626-7082

JESSAMINE COUNTY REGION 3

Central Kentucky Job Center
1055 Industry Rd. 2nd Floor
Lexington, KY 40505-3823
859-425-2180
Fax: 859-225-5106

JOHNSON COUNTY REGION 4

Office of Employment and Training
686 North Lake Drive
Prestonsburg, KY 41653
606-889-1772/1773
606-889-1776/1777
606-889-1778/1782
Fax: 606-889-1775

KENTON COUNTY REGION 3

Department for Employment Services
320 Garrard St.
Covington, KY 41011-1790
859-292-6666
UI Direct Line-889-292-6670
Fax: 859-292-6675

One-Stop Northern Kentucky
Greater Cincinnati/Northern KY
Airport Terminal 1
P.O. Box 75356
Cincinnati, KY 45275
859-767-9675
Fax: 859-767-6200

KNOTT COUNTY *SEE* PERRY
COUNTY

KNOX COUNTY *SEE* WHITLEY
COUNTY

LARUE COUNTY REGION 1

Lincoln Trail Career Center
916 North Mulberry St.

P.O. Box 1386
Elizabethtown, KY 42702-1386
270-766-5115
270-766-5110
1-800-455-5587
Fax: 270-766-5112
DCI Fax: 270-766-5183

LAUREL COUNTY REGION 1

Laurel Office
Regional S.O.B.
Room 133
85 State Police Rd.
London, KY 40741
606-330-2115
Fax: 606-330-2122

LAWRENCE COUNTY REGION 4

Ashland Career Center
1844 Carter Ave.
Ashland, KY 41101
606-920-2024
Fax: 606-920-2026

LEE COUNTY REGION 4

Hazard Office
742 High St.
Hazard, KY 41701
606-435-6038
606-435-6102
Fax: 606-435-6039

LESLIE COUNTY *SEE* WHITLEY COUNTY

LETCHER COUNTY

Whitesburg Call Center
65 North Webb St.
Whitesburg, KY 41858
606-633-3154
Fax: 606-633-3156

LEWIS COUNTY REGION 4

Marysville One-Stop Career Center
201 Government St., Suite 101

Marysville, 41056
606-564-3347
606-564-5513
Fax: 606-564-3829

LINCOLN COUNTY REGION 3

121 East Broadway
Danville, KY 40422
859-239-7411
Fax: 859-239-7541

LIVINGSTON COUNTY REGION 1

Paducah Career Center
416 South 6th St.
Paducah, KY 42003
270-575-7000
Fax: 270-575-7008

LOGAN COUNTY REGION 1

Bowling Green Career Center
803 Chestnut St.
P.O. Box 90003
Bowling Green, KY 42102
270-746-7425
Fax: 270-746-7825
DCI Fax: 270-746-7171

LYON COUNTY REGION 1

Breathitt Career Center
110 Riverfront Drive
P.O. Box 1128
Hopkinsville, KY 42241-1128
270-869-6509
Fax: 270-889-6599

MADISON COUNTY

Central Kentucky Job Center
595 South Keeneland Drive
Richmond, KY 40475
859-624-2564
Fax: 859-624-1075

MAGOFFIN COUNTY REGION 4

Office of Employment and Training
686 North Lake Drive

Prestonburg. KY 41653
606-889-1772/1773
606-889-1776/1777
606-889-1778/1782
Fax: 606-889-1775

MARION COUNTY REGION 1

Lincoln Trail Career Center
145 Cemetery Drive, Suite 4
Lebanon, KY 40033
270-575-7000
Fax: 270-575-7008

MARSHALL COUNTY REGION 1

Paducah Career Center
416 South 6th St.
Paducah, KY 42003
270-575-7000
Fax: 270-575-7008

MARTIN COUNTY REGION 4

Office of Employment and Training
686 North Lake Drive
Prestonsburg, KY 41653
606-889-1772/1773
606-889-1776/1777
606-889-1778/1782
Fax: 606-889-1775

MASON COUNTY REGION 4

Maryville One-Stop Career Center
201 Government St., Suite 101
Maryville, KY 41056
606-564-3347
606-564-5513
Fax: 606-564-3829

McCracken County Region 1
Paducah Career Center
416 South 6th St.
Paducah, KY 42003
270-575-7000
Fax: 270-575-7008

McCREARY COUNTY *SEE*
PULASKI COUNTY

McLEAN COUNTY *SEE*
DAVIESS COUNTY

MEADE COUNTY REGION 1

Meade Office
Fernando Arroyo
River Ridge Plaza
Brandenburg, KY 40108
270-422-4228
Fax: 270-422-1194

MENIFEE COUNTY REGION 4

Gateway Career Center
126 Bradley Ave.
Morehead, Ky 40351
606-783-8525
Fax: 606-783-8529
Fax: 606-783-8522

MERGER COUNTY *SEE* BOYLE
COUNTY

METCALFE COUNTY REGION 1

Glasgow Area Career Center
445 North Green St.
  Glasgow, KY 42141
270-651-2121
270-651-2111
Fax: 270-651-8916

MONROE COUNTY *SEE* BARREN
COUNTY

MONTGOMERY COUNTY REGION 4

Call Center
Elliott County Public Library
P.O. Box 750
Main St.
Sandy Hook, KY 41171
606-738-4704

Montgomery Local Office
Montgomery County Health and
  Civic Center

108 East Locust St.
Mt. Sterling, KY 40353
859-498-4418
Fax: 859-496-4782

MORGAN COUNTY REGION 4

Gateway Career Center
126 Bradley Ave.
Morehead, KY 40351
606-783-8525
Fax: 606-783-8522
Fax: 606-783-8529

MUHLENBERG COUNTY REGION 1

Muhlenberg Career
Leigh Douglas
50 Career Way
Central City, KY 42330
270-338-3654
Fax: 270-3384891

NELSON COUNTY REGION 1

Lincoln Trail Career Center
860 West Stephen Foster Blvd
Bardstown, KY 40004
502-348-2709
502-348-8662
Fax: 502-349-6608

NICHOLAS COUNTY REGION 3

Central KY Job Center
1000 West Main St., Suite 5
Georgetown, KY 40324
502-863-2402
Fax: 502-863-1966
Ohio County see Daviess County

OLDHAM COUNTY REGION 3

Oldham Office
202 South First St.
LaGrange, KY 40031
502-222-1581
Fax: 502-222-5590

OWEN COUNTY REGION 3

One-Stop Northern Kentucky
8020 Veterans Memorial Drive
Florence, KY 41042-1895
859-371-0808
Fax: 859-371-5103
Owsley County see Perry County

PENDLETON COUNTY REGION 3

500 Chapel St.
Falmouth, KY 41040
859-654-3325 Ext. 2607
Fax: 859-654-2402

PERRY COUNTY

Perry Job Sight Center
14 Logan Drive
P.O. Box340
Jeff, KY 41751
606-438-3161 Ext. 205

PIKE COUNTY REGION 4

Pike County Job Sight
120 South Riverfill Drive
Pikesville, KY 41501
606-218-1247
Fax: 606-218-2147

Pikeville Office
138 College St.
Pikesville, KY 41501-1783
606-433-7721
Fax: 606-433-7696

POWELL COUNTY REGION 3

Office and Employment and Training
15 West Lexington Ave.
Winchester, KY 40391
859-737-7793
Fax: 859-797-7310

PULASKI COUNTY REGION 1

Somerset Career Center
410 East Mt. Vernon

P.O. Box 29
Somerset, KY 42502
606-677-4124
606-677-4125
Fax: 606-677-4119

ROBERTSON COUNTY REGION 4

Marysville One-Stop Career Center
201 Government St., Suite 101
Marysville, KY 41056
606-564-3347
609-564-5513
Fax: 606-564-3829

ROCKCASTLE COUNTY REGION 1

Corbin Career Center
310 Roy Kidd Ave.
Corbin, KY 40701
606-528-3460
606-528-3421
Fax: 606-523-5642

ROWAN COUNTY REGION 4

Gateway Career Center
126 Bradley Ave.
Moreland, KY 40351
606-783-8525
Fax: 606-783-8529

RUSSELL COUNTY REGION 1

Russell County Career Center
848 West Steve
Warner Drive
Russell Springs, KY 42629
270-866-6733
Fax: 270-866-6780

SCOTT COUNTY REGION 3

Central Kentucky Job Center
West Main St., Suite 5
Georgetown, KY 40324
502-663-2402
Fax: 502-863-1966

SHELBY COUNTY REGION 3

Shelby Office
31 Mt. Rushmore Court
Shelbyville, KY 40065
502-633-5045
Fax: 502-633-1453

SIMPSON COUNTY *SEE* WARREN COUNTY

SPENCER COUNTY REGION 3

Kentuckiana Works One-Stop
600 West Cedar
Louisville, KY 40202
502-595-4166
502-595-3164
502-595-4636/4617
WIA: 502-595-0099
Fax: 502-595-4623
DCI: 502-595-4701
DCI Fax: 502-595-4859

TAYLOR COUNTY REGION 1

Campbellsville Career Center
1311 East Broadway, Suite C
Campbellsville, KY 42718
270-769-1352
WIA: 270-465-2335
Fax: 270-789-4082

TODD COUNTY REGION 1

Breathitt Career Center
110 Riverfront Drive
Hopkinsville, KY 42241-1128
270-889-6509
Fax: 270-889-6599

TRIGG COUNTY REGION 1

Breathitt Career Center
110 Riverfront Drive
P.O. Box 1128
Hopkinsville, KY 42241-1128
270-889-6509
Fax: 270-889-6599

TRIMBLE COUNTY REGION 3

Kentuckiana Works One-Stop
600 West Cedar
Louisville, KY 40202
502-595-4166
Fax: 502-595-4623
WIA: 502-595-0099
502-595-3164
502-595-4636/4617
DCI: 502-595-4701
DCI Fax: 502-595-4859

UNION COUNTY SEE HENDERSON
COUNTY

WARREN COUNTY REGION 1

Bowling Green Career Center
803 Chestnut St.
P.O. Box 90003
Bowling Green, KY 42102-9003
270-746-7425
Fax: 270-746-7825
DCI Fax: 270-746-7171

WASHINGTON COUNTY REGION 1

Washington Local Office
111 North Main St.
Springfield, KY 40069
859-336-3281
Fax: 859-336-3289

WAYNE COUNTY REGION 1

Wayne County Local Office
1500 North Main St., Suite 168

Monticello, KY 42633
606-348-6050
Fax: 606-348-0965

WEBSTER COUNTY SEE HENDER-
SON COUNTY

WHITLEY COUNTY REGION 1

Corbin Career Center
310 Roy Kidd Ave.
Corbin, KY 40701
606-528-3460
606-528-3421
Fax: 606-523-5642

WOLFE COUNTY SEE PERRY
COUNTY

WOODFORD COUNTY REGION 3

Department for Employment Services
1121 Louisville Rd., Suite 6
Frankfort, KY 40601
502-564-7046
502-564-3512
Fax: 502-564-7794

One-Stop Service Centers
Kentucky Department for Training
    and Re-Employment
275 E. Main St. 2CA
Frankfort, KY 40621
502-584-5360

LOUISIANA

CURE
P.O. Box 181
Baton Rouge, LA 70621
225-270-5245
FAX: 225-246-8731
checoyancy@yahho.com

www.curelouisana.org
CURE is a grassroots organization from top to bottom. It does not hire professional leaders. Instead, its leaders come from the ranks of people formerly in prison and family members of friends of prisoners. This organization offers assistance to ex-offenders.

Communities Industrialization Center, Inc. of Greater New Orleans
2701 Piety St.
New Orleans, LA 70126
504-949-4421

This organization offers job training and placement to the unemployed and under-employed into unsubsidized jobs in the New Orleans area.

Comprehensive One-Stop Career Centers by Region

ALEXANDRIA REGION

CENLA Community Action Committee
1335 Jackson St.
Alexandria, LA 71301
318-487-5878

Avoyelles Career Solutions Center
320 College St.
Marksville, LA 71351
318-240-8820

Avoyelles Progress Action Committee
641 Government
Marksville, LA 71351
318-253-6085

Beauregard CAA
204 West First St.
DeRidder, LA 70634
337-463-7895

Beauregard Career Solutions Center
1102 West First St.
DeRidder, LA 70634
337-462-5838

Business and Career Solutions Center
203 East Academy
Jennings, LA 70546
337-824-2797

Calcasieu Business and Career Solutions Center
4250 Fifth Ave.

Lake Charles, LA 70697
337-475-4800

Calcasieu Office of Community Services
2424 Third St.
Lake Charles, LA 70602
318-437-3467

Cameron CAA
723 Marchall St.
Cameron, LA 70631
318-775-5668

Catahoula Career Solutions Center
204 Sicily St.
Harrisburg, LA 71340
318-744-5445

Concordia Career Solutions Center
105 North E.E. Wallace Blvd.
Ferriday, LA 71334
318-757-9213

District 2 Hearing Office
3724 Government St.
Alexandria, LA 71302
318-487-5966

District 3 Hearing Office
4250 Fifth Ave.
Lake Charles, LA 70607
337-475-4882

Grant Career Solutions Center
207 Main St.
Colfax, LA 71417
318-627-5251

LaSalle CAA
204 Sicily St.
Harrisburg, LA 71340
318-744-5445

LaSalle Career Solutions Center
1050 Courthouse St.
Jena, LA 71342
318-992-8264

North Centralia, Inc.
215 Main St.

Colfax, LA 71417
318-627-3754

Rapides Business and Career Solutions Center
5610-B Coliseum Blvd.
Alexandria, LA 71303
318-487-5532

Vernon Career Solutions Center
1100 S. Third St.
Leesville, LA 71446-4902
337-238-4179

Vernon Community Action Council
408 W. Fertitta Blvd.
Leeville, LA 71496
318-239-4457

Winn Career Solutions Center
201 North Bevill St.
Winnfield, LA 71483
318-628-4641

BATON ROUGE REGION

Ascension Career Solutions Center
1721-D South Burnside Ave.
Gonzales, LA 70707
225-644-0335

City of Baton Rouge Division of
Human Development and Services
4523 Plank Rd.
Baton Rouge, LA 70805
225-358-4561

East and West Feliciana Career Solutions Center
5681 Commerce St.
St. Francisville, LA 70775
225-635-6635

East Baton Rouge North Career Solutions Center
4523 Plank Rd.
Baton Rouge, LA 70805
225-358-4579

East Baton Rouge South Career Solutions Center

1991 Wooddale Blvd.
Baton Rouge, LA 70806
225-925-4311

Iberville Career Solutions Center
23425 Railroad Ave.
Plaquemine, LA 70764
225-687-0969

Livington Career Solutions Center
9384 Florida Blvd.
Walker, LA 70785
225-667-1874

Pointe Coupee Career Solutions Center
305 E. Main St.
New Roads, LA 70760
225-638-6852

Tangipahoa Career Solutions Center
1745 S.W. Railroad Ave.
Hammond, LA 70403
985-902-4200

Washington Career Solutions Center
438 Ave. B
Bogalusa, LA 70427
985-732-6630

HOUMA REGION

Assumption Business and Career Solutions Center
4847A Highway 1, Suite C
Napoleonville, LA 70390
985-369-1810

Assumption Parish Police Jury
4813 Highway 1
Napoleonville, LA 70390
985-369-7435

Lafourche Career Solutions Center
1711 Ridgefield Rd.
Thibodaux, LA 70301
985-446-3016

Lafourche Office of Community Services
4777 Highway 1

Raceland, LA 70394
985-537-7603

Terrebonne Career Solutions Center
807 Barrow St.
Houma, LA 70360
985-876-8990

Workers Compensation
8026 Main St.
Houma, LA 70360
504-857-3775

LAFAYETTE REGION

Acadia Career Solutions Center
11 North Parkerson Ave.
Crowley, LA 70527
337-788-7550

Career Solutions Center, Acadiana
  Works
1301 Clover St., Room 109 (Media
  Tech Bldg)
Abbeville, LA 70510
337-893-1986

East St. Mary Career Solutions Center
7710 Hwy 182 East
Morgan City, LA 70381
985-380-2448

Evangeline CAA
403 West Magnolia St.
Ville Platte, LA 70586
318-363-1306

Evangeline Career Solutions Center
417 West Magnolia St.
Ville Platte, LA 70586
337-363-6241

Iberia Career Solution Center
124 East Main St.
New Iberia, LA 70560
337-373-0010

Lafayette Business and Career Solution Center
706 East Vermillion St.

Lafayette, LA 70501
337-262-5601

St. Landry CAA
Airport Rd.
Opelousas, LA 70571
337-948-3651

St. Landry Career Solutions Center
1305 Diesi St.
Opelousas, LA 70570
337-948-1330

St. Martin Career Solution Career
  Center
215 Evangeline Blvd.
St. Martinville, LA 70582
337-394-2205

St. Mary CAA, Inc.
1407 Barrow St.
Franklin, LA 70538
318-828-5703

S.M.I.L.E. CCA
501 St. John St.
Lafayette, LA 70501
337-234-3272

West St. Mary Career Solutions Center
600 Main St.
Franklin, LA 70538
337-828-0257

Workers Compensation Office District 4
556 Jefferson St., First Floor
Lafayette, LA 70501
337-262-1057

LAKE CHARLES REGION

Allen Action Agency, Inc.
106 S. Fourth St.
Oberlin, LA 70655
337-639-4348

Allen Career Solutions Center
602 Court St.

Oberlin, LA 70655
337-639-2175

MONROE REGION

Caldwell Parish Career Solutions
  Center
404 Wall St.
Columbia, LA 71418
318-649-5398

District 1E Hearing Office
1908 Stubbs
Monroe, LA 71201
318-362-3078
Delta CCA

611 North Center
Tallulah, LA 71284
318-574-2130

East Carroll CAA
209 Hood St.
Lake Providence, LA 71254
318-559-0004

East Carroll Parish Solutions Center
407 2nd St.
Lake Providence, LA 71254

Franklin Parish Career Solutions Center
3290 Front St.
Winnsboro, LA 71295
318-435-5687

Jackson Parish Career Solutions Center
182 Industrial Drive
Jonesboro, LA 71251
318-259-3801

Macon Economic Opportunity, Inc.
407 Kay St.
Oak Grove, LA 71263
318-428-4379

Madison Parish Career Solutions
  Center
405 North Cedar St.
Tallulah, LA 71284
318-574-0140

Morehouse Career Solutions Center
250 Holt Drive
Bastrop, LA 71270
318-283-0849

Ouachita Career Solutions Center
1301 Hudson Ave.
Monroe, LA 71201
318-362-5111

Ouachita Multi-Purpose CAP
315 Main St.
Monroe, LA 71210
318-322-7151

Pine Belt Multi-Purpose Agency, Inc.
710 Cooper St.
Jonesboro, LA 71251
318-259-6444

Richland Parish Career Solutions
  Center
146 Christian Drive
Rayville, LA 71269
318-728-3348

Tensas Parish Career Solutions Center
107 Arts Drive
St. Joseph, LA 71366

Union CAA
202 Water St.
Farmerville, LA 71241
318-368-9606

Union Career Solutions Center
303-B Water St.
Farmerville, LA 71241
318-368-9606

West Carroll Career Solutions Center
310 Skinner Lane
Oak Grove, LA 71263
318-428-8640

NEW ORLEANS REGION

Algiers
West Bank Orleans Career Solutions
  Center-Job 1 Algiers

3520 General DeGaulle Drive
Algiers, LA 70831
504-658-4580

Belle Chasse
Plaquemines Career Solutions Center
1112 Engineers Rd., Room 19
Belle Chasse, LA 70037
504-392-5803

Chalmette
St. Bernard Career Solutions Center
8201 W. Judge Perez Drive
Chalmette, LA 70043
504-355-4439

Gretna
West Jefferson Career Solutions Center
1900 Lafayette St.
Gretna, LA 70053
504-227-1283

LaPlace
St. John the Baptist Parish Career Solutions Center
975 Cambridge Drive
LaPlace, LA 70068
985-652-3471

Luling
St. Charles Career Solutions Center
737 Paul Maillard Rd.
Luling, LA 70057
985-783-5030

Lutcher
St. James Career Solutions Center
2289 Texas Ave.
Lutcher, LA 70071
225-869-9773

Metairie
East Jefferson Business and Career Solutions Center
1801 Airline Drive, Suite A
Metairie, LA 70001
504-838-5678-111

New Orleans
East Bank Orleans Career Solutions Center-Job 1
2330 Canal St.
New Orleans, LA 70119
504-658-4500

Slidell
St. Tammany Career Solutions Center
316 E. Howze Beach Lane
Slidell, LA 70461
985-646-6410

SHREVEPORT REGION

Arcadia Business and Career Solutions Center
1119 South RR Ave.
Arcadia, LA 71001
318-263-8456

Bienville Business and Career Solutions Center
2434 Manning St.
Ringgold, LA 71068
318-894-9173

Bossier Career Solutions Center
4000 Viking Drive, B-1
Bossier City, LA 71111
318-741-7360

Bossier Office of Community Services
700 Benton Rd.
Bossier, City, LA 71171
318-747-1045

Caddo CAA
4055 St. Vincent St.
Shreveport, LA 71103
318-861-4808

Caddo Business and Career Solutions Center
2900 Dowdell St.
Shreveport, LA 71133
318-676-7788

Claiborne Career Solutions Center
3940 Hwy 79

Homer, LA 71040
318-927-3338

Claiborne Parish Police Jury Office of
Community Services
621 South Main St.
Homer, LA 71040
318-927-3557

Desoto Career Solutions Center
142 Lake Rd.
Mansfield, LA 71052
318-871-2391

Desoto Office of Community Services
113 Franklin St.
Mansfield, LA 71052
318-872-0880

District 1W Hearing Office
9234 Linwood
Shreveport, LA 71106
318-676-5331

Humanitarian Enterprises of Lincoln
Parish
Courthouse Annex
Ruston, LA 71270
318-251-5136

Lincoln Business and Career Solutions
Center
307 North Homer St., Suite 306
Ruston, LA 71270
318-251-4175

Natchitoches East Business and Career Solutions Center

303 Bienville St.
Natchitoches, LA 71457
318-357-3145

Natchitoches Parish Police Jury-Office
of Community Service
415 Trudeau St.
Natchitoches, LA 71459
318-357-2220

Natchitoches West Business and Career Solutions Center
714 Fourth St.
Natchitoches, LA 71457

Red River Careers Solution Center
615 E. Carroll St.
Coushatta, LA 71019
318-932-9570

Sabine Career Solutions Center
1125 West Mississippi Ave., Suite A
Many, LA 71449
318-256-2698

Webster Career Solutions Center
310 Homer Rd.
Minden, LA 71058
318-371-3024

Webster Parish Office of Community
Services
208 Gleason St.
Minden, LA 71058
318-377-7022

MAINE

CURE
23 Washington St.
Sanford, ME 04073
kaymaine@yahoo.com
    *CURE is a grassroots organization from top
to bottom. It does not hire professional leaders.*

*Instead, its leaders come from the ranks of peo-
ple formerly in prison and family members of
friends of prisoners. This organization offers
assistance to ex-offenders.*

Set Free in Maine
18 Lithgow St.

Winslow, ME 04901
207-692-2128
sfme@mint.net

   This program provides employment and life-skills training, anger management groups, and housing Referrals to the program are made by religious organizations that operate within the prison system.

One-Stop Career Centers

www.mainecareercenter.com

Augusta Career Center
21 Enterprise Drive, Suite 2
State House Station 109
Augusta, ME 04333
207-624-5120

Bangor Career Center
45 Oak St., Suite 3
Bangor, ME 04401
207-561-4050

Bath Career Center
34 Wing Farm Pkwy
Bath, ME 04530
207-442-0300

Calais Career Center
One College Drive
Calais, ME 04619-0415
207-454-7551
800-543-0303

Houlton Career Center
91 Military St., Suite 2
Houlton, ME 04730
207-532-5300

Katahdin Region Career Center
One Dingo Drive, Suite 2
East Millinocket, ME 04430
207-746-9608 Ext. 227

Lewiston Career Center
5 Mollison Way
Lewiston, ME 04240-5805
207-753-9000

Machias Career Center
15 Prescott Drive, Suite 1
Machias, ME 04654
207-255-1900

Madawaska Career Center
86 Fox St.
Madawaska, ME 04756
207-726-6345

Portland Career Center
185 Lancaster St.
Portland, ME 04101-2453
207-771-5627

Presque Isle Career Center
66 Spruce St., Suite 1
Presque Isle, ME 04700-3222
207-760-6300

Rockland Career Center
91 Camden St., Suite 201
Rockland, ME 04841
207-596-2600

Rumford Career Center
60 Lowell St.
Rumford, ME 04276
207-364-3738

Skowhegan Career Center
98 North Ave., Suite 20
Skowhegan, ME 04976
207-474-4950

South Paris Career Center
232 Main St.
South Paris, ME 04101-2453
207-743-7763

Springvale Career Center
9 Bodwell Court
Springvale, ME 04083
207-324-5460

Wilton Career Center
865 U.S. Route 2E
Wilton, ME 04294
207-645-5800

MARYLAND

American Correctional Association
Publications Department
4380 Forbes Blvd.
Lanham, MD 20706
301-918-1800 or 800-ACA-JOIN
www.aca.org

This organization offers a parole-planning guide entitled "As Free as an Eagle" and sells self-help books. Write for more details about other available publications.

CURE
P.O. Box 23
Simpsonville, MD
21150
206-202-4872
mdcure@curenational.org
www.curenational.org/~mdcure

CURE is a grassroots organization from top to bottom. It does not hire professional leaders. Instead, its leaders come from the ranks of people formerly in prison and family members of friends of prisoners. This organization offers assistance to ex-offenders.

Division of Rehabilitation Services and Workforce Development

REGION 1: ALLEGANY, CARROLL, FREDERICK, GARRETT, AND WASHINGTON COUNTIES

Cumberland Office
138 Baltimore St.
Suite 201
McMullen Bldg.
Cumberland, MD 21502-2590
301=777-2119
1-800-244-4048
TTY: 301-777-2119
Fax: 301-777-2056
Cumberland@dors.state.md.us

Frederick County Business and Employment Center
5340 Spectrum Drive, Suite A
Frederick, MD 21703
301-600-3072
Fax: 301-600-2791

Frederick Office
100 E. All Saints St., Room 201
Frederick, MD 21701-5514
301-600-3075
1-888-523-0265
TTY: 301-600-3078
Fax: 301-600-3084
Frederick@dors.state.md.us

Hagerstown Local Office
Suite 411, Professional Arts Bldg. 5
    Public Square
Hagerstown, MD 21740-5583
301-791-4760
1-800-801-4297
TTY-301-791-4763
Fax: 301-739-8464
Hagerstown@dors.state.md.us

Hagerstown Regional Office
Suite 511, Professional Arts Bldg. 5
    Public Square
Hagerstown, MD 21740-5583
301-791-4764
1-877-516-5397
TTY: 301-791-4764
Fax: 301-739-8537
Region1@dors.state.md.us

Oakland Office
215 S. Third St.
P.O. Box 595
Oakland, MD 21550
301-334-7947
TTY: 301-334-7947
Fax: 301-334-7946
Oakland@dors.state.md.us

Westminster Office
1004 Littlestown Pike, Suite B1
Westminster, MD 21157
410-848-4456
1-866-819-2034
TTY: 410-848-4456
Fax: 410-857-1807
Westminster@dors.state.md.us

REGION 2: ANNE, ARUNDEL,
CALVERT, CHARLES, AND ST.
MARY'S COUNTIES

Annapolis Local Office
2001-A Commerce Park Dr., Suite 1
Annapolis, MD 21401-2913
410-974-7608
TTY: 410-974-7742
Fax: 410-974-7741
Annapolis@dors.state.md.us

Annapolis Regional Office
2001-A Commerce Park Dr., Suite 2
Annapolis, MD 21401-2913
410-974-7604
Fax: 410-974-7747
Region2@dors.state.md.us

Glen Burnie Office
7480 Baltimore-Annapolis Blvd. #100
Glen Burnie, MD 21061
410-424-3240
Fax: 410-508-2003
Glenburnie@dors.state.md.us

Leonardtown Office
23110 Leonard Hall Drive
P.O. Box 653
Leonardtown, MD 20650-0653
301-880-2790
Fax: 301-475-2541
Leonardtown@dors.state.md.us

Lexington Park Office
Jobs Connection/DORS
21783 North Coral Drive
Lexington Park, MD 20653

240-725-5785
Fax: 240-725-5787

Prince Frederick Office
200 Duke St., Suite 1000
Frederick, MD 20678-9303
443-550-6880
1-866-629-9882
TTY: 443-550-6885
Fax: 443-550-6890
princefrederick@dors.state.md.us

Waldorf Office
Smallwood Bldg., Suite 208
2670 Crain Highway
Waldorf, MD 20601-2806
301-645-8882
TTY: 301-645-8883
Fax: 301-645-2596
waldorf@dors.state.md.us

REGION 3: BALTIMORE CITY

Baltimore City (Northeast)
2301 Argonne Drive
Baltimore, MD 21218
410-261-2944
TTY: 410-261-2943
Fax: 410-261-2957

Baltimore Local Office
1010 Park Ave. Suite 102
Baltimore, MD 21201-5637
410-333-4926
Fax: 410-333-4926
ParkAverUnit37@dors.state.md.us

Baltimore Regional Office
1010 Park Ave. Suite 110
Baltimore, MD 21201-5637
410-333-6119
Fax: 410-333-7400
Region3@dors.state.md.us

Gaslight Square Office
1401 Severn St.
Baltimore, MD 21230
410-637-1699
Fax: 410-637-1688

REGION 4: CAROLINE, CECIL, DORCHESTER, KENT, QUEEN ANNE'S SOMERSET, TALBOT, WICOMICO, AND WORCESTER COUNTIES

Easton Office
8221 Teal Drive Unit 429
Easton, MD 21601-7212
410-822-1831
Dorchester County residents 410-476-5741
(Voice and TTY)-1-800-586-3824
Fax: 410-822-0562
Easton@dors.state.md.us

Elkton Office
Upper Chesapeake Corporate Center
103 Chesapeake Blvd. Suite B
Elkton, MD 21921-5945
410-996-0620
1-866-436-4087
TTY: 410-996-0625
Fax: 410-996-0626
elkton@dors.state.md.us

Salisbury Local Office
917 Mt. Hermon Rd., Suite 4
Salisbury, MD 21804-5105
410-548-7025
1-866-223-2661
TTY: 410-546-9171
Fax: 410-543-6725
Salisbury@dors.state.md.us

Salisbury Regional Office
917 Mt. Hermon Rd., Suite 4
Salisbury, MD 21804-5105
410-543-6906
1-866-223-2661
TTY: 410-546-9171
Fax: 410-543-6725
Region4@dors.state.md,us

REGION 5: BALTIMORE, HARFORD, AND HOWARD COUNTIES

Bel Air Office
Mary E. W. Risteau Center
2 S. Bond St.
Bel Air, MD 21014-3736
410-836-4590
Baltimore line 410-893-4920
TTY: 410-836-4590
Fax: 410-836-4584

Catonsville Office
Beltway West Corporate Center
Suite 214-216, 5740 Executive Drive
Catonsville, MD 21228-1758
410-744-8460
TTY: 410-744-8461
Fax: 410-744-9071
Catonsville@dors.state.md.us

Columbia Workforce Center
7161 Columbia gateway Drive, Suite D
Columbia, MD 21046
410-290-2640
Fax: 410-290-2651
Columbia@dors.state.md.us

Dundalk Office
1005 North Point Blvd., Suite 722
Dundalk, MD 21224-3415
410-285-7654
TTY: 410-285-7656
Fax: 410-285-4295
dundalk@dors.state.md.us

Towson Local Office
113 Towsontown Blvd, Suite B
Towson, MD 21286-5352
410-321-4044
TTY: 410-321-4035
Fax: 410-321-4281
towson@dors.state.md.us

Towson Regional Office
113 Towsontown Blvd., Suite A
Towson, MD 21286-5352
410-321-4035
TTY: 410-321-4035
Fax: 410-321-4281
towson@dors.state.md.us

REGION 6: MONTGOMERY AND PRINCE GEORGE'S COUNTIES

Germantown Office
20010 Century Blvd., Suite 400 Germantown, MD 20874
301-601-1500
TTY: 301-540-5694
Fax: 301-540-7026
Germantown@dors.state.md.us

Lanham Local Office
Metro Business Center
4451-Z Parliament Place
Lanham, MD 20706-1843
301-306-3600
TTY: 301-306-3645
Fax: 301-306-3640
lanham@dors.state.md.us

Lanham Regional Office
Metro Business Center
4451-Z Parliament Place
Lanham, MD 20706-1843
301-306-3600
TTY: 301-306-3645
Fax: 301-306-3641
Region6@dors.state.md.us

Oxon Hill Office
6188 Oxon Hill Rd., Suite 500

Oxon Hill, MD 20745
301-749-4660
TTY: 301-749-6759
Fax: 301-749-0348
oxonhill@dors.state.md.us

Prince George's Workforce Services Corp-Largo
1100 Mercantile Lane, Suite 100
Largo, MD 20774
301-618-8425 Ext.1054
Fax: 301-386-2419

Wheaton Office
11002 Veirs Mill Rd., Suite 408
Wheaton, MD 20902-1991
301-949-3750
TTY: 301-942-7513
Fax: 301-949-5876
wheaton@dors.state.md.us

Workforce and Technology Center
2301 Argonne Drive
Baltimore, MD 21218-1696
410-554-9100
1-888-200-7117
TTY: 410-554-9583
Fax: 410-554-9112
wtc@dors.state.md.us

MASSACHUSETTS

Aid to Incarcerated Mothers (AIM)
434 Massachusetts Ave. Suite 503
Boston, MA 02118
617-536-0058; Accept Collect Calls
M, W, Th

AIM provides services to incarcerated mothers and their children, as well as women who have had trouble with the law in the past and are trying to improve their lives upon re-entry into the community. While a woman is in prison, AIM attempts to prevent her from being permanently separated from the children. AIM

arranges foster care review with DSS, children's visitation, as well as counseling and support for children of incarcerated mothers. For women in transition, the RENEW program offers medical assistance, resource development (housing, education, jobs), parental assessment and 1-on-1 counseling. The CHARM (Comprehensive Health to At-Risk Mothers) program works with women on issues of self-esteem and domestic violence, and helps them teach back to the community. AIM also runs a support group for women who have returned to the community, working on habits that will keep them clean and legal. Referrals for services such as detox programs, shelters and sober houses are also available.

American Friends Service Committee (AFSC)
2161 Mass Ave.
Cambridge, MA 02140
617-661-6130

The AFSC Criminal Justice Program provides prisoners referrals for legal help available to prisoners and ex-offenders. Provides assistance to prisoner organizations in prison and community organizations working on prison issues. AFSC's quarterly newsletter, Outlook on Justice, is available to prisoners for $2 per year.

Community Resources for Justice (CRJ)
355 Boylston St.
Boston, MA 02116
617-482-2520
www.crjustice.org
crj@crjustice.org

Programs offered include education, counseling, assistance with employment and housing, and substance abuse treatment.

CURE
P.O. Box 67
Brookline, MA 02446
617-730-5814
FAX: 617-739-9191
jceltic@bellatlantic.net

CURE is a grassroots organization from top to bottom. It does not hire professional leaders. Instead, its leaders come from the ranks of people formerly in prison and family members of friends of prisoners. This organization offers assistance to ex-offenders.

First Incorporated
167 Centre St.
Roxbury, MA 02119
617-427-1588 No collect calls
And
37 Intervale St.
Roxbury, MA 02119
617-445-2291

Provides services for men who have been released from prison and have substance abuse concerns, sometimes in combination with mental health problems. The program is geared toward behavior modification through counseling and building structured living.

Health and Education Services-TIP
60 Merrimack St.
Haverhill, MA 01830

TIP helps HIV-positive inmates from Massachusetts make the transition back into the community, providing advocacy, counseling, crisis intervention and transportation to services. They also provide information and referrals to resources and services, e.g., medical care, housing, benefits, etc.

Massachusetts Department of Corrections
50 Maple St. Suite 3
Milford, MA 01757
508-422-3300

Provides children's center in visiting rooms, parent education, self-help support groups, information, referrals, case management, group activities for children, religious ministry, and family reunification support.

The Neil J. Houston House (NJHH)
9 Notre Dame St.
Roxbury, MA 02119
617-445-3066

The Neil J. Houston House- is a residential pre-release substance abuse treatment program, offering pregnant women in prison an alternative to incarceration, pre and post-natal medical services and early intervention services to their infants.

Prisoners Re-entry Working Group
c/o Community Change Inc.
14 Beacon St. Room 605
Boston, MA 02108
617-523-0555 ext. 4 or 617-236-1808

Publishes "Coming Home," a resource directory for prisoners returning to the greater Boston area; available for $40.

The Salvation Army-Harbor Light Center

83 Brookline St.
Boston, MA 02118
617-536-7469

Harbor Light provides both short-term and longer residential substance abuse treatment programs for individuals in transition from prison to community. Programs include 3 meals a day. 1-on-1 counseling, structured classes on behavior and life decision-making, referrals and assistance making community contacts (housing, employment, etc.). Inmates can contact Harbor Light in writing or through a case manager.

Span, Inc.
110 Arlington St.
Boston, MA 02116
617-423-0750 Collect calls accepted.

SPAN provides services to inmates and ex-inmates making the transition from prison to community living in Eastern and Central MA. Programs include release planning, substance abuse counseling, transitional housing assistance, health education, reintegration support, and a drop-in center. SPAN provides a wide range of services specific to people with HIV, such as management, transitional housing, medicine adherence assistance, etc. Agencies within SPAN include: Community Resource Center (CRC)-multi-service center for offenders and ex-offenders; Transitional Intervention Program for HIV-Positive Inmates (TIP). TIP covers all aspects of integration. They meet with inmates up to six months prior to release, and provide referrals to medical services as well as a number of social services. Housing Program for HIV-Positive Clients-Helps clients find housing and may pay rent up to six months at Sullivan House, a halfway house. Client Reintegration Support Group- provides case management for non–HIV clients.

Spectrum Health Systems
Central Office: 10 Mechanic St. Suite 302
Worcester, MA 01608
508-792-5400 No collect calls

Spectrum operates five major programs in behavioral health, correctional treatment services, adolescent services, women's services and prevention services.

Community Resource Centers (CRCs)

CRCs are state-funded multi-service center for offenders and ex-offenders. Services include work readiness classes, sex offender referral and support, thinking for a change classes, reintegration counseling groups, transitional intervention, transitional housing, and housing research.

Boston
110 Arlington St.
Boston, MA 02116-5377
617-423-0750 Collect calls accepted

Fall River
186 South Main St.
Fall River, MA 02721
508-676-3729 No Collect calls

Lowell
45 Merrimack St. Suite 500
Lowell, MA 01852
978-458-4286 No collect calls

Springfield
136 Williams St.
Springfield, MA 01105
413-737-9544 No Collect Calls

Worcester
324 Grove St.
Worcester, MA 01605
508-831-0050

Workforce Development Offices

Central Massachusetts Region

North Central Career Center
25 Main St.
Gardner, MA 01440
978-632-5050
TTY: 508-792-7571

North Central Career Center
100 Erdman Way
Leominster, MA 01453

978-534-1481
TTY: 978-534-1637

Workforce Central Career Center
425 Fortune Blvd, Suite 202
Milford, MA 01757
508-478-4300
TTY: 508-478-1887

Workforce Central Career Center
5 Optical Drive, Suite 200
Southbridge, MA 01550
508-765-6430
TTY: 508-765-6437

Workforce Central Career Center
44 Front St. 6th Floor
Worcester, MA 01608
508-799-1600

GREATER BOSTON REGION

Boston Career Link
1010 Harrison Ave.
Boston, MA 02119
617-536-1888
TTY: 617-867-4687

The Career Place
Trade Center Park
100 Sylvan Rd., Suite 6-100
Woburn, MA 01801
781-932-5500
888-273-WORK

Career Source
186 Alewife Brook Parkway
Cambridge, MA 02138
617-661-7867
888-454-9675
TTY: 800-439-2370

Employment and Training Resource
201 Boston Post Rd. West
Suite 200
Marlborough, MA 01752
508-786-0928

Employment and Training Resource
449 Newtonville Ave.

Newtonville, MA 02460
617-928-0530

Employment and Training Resource
275 Prospect St.
Norwood, MA 02062

Everett Career Source
1935 Reverse Beach Parkway
Everett, MA 02149
617-389-8025

JobNet
210 South St. 1st Floor
Boston, MA 02111
617-338-0809
800-5JOBNET
TTY: 711(state wide relay number)

The Work Place
19 Winter St. 4th Floor
Boston, MA 02108
617-737-0093
1-800-436-WORK (9675)
TTY: 617-428-0390

NORTHEASTERN MASSACHUSETTS
REGION

Career Center of Lowell
107 Merrimack St.
Lowell, MA 01852
978-458-2503
TTY: 978-805-4915

North Shore Career Center of
Gloucester
11-15 Parker St.
Gloucester, MA 01930
978-283-4772

North Shore Career Center of Lynn
181 Union St.
Lynn, MA 01901
781-593-0585

North Shore Career Center of Salem
70 Washington St.
Salem, MA 01970
978-825-7200

ValleyWorks Career Center
192 Merrimack St.
Haverhill, MA 01930
978-722-7000

ValleyWorks Career Center
Heritage Place
439 South Union St.-Building 2
Lawrence, MA 01843
978-722-7000

SOUTHEASTERN MASSACHUSETTS
REGION

Attleboro Career Center
67 Mechanic St.
Attleboro, MA 02703
508-222-1950

Career Opportunities Falmouth
205 Worchester Court Unit B-3
Falmouth, MA 02540
508-548-4828
TTY: 800-439-2370 Mass Relay 711

Career Opportunities Hyannis
372 North St.
Hyannis, MA 02601
508-771-JOBS (5627)
TTY: 508-862-6102

Career Opportunities Orleans
77 Finley Rd.
Orleans, MA 02653
508-240-1900
TTY: 800-439-2370

CareerWorks
34 School St.
Brockton, MA 02301
508-543-3400

Fall River Career Center
446 North Main St.
Fall River, MA 02720
508-730-5000

Greater New Bedford Career Center
618 Acushnet Ave.

New Bedford, MA 02740
508-990-4000

Plymouth Career Center
36 Cordage Park Circle-Suite 200
Plymouth, MA 02360
508-732-5300
TTY: 508-732-5300

Quincy Career Center
152 Parkingway
Quincy, MA 02169
617-745-4000

Taunton Career Center
72 School St.
Taunton, MA 02780
508-977-1400

Wareham Career Center
48 Marion Rd. Route 6
Wareham, MA 02571
508-291-7062

WESTERN MASSACHUSETTS
REGION

BerkshireWorks Career Center
37 Main St.
North Adams, MA 01247
413-663-1111
TTY: 413-663-5442

BerkshireWorks Career Center
160 North St.
Pittsfield, MA 01201
413-499-2220
TTY: 413-499-7306

CareerPoint
850 High St.
Holyoke, MA 01040
413-532-4900
TTY: 413-535-3098

Franklin/Hampshire Career Center
One Arch Place
Greenfield, MA 01301
413-774-4361
TTY: 413-772-2174

Franklin/Hampshire Career Center
178 Industrial Drive, Suite 1
Northhampton, MA 01060
413-586-6506
TTY: 413-586-4921

FutureWorks
One Federal St. Bldg. 103-3
Springfield, MA 01105
413-858-2800
TTY: 413-858-2800

MICHIGAN

CURE
P.O. Box 2736
Kalamazoo, MI 49003-2736
269-383-0028
FAX: 269-373-2545
kayperry@aol.com

CURE is a grassroots organization from top to bottom. It does not hire professional leaders. Instead, its leaders come from the ranks of people formerly in prison and family members of-friends of prisoners. This organization offers assistance to ex-offenders.

MCM Ministers
1260 28th SE
Grand Rapids, Michigan 49508
616-475-5787
*http://newcreationsmin.net/joegerkins@s
    bcglobal*

MCM ministers to the spiritual needs of in-mates and at risk adolescents through bible studies and small group ministries.

VIP/Volunteers in Prevention, Proba-
    tion, and Prison, Inc.
163 Madison Ave.
Detroit, MI 48226
313-964-1110

Helps with effective transition back into the community for ex-offenders.

Michigan Works! Career Centers

www.michiganworks.org

Alcona Service Center
202 South 2nd St., Suite B
P.O. Box 316

Lincoln, MI 48742
969-736-6082

Allegan County Service Center
2891 116th Ave.
Allegan, MI 49010
269-686-5079

Alma Service Center
327 East Center St.
Alma, Mi 48801
969-466-4832

Alpena County Service Center
315 West Chisholm
Alpena, MI 49707
969-356-3339

Arenac County Service Center
4480 West M-61
Standish, Mi 48658
989-846-2111

Baraga County
115 North Front St.
L'Anse, MI 49946
906-524-5300

Battle Creek Service Center
135 West Hamblin Ave.
Battle Creek, MI 49017
269-962-5411

Bay Rd. (Saginaw) Service Center
541 East Slocum St.
Whitehall, MI 49461
231-893-1091

Benton Harbor
409 W. Main St.

Benton Harbor, MI 49022
269-927-1799

Buchanan Service Center
400 E. Front St., Suite B
Buchanan, MI 49107
269-697-8736

Capitol Area Service Center
2110 S. Cedar St.
Lansing, MI 48801
517-492-5500

Capitol Area Service Center, Eaton
    County
311 West First St.
Charlotte, MI 48813
517-543-5278

Cheboygan Service Center
11153 N. Straits Hwy
Cheboygan, MI 49721
231-627-4303

Chippewa Service Center
1118 East Easterday Ave.
Sault Suite Marie, MI 49783
906-635-1752

Detroit Department of Workforce
    Development
455 W. Fort St.
Detroit, MI 48226
313-962-9675 Ext. 527

Detroit One-Stop Service Center
5555 Conner Ave.
Detroit, MI 48213
313-579-4925

Detroit Workforce Development De-
    partment
707 W. Milwaukee
Detroit, MI 48202
313-873-9675 Ext. 527

Dowagiac
601 D North Front St.
Dowagiac, MI 49047
269-782-9664

Elkland Service Center
12519 State St.
P.O. Box 836
Atlanta, MI 49709
969-785-4054

Family Workforce Development Center
1516 Peck St.
Muskegon, MI 49441
231-726-2626

Gladwin County Service Center
150 Commerce Court
Gladwin, MI 48624
969-426-8571

Gogebic County
100 West Cleveland Drive
Ironwood, MI 49938
906-932-4059

Goodwill Industrial Workforce Devel-
    opment Center
950 West Norton Ave., Suite C
Muskegon, MI 49441
231-739-9010

Hastings Service Center
535 West Woodlawn
Hastings, MI 49058
269-945-9545 Ext. 144

Highland Career Center
2218 S. Milford Rd.
Highland, MI 48357

Hillsdale Service Center
21 Care Drive
Hillsdale, Mi 49242
517-437-3381

Houghton County Service Center
902 Razorback Drive, Suite 6
Houghton, MI 49931
906-482-6916

Ionia Service Center
307 West Adams St.
Ionia, MI 48846
616-527-2360

Iosco County Service Center
1230 East U.S. 23
East Tawas, MI 48730
989-362-6407

Iron County Service Center
237 East Caspian Ave.
P.O. Box 670
Caspian, MI 49915
906-265-0532

Isabelle Service Center
1803 South Mission St.
Mt. Pleasant, MI 48858
969-722-5304

The Job Force
114 W. Superior
Munising, Mi 49862
906-387-4937

Joblink Service Center
1847 N. Perry
Pontiac, MI 48340
248-276-1777

Leonard Service Center
1560 Leonard NE
Grand Rapids, MI 49505
989-879-6640

Livonia Service Center
30246 Plymouth Rd.
Livonia, MI 48150
734-513-4900

Kalamazoo-St. Joseph
1601 S. Burdick St.
Kalamazoo, MI 49001-4614
269-383-2536

M. TECH Service Center
622 Godfrey SW
Grand Rapids, MI 49503
616-234-3398

Montcalm Service Center
114 South Greenville West Drive
Gladwin, MI 48624
989-426-8571

Macomb Service Center, Clinton
Township
Clinton Township
43630 Hayes Rd., Suite 100
Clinton Township, MI 48038
586-263-1501

Macomb Service Center
75 North River Rd.
Mt. Clemons, Mi 48043
586-783-8700

Macomb Service Center
15950 Twelve Mile Rd.
Roseville, MI 48066
586-447-9200

North Ottawa County Job Connection
1830-G 172nd Ave.
Grand Haven, MI 49417-8931
616-296-0776

Novi Service Center
31186 Beck Rd.
Novi, MI 48377
248-926-1820

Oak Park Career Center
22180 Parklawn
Oak Park, MI 48237
246-691-8437

Ogemaw County Service Center
2389 South M-76
West Branch, MI 48661
989-345-1090

Ontonagon County
429 River St.
Ontonagon, MI 49953
906-884-4753

Osceola Service Center
240 East Church St.
Reed City, MI 49677
231-832-3131

Otsego Service Center
2927 D&M Drive

Gaylord, MI 49735
969-732-3886

Paw Paw Service Center
32849 Red Arrow Highway, Suite 200
Paw Paw, MI 49079
269-657-7014

Pinconning Service Center
625 S. Maple
Pinconning, MI 48650
989-879-6640

SER Metro-Detroit
9301 Michigan Ave.
Detroit, MI 48210
313-846-5447

Shiawassee Service Center
1975 West Main St.
Owosso, MI 48867
969-729-6663

St. Clair Service Center
100 McMorran, 6th Floor
Port Huron, MI 48060
810-966-3300

South Haven
125 Veterans Blvd., Suite 123
South Haven, MI 49090
269-637-4020

South Ottawa County Service Center
121 Clover Ave.
Holland, MI 49423
616-396-2154

Sylvester Broome Jr. Training and
    Technology Center
4119 North Saginaw St.
Flint, MI 48505

810-787-7995
800-551-3575

Thumb Area Tuscola County Service
    Center
1184 Cleaver Rd.
Caro, Mi 48723
969-673-8103

ThumbWorks: A Michigan Works
    Service
614 N. Port Crescent
Bad Axe, MI 48413
969-269-2311

Three Rivers Service Center
16587 Enterprise Drive
Three Rivers, MI 49093
269-273-2717

Troy Service Center
550 Stephenson Highway, Suite 400
Troy, Mi 48083
248-823-5101

West Central-Newaygo County
4747 West 48th St., Suite 162
Fremont, MI 49412
231-924-3230

West Central Mason County
5722 W. U.S. 10
Ludington, MI 49431
231-845-2563

White Lake Workforce Development
    Center
541 East Slocum St.
Whitehall, Mi 49461
231-893-1091

MINNESOTA

Amicus
100 N. Sixth St. Suite 529-B
Minneapolis, MN 55403

612-348-8570
www.amicus.org
staff@amicususa.org

This organization assists former prisoners with housing, clothing, and employment. They also offer scholarships and pre/post release programs.

Minnesota Workforce Centers

Albert Lea
1649 West Main St.
Albert Lea, MN 56007-1868
507-379-3409

Alexandra
303 22nd Ave. W. Suite 107
Alexandra, MN 56308
320-762-7800

Anoka County
1201 89th Ave. NE., Suite 235
Blaine, MN 55434
763-783-4800

Austin
1600 8th Ave., NW
Riverland Community College
Austin, MN 55912-1400
507-433-0555

Bemidji
616 America Ave. NW
Bemidji, MN 566601
218-333-8200

Brainerd
204 Laurel St., Suite 21
Brainerd, Mn 56401
218-828-2450

Cambridge
140 Buchanan St. N. Suite 152
Cambridge, MN 55008-1756
763-279-4492

Cloquet
715 Cloquet Ave.
Cloquet, MN 55720-1629
218-878-4414

Crookston
1730 University Ave.

Crookston, MN 56716-1112
218-281-6020

Dakota County-Northern Area
1 Mendota Rd. W. Suite 170
West St. Paul, MN 55118-4768

Dakota County-Western Area
2900 W. County Rd. 42, Suite 140
Burnsville, MN 55337
952-895-7600

Detroit lakes
801 Roosevelt Ave.
P.O. Box 1108
Detroit Lakes, MN 56502
218-846-7377

Duluth
320 West Second St., Room 206
Government Service Center
Duluth, MN 55802
218-723-4730

Fairmont
412 South State St.
Fairmont, MN 56301-0767
507-235-5518

Faribault
201 South Lyndale Ave. S-1
Faribo Town Square
Faribault, MN 55021-0009
507-333-2047

Fergus Falls
125 West Lincoln Ave., Suite 1
P.O. Box 161
Fergus Falls, MN 56537

Grand Rapids
1216 SE 2nd Ave.
Itasca Resource Center
Grand Rapids, MN 55744-3982
218-327-4460

Hennepin North
7115 Northland Terrace, Suite 100
Brooklyn Park, MN 55428
763-536-6000

Hennepin South
4220 West Old Shakopee Rd.
Bloomington, MN 55437
952-346-4000 Ext.4045

Hibbing
3920 13th Ave. East
Hibbing, MN 55746-0068
218-262-6777

Hutchinson
2 Century Ave.
P.O. Box 550
Hutchinson, MN 55350-0550
320-587-4740

International Falls
1501 Highway 71, Room SC 128
International Falls, MN 56649
218-283-9427

Litchfield
114 North Holcomb Ave., Suite 170
Litchfield, MN 55355-2273
320-693-2859

Little Falls
315 12th St. NE.
Little Falls, MN 56345-2910

Mankato
12 Civic Center Plz., Suite 1600A
Mankato, MN 56001-7796
507-389-6723

Marshall
607 West Main St.
Marshall, MN 56258-3099
507-537-6236

Minnesota North
1200 Plymouth Ave. North
Minnesota, MN 55411-0040
612-520-3500

Minnesota South
777 E. Lake St.
Minnesota, MN 55407-1546

Montevideo
202 North 1st St., Suite 100

Montevideo, MN 56265
320-269-8819

Monticello
406 E. 7th St.
P.O. Box 720
Monticello, MN 55362
763-271-3700

Moorhead
715 11th St. N. Suite 302
Moorhead, MN 56560
218-287-5060

More
903 E. Forest Ave.
More, MN 55051-1617
320-679-6484

New Ulm
1618 South Broadway, Suite 203
New Ulm, MN 56073-3756
507-354-3138

Owatonna
631 N. Cedar
Owatonna, MN 55060-2328
507-446-1470

Ramsey County-North St. Paul
2008 11th Ave.
North St. Paul, MN 55109-5100
651-779-5666

Ramsey County St. Paul
540 Fairview Ave. N
St. Paul, MN 55104
651-642-0383

Red Wing
1606 West Third St.
Red Wing, MN 55066-0033
651-385-6460

Rochester
300 11th Ave. N.W., Suite 112
Rochester, MN 55901
507-285-7315

St. Cloud
1542 Northway Dr. Door 2

St. Cloud, MN 56303
320-308-5320

Scott County
752 Canterbury Rd. South
Shakopee, MN 55379
952-496-8686

Thief River Falls
1301 Highway 1 E
Thief River Falls, MN 56701-2500
218-681-0909

Virginia
820 North 9th St., Olcott Plazas
Virginia, MN 55792-2345
218-748-2200

Wadena
124 SE. 1st, Suite 3
Wadena, MN 56482-0643
218-631-7660

Washington County Woodbury
2150 Radio Drive
Woodbury, MN 55125
651-275-8850

Willmar
2200 23rd St NE., Suite 2040
Willmar, MN 56201-9423
320-231-5174

Winona
1250 Homer Rd., Suite 200
Winona, MN 55987-4842
507-453-2920

Worthington
318 Ninth St.
P.O. Box 816
Worthington, MN 56187
507-376-3116

MISSISSIPPI

CURE
P.O. Box 1620
Philadelphia, MS 39350-9996
TOLL FREE 877-819-9663
www.mississippicure.org
patticake1954@bellsouth.net

CURE is a grassroots organization from top to bottom. It does not hire professional leaders. Instead, its leaders come from the ranks of people formerly in prison and family members of friends of prisoners. This organization offers assistance to ex-offenders.

Goodwill of South Mississippi, Inc.
Gulfport:
2407 31 St.
Gulfport, MS 39501
228-863-2323

Ridgeland
104 E. State St.
Ridgeland, MS 39157
601-853-8110

Provides training, vocational rehabilitation, skill development and work opportunities.

WIN Job Centers

Amory
1619 Highland Drive
Amory, MS 38821
662-256-2618

Batesville
103-16 Woodland Rd.
Tylertown Plaza
Batesville, MS 38606
662-563-7318

Biloxi
2306 Pass Rd.
Biloxi, MS 39535-4647
228-388-7997

Carthage
202 C. O. Brooks St.

Carthage, MS 39051
601-267-9282

Clarksdale
236 Sharkey Ave.
Clarksville, MS 38614
662-624-9001

Cleveland
119 North Commerce Ave.
Cleveland, MS 38732
662-843-2704

Columbia
1111 Highway 98
Columbus, MS 39429
601-736-2628

Corinth
2759 South Harper Rd.
Corinth, MS 38834
622-696-2336
622-287-3247

De Soto County
7320 Hwy 51 N.
Southhaven, MS 38671
662-342-4002

Forest
536 Deer Field Drive
Forest, MS 39074
601-469-2851

Fulton
201 W. Main St.
Fulton, MS 38843
662-862-3824

Golden Triangle
5000 North Frontage Rd.
Columbus, MS 39701
662-328-6876

Greenville
800 Dr. Martin Luther King Jr. Blvd
Delta Plaza
Greenville, MS 38703
662-332-8101

Greenwood
313 Lamar St.
Greenwood, MS 38935
662-453-7141

Grenada
1229-A Sunset Drive
Grenada, MS 38902
662-226-2911

Gulfport
12121 Highway 49 N.
Gulfport, MS 39505-2849
228-539-6800

Hattiesburg
1911 Arcadia St.
Hattiesburg, MS 39401
601-584-1202

Holly Springs
1180 Hwy 311
Holly Springs, MS 38635
662-252-1488

Houston
665 North Jefferson St.
Houston, MS 38851
662-456-3563

Indianola
226 North Martin Luther King Drive
Indianola, MS 38751
662-887-2502

Iuka
1107 Maria Lane
Iuka, MS 38852
662-423-9231

Jackson
5959 I-55 N. Frontage Rd.
Suite C
Jackson, MS 39211
601-321-7931

Kosciusko
Highway 12 E. 127
Northside Shopping Center

Kosciusko, MS 39090
662-289-3700

Laurel
1721 B-West 10th St.
Laurel, MS 39441
601-399-4000

Louisville
600 North Court Ave., Suite B
Louisville, MS 39339
662-773-5051

Madison County
152 Watford Parkway Dr., Suite B
Canton, MS 39046
601-859-7609

Meridian
2000 Highway 19 N.
Meridian, MS 39307
601-483-1406

New Albany
301 North St.
New Albany, MS 38652-3008
662-692-1502

Northeast Corinth
2759 South Harper Rd.
Corinth, MS 38834
662-287-3247

Oxford
204 Colonnade Cove, Suite 1

Oxford, MS 38655
662-234-3231

Pascagoula
1604 Denny Ave.
Pascagoula, MS 39569
228-762-3726

Philadelphia
1120 East Main St., Suite 11
Philadelphia, MS 39350-0549
601-656-2811

Picayune
2005 Wildwood Rd.
Picayune, MS 39466
601-798-3472

Ripley
111 East Spring St.
Ripley, MS 38663
662-837-7411

Tunica
1054 South Fitzgerald Blvd.
Robinsonville, MS 38664
662-842-4371

Winona
109 Liberty St.
Winona, MS 38967
662-283-4105

MISSOURI

Association of Gospel Rescue Missions
1045 Swift St.
North Kansas City, MO 64116-4127
816-471-8020; 800-624-5156
   Have residential programs in some cities for ex-offenders

Center for Women in Transition
6400 Minnesota
St. Louis, MO 63111

314-771-5207
www.cwitstl.org
cwit@cwitstl.org
   This program offers mentoring for women making the transition back into society and is involved with prison advocacy.

Child Evangelism Fellowship
P.O. Box 348
Warrenton, MO 63383-0348
800-300-4033

http://www.cefonline.com/cefexecutive-offices@ceonline.com

CEF provides a free correspondence Bible study for children of those incarcerated and for juveniles entitled, "The Mailbox Club." The material is age appropriate and parents can also sign up.

CURE
P.O. Box 6034
Chesterfield, MO 63006
816-413-0186
www.Mocure.org
missouricure@hotmail.com

CURE is a grassroots organization from top to bottom. It does not hire professional leaders. Instead, its leaders come from the ranks of people formerly in prison and family members of friends of prisoners. This organization offers assistance to ex-offenders.

Employment Connection
4000 Laclede Ave.
St. Louis, MO 63108
www.employmentstl.org

This organization offers intensive job acquisition skill training and employment placement assistance to persons with criminal records.

Jail Ministry Outreach
Lutheran Ministries Association
8631 Delmar Suite 306
St. Louis, MO 63124
314-754-2821
sbarnes@imaonline.org

Provides restorative justice through community services. This program is based around love, resource awareness for a positive re-entry, and individual and group support sessions.

Our Savior Lutheran Prison Ministry
Service Group
1500 San Simeon Way
Fenton, MO 63026
636-343-2192

Networks with other agencies to provide jobs, clothing, food and housing for recently released ex-offenders.

Project Cope
3529 Marcus Ave.
St. Louis, MO 63115
314-389-4804
www.projcope.org
office@projcope.org

This project offers re-entry support through faith-based partnership teams and transitional housing for some, to former prisoners of the St. Louis Community.

Workforce Investment Board:
Central Region
1202 Forum Dr.
Rolla, MO 65401
WIB Chair-Jim Dickerson
573-364-7030 Ext. 133
Fax: 573-364-7130
jvaughn@copic.ext.missouri.edu

Work Force Investment Board:
City of Springfield
Department of Workforce Development
Bill Dowling, Director
1514 South Glenstone
Springfield, MO 65804
WIB Chair-William Skains
417-887-4343
Fax: 417-887-1892
bdowling@jcocmis.org

Workforce Investment Board:
City of St. Louis
St. Louis Agency on Training and Employment (SLATE)
Mike Holmes, Director
1017 Olive St.
St. Louis, MO 63101
WIB Chair-Janice Rhodes
314-589-8101
Fax: 314-622-3553
mholmes@stlworks.com

Workforce Investment Board:
Eastern Jackson County
Employment Council
Clyde McQueen, President and CEO

1740 Paseo, Suite D
Kansas City, MO 64106

WIB Acting-Chair-Betty Freeman-
  Boots
816-471-2330
816-471-0132
cmcqueen@feckc.org

Workforce Investment Board: Jefferson-
  Franklin Consortium
Office of Job Training
Shirley Wilson, One-Stop Coordinator
Jefferson-Franklin Counties, Inc
P.O. Box 350
Hillsboro, MO 63050
WIB Chair-John Rhodes
636-287-8909
Fax: 636-287-1245
Swilson.ojtp@sbcglobal.net

Workforce Investment Board: Kansas
  City
Full Employment Council, Inc.
Clyde McQueen, Director
1740 Pasco, Suite D
Kansas City, MO 64108
WIB Chair-Barbara Curry
816-471-2330 Ext 267
Fax: 816-471-0132
cmcqueen@feckc.org

Workforce Investment Board: Northeast Region
NEMO Workforce Investment Board,
  Inc.
Mark Fuqua, Director
111 E. Monroe
Paris, MO 65275
WIB Chair-Virgil (Sonny) Raines
660-327-5125
660-327-5128
mfuqua@nemowib.org

Workforce Investment Board: Northwest Region
NW Workforce Investment Board

Becky Steele, Director
North Central Missouri College
912 Main St.
Trenton, MO 64683
WIB Chair-Lisa McGhee
660-359-3622 Ext 17
Fax: 660-359-3082
bsteele@mail.ncmissouri.edu

Workforce Investment Board: St.
  Charles County
Donald N. Holt, Executive Director
212 Turner Rd.
St. Peters, MO 63376-1079
WIB Chair-Walter Tate
636-278-1360
Fax: 636-278-1843
dholt@saintcharlescounty.org

Workforce Investment Board: St.
  Louis County
26 North Oaks Plaza
St. Louis, Mo 63121
WIB Chair-Fredrick Douglas
314-679-3300
Fax: 314-679-3301
ggordon@stlouisco.com

Workforce Investment Board: South
  Central Region
Tana Hokler, Director
1105 Independence Drive
P.O. Box 88
West Plains, MO 65775
WIB Chair-Garland Barton
417-257-2630
417-257-2633
tholder@centurytel.net

Workforce Investment Board: South-
  east Region
June O'Dell, President/COO
Eagle Park Building
760 S. Kings Highway, Suite C
Cape Girardeau, MO 63703
WIB Chair-John Moorman
573-334-0990 Ext. 100

Fax: 573-334-0335
june@job4you.org

Workforce Investment Board: Southwest Region
Jasen Jones, Executive Director
105 Rangeline Rd.
P.O. Box 1706
Joplin, MO 64802
WIB Chair-Gary Little
417-206-1717 Ext 224
Fax: 417-206-0022
ceo@workforcezone.net

Workforce Investment Board: West Central Region
Workforce Development Board of Western Missouri, Inc.
Patti Carter, Director
2905 West Broadway
Sedalia, MO 65301
WIB Chair-Randy Lee
660-827-3722
Fax: 660-827-3789
wdbpc@iland.net

MONTANA

One-Stop Job Service Workforce Centers

Anaconda
307 East Park St.
Anaconda, MT 59711
406-563-3444

Billings
2121 Rosebud Drive, Stop B
Billings, MT 59102-6274

Bitterroot
333 West Main St.
Hamilton, MT 59840
406-363-1822

Bozeman
121 North Wilson
Bozeman, MT 59715
406-582-9200

Butte
2201 White Blvd.
Butte, MT 59701
406-494-0300

Cut Bank
501 East Main
Cut Bank, MT 59427-3015
406-873-2191

Dillon
730 North Montana St., Suite 4
Dillon, MT 59701
406-683-4259

Flathead
427 First Ave. East
Kalispell, MT 59901
406-758-6200

Glendive
221 South Kendrick Ave.
Glendive, MT 59330
406-337-3314

Great Falls
1018 7th St. South
Great Falls, MT 59405
406-791-5800

Havre
160 First Ave.
Havre, MT 59501
406-265-5847
866-288-9642

Helena
715 Front St.
Helena, MT 59620-1505
406-447-3200

Kootenai
417 Mineral Ave., Suite 4
Libby, MT 59923
406-293-6282

Lewistown
300 First Ave. North
Lewistown, MT 59457
406-538-8701

Livingston
220 East Park St.
Livingston, MT 59047
406-222-0520

Miles City
12 North 10th St.
Miles City, MT 59301
406-232-8340

Mission Valley, Lake County
417-B Main St.
Polson, MT 59860
406-883-7880

Missoula
539 South 3rd St.
Missoula, MT 59806
406-728-7060

Northeast Montana
201 Main St.
Wolf Point, MT 59201
406-653-1720

Sanders County
2504 Tradewinds Way
Thompson Falls, MT 59873
406-827-3472

Shelby
202 Main St.
Shelby, MT 59474
406-434-5161

Sidney
221 North Central
Sidney, MT 59270
406-433-1204

NEBRASKA

CEGA Services, Offender Referrals
P.O. Box 81826
Lincoln, NE 68501
402-464-0602

This organization offers pre-release referrals for housing, employment, and substance abuse treatment programs. They charge a $15 fee for each city's list of referrals.

Workforce Development Centers

Alliance
302 Box Butte
Alliance, NE 69301-3342
308-763-2935

Beatrice
5109 West Scott Rd., Suite 413

Beatrice, NE 68310-1408
402-223-6060

Columbus
3020 18th St., Suite 1
Columbus, NE 68601-4918
402-564-7160

Hastings
2727 West 2nd St., Suite 338, Landmark Center
Hastings, NE68901-4663
402-462-1867

Lexington
1308 North Adams St.
Lexington, NE 68850-1212
308-324-2064

McCook
220 West 1st St.

McCook, NE 69001
308-345-8470

Nebraska City
917 Wildwood Lane, Suite 3
Nebraska City, NE 68410
402-873-3384

Nebraska Department of Labor, Fremont Career Center
835 N. Broad St.
Fremont, NE 68025-5136
402-727-3250

Nebraska Department of Labor, Grand Island
1306 West 3rg St.
Grand Rapids, NE 68801
308-385-6300

Nebraska Department of Labor, Lincoln Career Center
1010 N St. Box 194
Lincoln, NE 68508
402-471-2275

Nebraska Department of Labor, York Career Center
510 Lincoln Ave.
York, NE 68467-2997
402-362-5891

Norfolk
105 East Norfolk Ave., Suite 100
Norfolk, NE 68701
402-370-3430

North Platte
306 E. 6th St.
North Platte, NE 69101
308-535-8320

Omaha
5717 F St.
Omaha, NE 68117-2822
402-595-3000

Omaha
2421 North 24th St.
Omaha, NE 68110-2216
402-444-4700

Scottsbluff
1930 E. 20th Place, Suite 200
Scottsbluff, NE 69361-2708
308-632-1420

Sidney
923 8th Ave.
Sidney, NE 69162-1418
308-254-6937

NEVADA

CURE
21 Shirley Lane
Yerington, NV 89447

CURE is a grassroots organization from top to bottom. It does not hire professional leaders. Instead, its leaders come from the ranks of people formerly in prison and family members of friends of prisoners. This organization offers assistance to ex-offenders.

EVOLVE
1951 Stella Lake Drive
Las Vegas, NV 89503

702-638-6371

Vocational training, counseling, and case management, for people with criminal histories.

Nevada AIDS Foundation
900 W. 1st Suite 200
Reno, NV 89503
775-348-9888

This organization attempts to find housing for prisoners upon release and maintains a food bank that is also geared towards HIV positive former prisoners.

Ridge House
900 W. 1st Suite 200
Reno, NV 89503
775-322-8941
Substance abuse treatment programs, and residential programs with career counseling.

Nevada Job Connect Career Centers

Carson City
1929 North Carson St.
Carson City, NV 89701
775-684-0441

CHR, Inc.
2980 South Jones, Suite H
Las Vegas, NV 89146
702-889-4466

Elko
172 6th St.
Elko, NV 89801
775-753-1900

Ely
1500 Ave. F, Suite 1
Ely, NV 89301-1908
775-289-1616

Fallon
121 Industrial Way
Fallon, NV 89406
775-423-5115

Great Basin College Career Connection Center
1541 West Basin, Suites 1-3
Pahrump, NV 89048
775-537-2323

Henderson Job Connect
119 S. Water St.
Henderson, NV 89015
702-486-0300

North Las Vegas
2827 Las Vegas Blvd. North
North Las Vegas, NV 89030
702-486-0200

Maryland Parkway
3405 S. Maryland Parkway
Las Vegas, NV 89169
702-486-0100

Reno
4001 South Virginia St., Suite H
Reno, NV 89146
775-834-1970

Sparks
1675 E. Prater Way, Suite 103
Sparks, NV 89434
775-336-5400

Winnemucca
475 West Haskell 1
Winnemucca, NV 89445
775-623-6520

NEW HAMPSHIRE

CURE
P.O. Box 3594
Nashua, NH 03061-3594
603-664-6952
Juoliver@aol.com

CURE is a grassroots organization from top to bottom. It does not hire professional leaders. Instead, its leaders come from the ranks of peo- ple formerly in prison and family members of friends of prisoners. This organization offers assistance to ex-offenders.

Mettanokit Outreach
167 Merriam Hill Rd.
Greenville, NH 03048
603-878-2310
603-878-2310

Native American circles in 9 prisons in New England. Booklet describing the program and post-prison group called Ending Violent Crime.

New Hampshire Department Employment Security
32 South Main St.
Concord, NH 03301
603-224-3311 or 800-852-3400

Provides a space for job searches and trains in job skills.

Workforce Opportunity Councils, Inc.
64 Old Suncook Rd.
Concord, NH 03301
603-228-9500 or 866-NHWORKS
www.nhworks.org
info@nhworks.org

13 locations allow you to search for jobs and get help with the application process.

New Hampshire WORKS Career Centers

Concord
10 West St.
Concord, NH 03302-1140
603-228-4100 Ext. 34117

Berlin
151 Pleasant St.
Berlin, NH 03570-0159
603-752-5500 Ext. 92304

Claremont
404 Washington St.
Claremont, NH 03743-4205
603-543-3111 Ext. 93201

Conway
518 White Mountain Highway
Conway, NH 03818-4205
603-447-5924 Ext. 95222

Keene
109 Key Rd.
Keene, NH 03431-3926
603-352-1904

Laconia
426 Union Ave.
Laconia, NH 03246
603-524-3960

Lebanon
85 Mechanic St., Suite 4
Lebanon, NH 03766-1506
603-448-6340

Littleton
646 Union St., Suite 100
Littleton, NH 03561-0318
603-444-2971

Manchester
300 Hanover St.
Manchester, NH 03104
603-627-7841

Nashua
6 Townsend West
Nashua, NH 03063
603-822-5177 Ext. 66649

Portsmouth
2000 Lafayette Rd.
Portsmouth, NH 03801-5673
603-436-3702

Salem
29 South Broadway
Salem, NH 03079-3026
603-893-9185

Somersworth
6 March Brook Drive
Somersworth, NH 03878
603-742-3600

NEW JERSEY

American Friends Service Committee
Prisoners Resource Center

89 Market St. 6th Floor
Newark, NJ 07102

973-643 — 2205
973-643-8924
http://www.afsc.org
   Has criminal justice programs in various states. Parole and Post-release services offered.

Garden State CURE
P.O. Box 77116
Trenton, NJ 08628
206-350-6337
206-350-6337
info@GardenStateCure.org
www.GardenStateCURE.org
GardenStateCURE@yahoogroups.com
   CURE is a grassroots organization from top to bottom. It does not hire professional leaders. Instead, its leaders come from the ranks of people formerly in prison and family members if friends of prisoners. This organization offers assistance to ex-offenders.

New Jersey Association on Corrections
986 South Broad St.
Trenton, NJ 08611
609-396-8900
www.njaponline.org
tparsons@njaonline.org
   Advocacy, legislation oversight, and post release programs.

Offenders Aid and Restoration of Essex County
535 Martin Luther King Jr. Blvd.
Newark, NJ 07102
973-624-6610
Email: offendersaid@aol.com
   In addition to helping clients acquire current forms of identification, OAR provides job development and placement services. Weekly job workshops are held to mact employers with individuals with criminal histories. Other services include transportation support and referrals for substance abuse treatment.

One-Stop Career Centers

Atlantic County
44 N. White Horse Pike, Suite A
Hammonton, NJ 08037-1860
609-561-8800
Atlantic County
2 South Main St., Suite 1
Pleasantville, NJ 09232-2728
609-813-3900

Atlantic County Department of Family and Community Development
1333 Atlantic Ave
Atlantic City, NJ 08401
609-348-3001 Ext. 2806

Bayonne One-Stop Affiliate Career Center
690 Broadway
Bayonne, NJ 07002
201-858-3037

Bergen
60 State St.
Hackensack, NJ 07601-5427
201-329-9600

Burlington County
795 Woodlane Rd., 2nd Floor
Westhampton, NJ 08060
609-518-3900

Camden County
2600 Mount Ephraim Ave., Suite 407
Camden, NJ 08104-3290
856-614-3150

Cape May County
3810 New Jersey Ave
Wildwood, NJ 08260
609-729-0997

Cumberland County
275 North Delsea Drive, 2nd Floor
Vineland, NJ 08360-8067
856-696-6600

Essex County
50 S. Clinton St.
East Orange, NJ 07018-3120
973-395-3230
973-395-8609

Flemington One-Stop Affiliate Career
Center
215 Sand Hill Rd.
Flemington, NJ 08822-1787
908-782-2371

Gloucester County
215 Crown Point, Suite 200
Thorofare, NJ 08086
856-384-3700

Hudson County
4800 Broadway
Union City, NJ 07087
201-866-4100

Jersey City
438 Summit Ave., 2nd Floor
Jersey City, NJ 07306-3175
201-795-8800

Lakewood Job Link
231 3rd St. 2nd Floor
Lakewood, NJ 08701
732-905-5996

Mercer County
26 Yard Ave., First Floor Station Plaza 4
Jersey City, NJ 08625-0954
609-989-6824

Middlesex County
506 Jersey Ave.
New Brunswick, NJ 08901-1392
732-937-6200

Middlesex County
161 New Brunswick Ave.
Perth Amboy, NJ 08861-4193
732-293-5016

Monmouth County
145 Wyckoff Rd.
Eatontown, NJ 07753-4844
732-775-1566

Morris County, Dover
107 Bassett Highway
Dover, NJ 07801-3696
973-361-8050

Morris County
30 Schuyler Place
Morristown, NJ 07960-3834
973-631-6321

Newark
990 Broad St., 1st Floor
Newark, NJ 07102
973-648-3370

Ocean County
1027 Hooper Ave., Building 6
Toms River, NJ 08753-8392
732-286-5616

Passaic County
52 Church St.
Paterson, NJ 07505
973-340-3400 Ext. 7200

Passaic County
25 Howe Ave.
Passaic, NJ 07055-4007
973-916-2645

Passaic County Affiliate
388 Lakeview Ave
Clifton, NJ 07011
973-340-3400 Ext. 7129

Salem County
174 East Broadway, 2nd Floor
Salem, NJ 08079
856-935-7007

Somerset County
75 Veterans Memorial Drive
East, Suite 102
Somerville, NJ 08876-2950
908-704-3000

Sussex County
12 Munsonhurst Rd.
Franklin, NJ 07416
973-209-0795

Sussex County
Route 206, Sussex County Mall
Newton, NJ 07860-1818
973-383-2775

Union County
921 Elizabeth Ave.
Elizabeth, NJ 07201-2306
908-558-8000

Union County
921 West 2nd St., 2nd Floor
Plainfield, NJ 07060-1218
908-412-7980

Union County One-Stop Affiliate
125 Broad St.
Elizabeth, NJ 07201
908-558-8000

Warren County
75 South Main St.
Phillipsburg, NJ 08865
908-859-0400

NEW MEXICO

Coalition for Prisoner's Rights
Prison Project of Santa Fe
P.O. Box 1911 Santa Fe, NM 87504
505-982-9520

Monthly newsletter free to currently and formally incarcerated individual and family members. Stamps and donations needed.

CURE
P.O. Box 543
Deming, NM 89447

This organization is a grassroots organization from top to bottom. It does not hire professional leaders. Instead, its leaders come from the ranks of people formerly in prison and family members of friends of prisoners. This organization offers assistance to ex-offenders.

PBJ, Inc./Project IMPACT
1101 Lopez Rd. SW
Albuquerque, NM 87105
505-877-7060 or 505-877-7010
www.pbjfamilyservices.org
Susannah@pbjfamilyservices.org

This organization offers a variety of services to reconnect incarcerated parents with their children and ease former prisoner's transition back into daily family life, including educational programs to help parents improve parenting skills.

Wings Ministry
2270 D Wyoming Blvd. NE #130
Albuquerque, NM 87112-2620
505-291-6412

http://www.wingministry.org/
This ministry is for family members of inmates. The goal of the Wing Ministry is to connect spouses, caregivers, and children of inmates with the nurturing and supporting relationships of Christian people in local churches.

One-Stop, Workforce Connection, and Workforce Development Centers

Alamogordo
901 Alaska Ave.
Alamogordo, NM 88310
575-437-9210

Albuquerque
501 Mountain Rd. NE
Albuquerque, NM 87102
505-843-1900

Artesia
704 West Main St.
Artesia, NM 88210
575-748-1303

Carlsbad
323 South Halagueno
Carlsbad, NM 88220
575-887-1174

Chavez County
2110 Main St. South
Roswell, NM 88203
575-624-6040

Central-Affiliate
221 S. Main St., Suite 209
Belen NM 87002
505-861-2144

Curry County
111 N, Main
Clovis, NM 88101
575-762-4571

De Baca County
537 North Tenth St.
Fort Sumner, NM 88119
575-355-2223

Deming
322 East Oak
Deming, NM 88030
575-546-0192

Eddy County
704 W. Main
Artesia, NM 88210
575-748-1303

Eddy County
323 N. Halagueno
Carlsbad, NM 88220
575-887-1040

Espanola
319 Onate St.
Espanola, NM 87532
505-753-2285

Farmington
600 West Arrington
Farmington, NM 87401
505-566-5800

Gallup
506 West 66th
Gallop, NM 87301
505-863-8884

Grants
551 Washington
Grants, NM 87020
505-285-3542

Guadalupe County
620 Historic Route 66
Santa Rosa, NM 88435
575-472-2555

Hobbs
204 West Park
Hobbs, NM 88240
575-393-5188

Las Cruces
226 South Alameda St.
Las Cruces, NM 88005
575-524-6250

Las Vegas
833 Grand Ave.
Las Vegas, NM 87701
505-425-6451

Lea County-Affiliate
204 West Park
Hobbs, NM 88240
575-393-5188

Lincoln County
707 Mechern Drive
Ruidoso, NM 88345
575-630-8181

Otero County
901 Alaska Ave.
Alamogordo, NM 88310
575-443-6196

Quay County
615 S. 2nd St.
Tucumcari, NM 88401
575-461-1154

Raton
1144 S. 2nd St., Suite A
Raton, NM 87740
575-445-2874

Rio Rancho
661 Quantum Rd.
Rio Rancho, NM 87124
505-896-1765

Roosevelt County
100 South Ave. A, Suite 110
Portales, NM 88130
575-356-5408

Santa Fe
301 West DeVargas
Santa Fe, NM 87501
505-827-7434

Silver City
410 West Broadway
Silver City, NM 88061
575-538-3737

Socorro
109 Faulkner
Socorro, NM 87801
575-835-0067

Sunland Park-Affiliate
141 Quinella Rd.

Sunland Park, NM 88063
575-589-0377
575-589-0382

Taos
1036
Salazar Rd.
Taos, NM 87571
575-758-4219

Truth or Consequences-Affiliate
1301 N. Pershing
Truth or Consequences, NM 87901
575-894-1263

Union County and Harding County
834 Main St.
Clayton, NM 88415
575-374-0183

NEW YORK

AIDS in Prison Project of the Osborne Association
809 Westchester Ave.
Bronx, NY 10455
718-378-7022
Email:info@osbomeny.org
*www.osbormeny.org/aids_in_prison_pro
   ject.htm*

*This organization assists pre-release HIV
positive prisoners that intend to parole to New
York with discharge planning.*

Catholic Charities
1011 First Ave.
New York, NY 10022
888-744-7900
www.catholiccharitiesny.org

*Available to persons about to be released or
newly released from New York City or New
York State correctional facilities. A comprehensive program including: clothing, bail fund
and referrals (including job referrals). Services*

*are also available to families of offenders. Re-
lease papers may be required. Call first Mon-
day-Friday 9-4:30. Accessible to people with
disabilities.*

Center for Employment Opportunities
32Broadway (between Exchange Plaza
   and Morris St.) 15th Floor
New York, NY 10004
212-422-4430

*Provides on-the-job work experience for per-
sons on parole, probation, or in work-release
programs. Must be referred by a parole or probation officer.*

The CUNY (City University of New
   York) Catch Program in Brooklyn:
Medger Evars College
718-270-6405

In the Bronx: Bronx Community
   College, 718-289-5852

In Queens: La Guardia Community
   College, 718-482-5100

Once enrolled, the program offers a career development services, job search skills, and assistance in housing family, and entitlement issues, assistance in entry job skills training, GED, substance abuse, and education programs for people 17 to 20 years old. It offers referrals for older people.

CURE
P.O. Box 1314
Wappinger Falls, NY 12590
845-298-7592
Goluis52@yahoo.com
www.bestweb.net/~cureny

CURE is a grassroots organization from top to bottom. It does not hire professional leaders. Instead, its leaders come from the ranks of people formerly in prison and family members of friends of prisoners. This organization offers assistance to ex-offenders.

Delancy St.
100 Turk Hill Rd.
Brewster, NY 10609
845-278-6181

Delancy St. provides, in a two- to four-year reintegration program, counseling and training in moving and trucking, para-transit services, a restaurant and catering service, a print and copy shop, retail; and wholesale sales, advertising specialties sales, and an automotive service center.

Exponents, Inc.
Case Management Connection
151 West 26th St. 3rd Floor
New York, NY 10001
212-243-3434
www.exponents.org
info@exponents.org

Offers a long-term case management program for HIV-Positive individuals who are in transition from correctional facilities back to the community. Services include, entitlements, housing, primary care, recovery/harm reduction, peer support, and HIV counseling and education. No referrals Provides foster care for children of incarcerated women. Works with incarcerated mothers and their children to strengthen family ties through parent educa-

tion, enhanced visiting, transportation assistance, advocacy. Five community residential programs for women and ex-prisoners and their children.

Fast Forward
500 8th Ave., Suite 1207
New York, NY 10018
212-714-0600

Designed especially for persons coming out of New York City Correctional Facilities. Offers vocational and education assessment, including college programs, job placement, and individual counseling.

Fortune Society
53 West 23rd St. 8th Floor
New York, 10011
212-691-7554
www.fortunesociety.org

The Fortune Society provides an educational program, counseling advocacy around HIV/AIDS, and court advocacy.

Harlem Restoration Project, Inc.
461 West 125th
New York, NY 10027
212-622-8186

Gives preferences to ex-offenders with any openings it may have in its office or its building renovation projects. All levels of people are hired, from labors to administrators. On occasion, housing is available to ex-offenders and their families.

Hour Children, Inc.
36-11A 12th St.
Long Island, NY 11106
718-433-4724
http://www.hourchildren.org/

Legal Action Center
225 Varick St. 4th Floor
New York, NY 10014
www.lac.org

Non-profit organization providing free legal services to formerly incarcerated people, recovering alcoholics, substance abusers, and people with HIV.

The Osborne Association
36-31 38th St.
Long Island City, NY 11101
718-707-2600
www.osborney.org
info@osborney.org
This organization assists pre-release HIV positive prisoners that intend to parole to New York with discharge planning. It also offers re-entry programs, employment programs, and family services.

Palladia (formerly Project Return)
10 Astor Place, 7th Floor
New York, NY 10003-6935
212-979-8800
http://www.projectreturn.org
Parole transition programs, employment readiness and job placement, residential treatment, and case management services.

Palladia, Inc.
Project Return
2006 Madison Ave. (at 128th St.)
New York, NY 10035
212-979-8600
Helps parolees with employment readiness, job placement, individual and family counseling, as well as recreational and community services activities.

Project Green Hope: Services for Women, Inc.
448 East 119th St.
New York, NY 10035
212-369-5100
Residence for women which offers personal counseling, individual and group therapy, vocational workshops, assistance in vocational placement, substance abuse support groups, parenting information and advocacy in areas such as foster care.

Providence House-Transitional Housing Program
703 Lexington Ave.
Brooklyn, NY 11221
718-455-0197
www.providencehouse.org

A community based residential program for women who are on New York State parole and who cannot return to their place of residence after they are released from prison. Each of the two houses, one in Brooklyn and one in Queens, has a core community of volunteers who live permanently in the house and who participate in the communal life with the residence. There is also paid staff who assist with referral services and housing. Length of stay: from 3 months to a year.

Reality House
637 West 125th St.
New York, NY 10027
212-666-8000 or 800-427-3254
Provides group therapy and counseling services to recent releases with a history of drug addiction. After-care services are available in the community facility. Services include counseling, vocational guidance, education, medical and social services. They also provide recently released detainees/inmates of the NYC Department of Corrections at Riker's Island with community-based substance abuse treatment (age 18+) and HIV primary care (e.g., counseling, HIV testing, medical evaluation, monitoring, case management, etc.)

Rogers House
934 Culver Rd.
Rochester, NY 14609
716-482-2694
Provides prisoner re-integration, mentoring, and assistance with housing and employment.

St. Patrick Friary
102 Seymore St.
Buffalo, NY 14210
716-856-6131
Group counseling provided at Attica, Wyoming, Collins, New Orleans, Albion, Groveland, Gowanda, and Rochester, prisons. Post-release services include housing for parolees and job training. They also offer assistance with educational opportunities, transportation, and job opportunities.

South Forty Employment and Training Services

36-31 38th St.
Long Island City, NY 11101
718-707-2600
www.osbormeny.org/south_forty/htm

This organization offers vocational services to people with criminal records; providing assessment, testing, career and educational counseling, job-readiness workshops, job training, and post-employment support in adjusting to the demands of the workplace and staying employed.

Stand Up, Harlem
145 West 130th St.
New York, NY 10027
212-926-4072

Has emergency overnight stays, transitional housing for the HIV positive, case management, health and holistic services. They also have a support group called YES TO LIFE designed for ex-offenders.

The Verite Program
810 Classon Ave.
Brooklyn, NY 11238
718-230-5100

Includes and ex-offender support group, as well as support groups around issues such as substance abuse, relapse and recovery, HIV/AIDS, men's sexually, stress, and anger management. Also, offers mental health therapy.

WomenCare, Inc.
105 Chambers St., 2nd Floor
New York, NY 10007
212-463-9500

Mentoring service for women making the transition from prison back to the community. Comprehensive resources and referrals in many fields, including housing, employment, and parenting issues. Must be a female ex-offender to qualify.

Women's Prison Association
110 Second Ave.
New York, NY 10027
212-674-1163
www.wpaonline.org
ajacobe@wpaonline.org

This organization works with women in county, state, and federal prisons throughout New York and provides a variety of services to help women transition back into the community. These services include transitional case management, two residential houses that allow women to bring their children, HIV prevention classes, life skills workshops, assistance with reunification and other custody issues.

One-Stop Workforce Career Centers

Allegany Co. Employment and Training One-Stop Center
7 Wells Lane
Belmont, NY 14813
585-268-9237

Amsterdam Workforce Solutions
2620 Riverfront Center
Amsterdam, NY 12010
518-842-2240 Ext. 3030

Bath Career Center
117 East Steuben St.
Bath, NY 14810
607-776-7712
1-800-553-2033 Ext. 152

Brooklyn Career and Educational Consultants
270 Flatbush Ave. Extension
Brooklyn, NY 11201
718-858-8500 Ext. 17

Brooklyn Workforce 1 Career Center
9 Bond St., 5th Floor
Brooklyn, NY 11201
718-246-5219 Ext. 2060

Broome-Tioga Workforce
171 Front St.
Binghamton, NY 13905
607-778-2136

Buffalo Employment and Training Center
77 Goodell St.
Buffalo, NY 14203
716-856-5627

Buffalo Employment Office
204 Main St.
Buffalo, NY 14202
716-851-2600

Cattaraugus One-Stop
175 North Union St.
Olean, NY 14760
716-373-1880

Cayuga Works Career Center
199 Franklin St., Suite 204
Auburn, NY 13021
315-253-1590

CDO Workforce
1 Gallant Ave., Suite 1
Delhi, NY 13753
607-746-7477

CDO Workforce
1 O'Hara Drive
Norwich, NY 13815
607-334-2201 Ext. 128

CDO Workforce Center
12 Dietz St.
Oneonta, NY 13820
607-432-4800 Ext. 115

CDO Workforce Center
21 Liberty St., Sidney Civic Center,
    Room 221
Sidney, NY 13838
607-561-7550

Chautauqua Works
323 Central Ave.
Dunkirk, NY 14048
716-366-9015

Chautauqua Works
23 E. 3rd St.
Jamestown, NY 14701
716-661-9553

Chemung/Schuyler/Steuben Work-
    force Development
318 Madison Ave.

Elmira, NY 14901
607-733-7131 Ext. 2131

CNY Works Incorporated
443 North Franklin St., Lower Level
Syracuse, NY 13204
315-473-8250

Cobleskill Workforce Solutions Center
795 E. Main St., Suite 4
Cobleskill, NY 12043
518-234-4254
Columbia Greene Workforce

4400 Route 23, Professional Aca-
    demic Center
Hudson, NY 12535
518-828-4181 Ext. 3109

Consortium for Worker Education
272 7th Ave.
New York, NY 10001
212-647-1900

Corning Career Center
20 Denison Parkway West
Corning, NY 14830
607-937-8337

Cortland Works Career Center
99 Main St.
Cortland, NY 13045
607-756-7585

Division of Employment and Work-
    force Solutions
75 Varick St. 7th Floor
New York, NY 10013
212-775-3769

Division of Employment and Work-
    force Solutions
160 South Ocean Ave.
Patchogue, NY 11772-3719
631-687-4819

Dutchess WORKS One-Stop
233 Main St.
Poughkeepsie, NY 12601
845-485-2660 Ext. 3002

Elizabethtown One Work Source
Center
103 Hand Ave.
Elizabethtown, NY 12932
518-873-2341
1-800-675-2668

Erie Community College One-Stop
Center
3176 Abbott Rd.
Orchard Park, NY 14127
716-270-4444

FEGS-Bronx
412 E. 147th St.
Bronx, NY 10455
212-336-8539 (HR Dynamics)

FEGS-Brooklyn
199 J St.
Brooklyn, NY 11201
718-488-0100

Finger Lakes Works
70 Elizabeth Blackwell St.
Geneva, NY 14456
315-789-1771

Finger Lakes Works
1519 Nye Rd., Suite 601
Lyons, NY 14489
315-946-7270

Finger Lakes Works
3010 County Complex Drive
Canandaigua, NY 14424
585-396-4020

Finger Lakes Works
1 Dr Pronio Dr
Waterloo, NY 13165
315-539-1905

Genesee County Career Center
Eastown Plaza
587 East Main St., Suite 100
Batavia, NY 14020
585-334-2042

Gloversville Workforce Solutions
199 South Main St.

Gloversville, NY 12078
518-725-6573 Ext. 3032

Hempstead Career Center
50 Clinton St., Suite 400
Hampstead Executive Plaza
Hampstead, NY 11550
515-485-5000

Hicksville Career Center
301 West Old Country Rd.
Hicksville, NY 11801
516-934-8517
516-934-8547

Hornell Career Center
107 Broadway
Hornell, NY 14843
607-324-8388

LaGuardia Workforce Office of Workforce Development
29-10 Thompson Ave.
Long Island, NY 11101
718-609-2130

Livingston County Office of Workforce Development
6 Court St., Room 105
Geneseo, NY 14454

Lockport Workforce One Center
81 Walnut St.
Lockport, NY 14094
716-433-14094

Malone One Work Source Center
158 Finney Blvd.
Malone, NY 12953
518-481-5755 Ext. 3033
1-877-410-5751

Montour Falls Career Center
323 Owego St. Unit 11
Montour, NY 14865
607-535-6840

New York Jobs Program-Delhi-Affiliate
111 Main St.
Delhi, NY 607-746-6381

Non Profit Assistance Corporation
Citizens Active Bureau-Bronx Works-
    Affiliate
391 West 14th St., 520
Bronx, NY 10455
718-993-8880

NYC Workforce 1 Career Center
358 East 149th St., 2nd Floor
Bronx, NY 10455
718-960-7901

NYC Workforce Career Center,
    Upper Manhattan
215 West 125th St., 6th Floor
New York, NY 10027
917-493-7000

NYS Department of Labor, Division
    of Employment
60 Bay St. 1st Floor
Station Island, NY 10301
718-285-8399

NYS Department of Labor, Division
    of Employment Services-Affiliate
621 Fulton St.-Fourth Floor
Brooklyn, NY 11201
718-780-9312

One-Stop Career Center
175 Central Ave.
Albany, NY 12206
518-462-7600

One-Stop of Washington County
383 Broadway
Fort Edward, NY 12828
518-746-2391

One Work Source
194 U.S. Oval
Plattsburgh, NY 12903
518-561-0430
1-866-967-5768

Orange Works Middletown-Affiliate
    Career Center
33 Fulton St.

Middleton, NY 10940
845-346-1100

Orange Works Newburgh Career
    Center
3 Washington Center, The Maple
    Bldg., 4th Floor
Newsburgh, NY 12550
845-568-5090
845-568-5377

Orange Works Port Jervis-Affiliate
    Career Center
150 Pike St.
Port Jervis, NY 12771
845-858-1455

Orleans Center for Workforce Devel-
    opment
458 West Ave.
Albion, NY 14411
585-589-5335

Oswego County Workforce
200 North Second St.
Fulton, NY 13069
315-591-9000

Queens Workforce Career Center
168-25 Jamaica Ave., 2nd Floor
Jamaica, NY 11432
718-557-6755
718-557-6760
718-557-6797

Rensselaer County One-Stop
1600 7th Ave., Ned Pattison Office
    Bldg, 4th Floor
Troy, NY 12180
518-270-2860

Rochester Works! Career Center
255 North Goodman St.
Rochester, NY 14607
585-258-3500

Rochester Works! Career Center
Department of Labor
276 Waring Rd.

Rochester, NY 14609
585-266-7760

Rome Working Solution
153 Brooks Rd., South West Entrance
Rome, NY 13441
315-356=0662

Saratoga County Employment and
Training
152 West High St.
Ballston, Spa, NY 12020
518-884-4170

Schenectady Job Training
797 Broadway
Schenectady, NY 12305
518-344-2735
518-334-4400
518-344-2756

Schuyler County JOBS Department
of Social Services
Watkins Glen-Affiliate
323 Owego St.
Montour Falls, NY 14865
607-535-8303

St. Lawrence County One-Stop Career Center
80 State Highway 310, Suite B
Canton, NY 13617-1498
315-386-3276

St. Nicholas Alliance Workforce De-
velopment-Affiliate
790 Broadway Ave.
Brooklyn, NY 11206
718-302-2057

Station Island Department of Labor
60 Bay St.
Staten Island, NY 10301
718-285-8388

Steuben County JOBS-Bath
3 E. Pulteney Square
Bath, NY 14810
607-776-7611

Suffolk County Department of Labor
Suffolk Works Employment Program-
Affiliate
395 Oser Ave.
Hauppauge, NY 11788
631-853-3809

Sullivan Work Stop Employment
Center
Suffolk County Department of Labor
725 Veterans Memorial Highway
Hauppauge, NY 11788
631-853-6600

The Work Place
1000 Coffeen St.
Watertown, NY 13601
315-782-9252

The Workplace, Lewis County
5274 Outer Stowe St.
Lowville, NY 13367
315-376-5800

Tioga Employment One-Stop Center
Broome-Tioga Workforce
1062 State Route 38
Owego, NY 13827
667-687-8500

Tomorrow's Workplace
1 Periman Drive
Spring Valley, NY 10977
845-356-6106
845-356-5100

Tompkins Workforce New York Career Center
171 East State St., Center
Ithaca, Suite 241
Ithaca, NY 14850
607-272-7570 Ext. 129

Trout ACCESS Center
Niagara County Employment and
Training
1001 11th St.
Niagara, Falls, NY 14301

716-278-8108
716-278-8281

Ulster County One-Stop Center
601 Development Court
Kingston, NY 12401
845-340-3170

Warren County One-Stop Career
   Center
Northway Plaza, Suite 13C
Queensbury, NY 12804
518-743-0925

Warsaw One-Stop-Affiliate
448 North Main St.
Warsaw, NY 14569
585-786-3145

Westchester County One-Stop Employment Center
120 Bloomingdale Rd.
White Plains, NY 10605
914-995-3910

Westchester/Putman One-Stop
110 Old Route 6, Building 3
Carment, NY 10512
845-225-7043 Ext. 46604

Williamsville One-Stop Center-Affiliate
4175 Transit Rd.
Williamsville, NY 14221
716-634-9081

Workforce 1 Career Center
NYS Department of Labor Office
138-60 Barclay Ave., 2nd Floor
Flushing, NY 11355
718-321-6307

Working Solutions One-Stop Career
   Center
320 N. Prospect St.
Herkimer, NY 13358
315-867-1400

Workforce Center-Affiliate
977 Hicksville Rd.
Massapequa, NY 11758
516-797-4560

Workforce Center 1 Career Center
1029 E. 163rd St., 3rd Floor
Bronx, NY 10459
718-542-6777

Working Solutions One-Stop Career
   Center
1006 Oneida Plaza Drive
Oneida, NY 13421
315-363-2400

Working Solutions One-Stop Center
207 Genesee St.
Utica, NY 13501
315-793-5300
315-793-2229

Wyoming County Community Action-Affiliate
6470 Rt. 20A
Perry, NY 14530
585-237-2600

Yonkers Employment Center
20 South Broadway, 12th Floor
Yonkers, NY 10701
914-965-9500 Ext. 111

NORTH CAROLINA

CURE
P.O. Box 49572
Charlotte, NC 28277
northcarolinacure@yahoo.com

CURE is a grassroots organization from top to bottom. It does not hire professional leaders. Instead, its leaders come from the ranks of people formerly in prison and family members of friends of prisoners. This organization offers assistance to ex-offenders.

Energy Committed to Offenders
(EGO)
P.O. Box 33533
Charlotte, NC 28233
704-374-0762
www.ecocharlotte.org
ecoclark@bellsouth.net

Provides emergency referrals, employment preparation and counseling, individual and group support, post-release services and referrals, and advocacy to persons recently released from prison.

Forgiven Ministry
P.O. Box 117
Taylorsville, NC 28681
828-632-6424
http://www.forgivenministry.org/
Scottie@forgiveministry.org

Forgiven Ministry conducts a parent/child in-prison camp, titled One Day with God Camp. These camps bring children inside the prison walls to spend a day of structured activities with their incarcerated parent. The objective is to help bring reconciliation and restoration of relationships, and to help break the cycle of incarceration that often follows from generation to generation.

Urban Ministry Center
945 North College St.
Charlotte, NC 28206
704-347-0278
www.urbanministrycenter.org

This is an intercept organization that offers food, laundry facilities, referrals, and employment counseling.

Job Link Career Centers

Alamance County
2720 South Mebane St.
Burlington, NC 27215
336-570-6800

Anson County
116 West Wade St.

Wadesboro, NC 28170-2137
704-694-6551 Ext. 211

Ashe County
626 Ashe Central School Rd., Unit 5
Jefferson, NC 28640
336-982-5627

Beaufort County
1385 John Small Ave.
Washington, NC 27889
252-946-3116

Bertie County
1001 South King St.
Windsor, NC 27983
252-794-5616

Bladen County
401 Mercer Mill Rd.
Elizabethtown, NC 28337
910-862-3255

Brunswick County
5300-7 Main St.
Shallotte, NC 28470
910-754-6120

Buncombe County
A-B Tech Campus
340 Victoria Rd., Maple Building
Asheville, NC 28801
828-250-4761

Burke County
720 East Union St.
Morganton, NC 28655
828-438-6161 Ext. 201

Cabarrus County
2275 Kannapolis Highway
Concord, NC 28027
704-786-3183 Ext. 214

Caldwell County
2855 Hickory Blvd.
Hudson, NC 28638
828-759-4680

Capital Area, Clayton Corners
11671 U.S. Hwy 70

Clayton, NC 27520
919-585-4805

Capital Area, Cary ESC
742-F East Chatham St.
Cary, NC 27511
919-469-1406

Capital Area, Eastern Regional Center
1002 Dogwood Drive
Zebulon, NC 27597
919-404-3900

Capital Area, Johnson Community
    College
245 College Rd.
Smithfield, NC 27577
919-209-2094

Capital Area, Smithfield ESC
224 Peedin Rd.
Smithfield, NC 27577-4718
919-934-0536

Capital Area, Southern Regional Center
130 N. Judd Parkway, S.E.
Fuquay Varina, NC 27526
919-557-1121

Capital Area, Raleigh ESC
3351 Carl Sandburg Court
Raleigh, NC 27610
919-212-3849

Carteret County
309 Commerce Ave.
Morehead City, NC 28557
252-726-7151

Caswell
331 Piedmont Drive
Yanceyville, NC 27379
336-694-5707 Ext. 247

Catawba County
2760 Hwy 70 SE
Hickory, NC 28602
828-324-5650

Charlotte-Mecklenburg, Arrowood
7140 Forest Point Blvd., Suite A

Charlotte, NC 28217
704-565-6865

Charlotte-Mecklenburg, Monroe Rd.
10801 Monroe Rd., Suite A
Matthews, NC 28105
704-847-2660 Ext. 223

Charlotte-Mecklenburg, North Tryon
4045 N. Tryon St.
Charlotte, NC 28206
704-597-8097 Ext. 2222

Charlotte-Mecklenburg, South Blvd.
5125-A South Blvd.
Charlotte, NC 28217
704-527-3195 Ext. 6506

Chowan County
1316-C North Broad St.
Edenton, NC 27932
252-482-2195

Cleveland County
404 East Marion St.
Shelby, NC 28150
704-480-5414 Ext. 217

Columbus County
4564 Chadbourn Highway
Whiteville, NC 28560
910-642-7141

Craven County
1305 Simmons St.
New Bern, NC 28560
252-514-4828

Cumberland County
414 Bay Ave.
Fayetteville, NC 28301
910-486-1010

Dare County
2522 South Croatan Highway
Nags Head, NC 27959
252-480-3500

Davis County
1211 Salisbury Rd. Room 109

Mocksville, NC 27028-9342
336-751-5903

Duplin County
192 Magnolia Extension
Kenansville, NC 28349
910-296-1478

Durham
1105 South Briggs Ave.
Durham, NC 27703
919-560-6880 Ext. 229

Edgecombe/Nash
121 South Fairview Rd.
Rocky Mount, NC 27801
252-977-3306, Ext. 202

Forsyth County
Employment Security Commission
450 West Hanes Mill Rd., Suite 101
Winston, NC 27105
336-776-6720 Ext. 6725

Forsyth County
Forsyth Technical Community College
1300 Bolton St.
Winston Salem, NC 27103
336-734-7748 Ext. 7760

Franklin County
98 Tanglewood Drive
Louisburg, NC 27549
919-496-6250

Gaston County
7220 Wilkinson Blvd.
Belmont, NC 28012
704-266-5005

Gaston County
1391 Bessemer Drive
Gastonia, NC 28052
704-853-5328 Ext. 218
Granville County

518 Lewis County Career Center
Oxford, NC 27565
919-693-2686

Greene County
818 Hwy 91 North
Snow Hill, NC 28580
252-747-5689

Greensboro/High Point Guilford
  County
303 North Raleigh St.
Greensboro, NC 27401
336-373-5922

Halifax/Northampton
945 Park Ave.
Roanoke Rapids, NC 27870
252-537-4188

Harnett County, Dunn
101 Hunt Valley Dr.
Dunn, NC 28334
910-891-2925

Harnett County
1137 East Cornelius Harnett Blvd.
Lillington, NC 27546
910-893-2191

Haywood County
1170 North Main St.
Waynesville, NC 28786
828-456-6061

Henderson County
College Drive
Flat Rock, NC 28731
828-694-1755

Hendersonville
Employment Security Commission
26 Francis Rd.
Hendersonville, NC 28792
828-693-1703

High Point
919 Phillips Ave., Suite 107
High Point, NC 27262
336-882-4141

Hoke County
310 Birch St.

Raeford, NC 28376
910-875-5059

Iredell County
Employment Security Commission
1907 Newton Drive
Statesville, NC 28677-4843
704-878-4241

Iredell County
470 A North Broad St.
Mooresville, NC 28115-9551
704-664-4225

Jackson County
26 Ridgeway St.
Sylva, NC 28779
828-586-4063

Jones County
509 Highway 58 North
Trenton, NC 28585
252-448-5021

Lee County
1909 Lee Ave.
Sanford, NC 27330
919-775-2241

Lenoir County
231 Highway 58 South
Kinston, NC 28502
252-527-6223 Ext. 126

Lincoln County
529 North Aspen St.
Lincolnton, NC 28092-2105
704-735-8035 Ext. 219

Macon County
427 Harrison Ave.
Franklin, NC 28734
828-369-9534

Madison County
4646 U.S. Highway 25-70
Marshall, NC 28753

Martin County
407 East Blvd.

Williamston, NC 27892
252-792-7816

McDowell County
316 Baldwin Ave.
Marion, NC 28752
828-659-6001

Mitchell County
100 Kim Thickets Rd.
Spruce Pine, NC 28777
828-765-7758
828-765-7378

Montgomery County
1011 Page St.
Troy, NC 27371
910-572-3641

Moore County
245 Shepherd Trail
Aberdeen, NC 28315
910-944-7697

New Hanover County Career Center
717 Market St.
Wilmington, NC 28401
910-251-5777 Ext. 229

Onslow County
461 Western Blvd., Suite 106
Jacksonville, NC 28546
910-347-2121

Orange County
503 West Franklin St.
Chapel Hill, NC 27909
919-969-3032 Ext. 229

Pamlico County
705 Main St.
Bayboro, NC 28515
252-745-9931
252-745-9934

Pasquotank County
422 McArthur St.
Elizabeth City, NC 27909
252-331-4798

Pender County
904-A S. Walker St.
Burgaw, NC 28425
910-259-0240

Person County
145 Weeks Drive
Roxboro, NC 27573
336-599-3109

Randolph County
629 Industrial Park Ave.
Asheboro, NC 27205
336-633-0304

Richmond County
115 West Franklin St.
Rockingham, NC 28358
910-997-9180

Robeson County
289 Corporate Dr., Suite B
Lumberton, NC 28358
910-618-5500

Rockingham County
8340 NC Highway 87
Reidsville, NC 27320
336-634-5600

Rowan County
1904 South Main St.
Salisbury, NC 28144-6714
704-639-7529 Ext. 202

Rutherford County
Employment Security Commission
139 East Trade St.
Forest City, NC 28043
828-245-9841

Sampson County
115 North Blvd.
Clinton, NC 28328
910-592-5756

Scotland County
303 North Main St.
Laurinburg, NC 28352
910-276-4260

Stanly County
2215 U.S. Highway 52 South
Albemarle, NC 28001-9510
704-982-2183 Ext. 204

Stokes County
904 North Main St.
Walnut Cove, NC 27052
336-591-4074

Surry County
541 West Pine St., Suite 300
Mount Airy, NC 27030
336-786-4169

Thomasville
211 West Colonial Drive
Thomasville, NC 27360
336-474-2655

Transylvania County
98 E. Morgan St., Suite 290
Brevard, NC 28712
828-884-3214

Tri County
642 Andrews Rd.
Murphy, NC 28906
878-837-7407 Ext. 203

Union County
1125 Skyway Drive
Monroe, NC 28110
704-283-7541

Vance County
945-G West Andrews Ave.
Henderson, NC 27536
252-438-6129

Warren County
309 North Main St., Room 123
Warrenton, NC 27589
252-257-3230

Wayne County
309 North William St.
Goldsboro, NC 27530
919-731-7950 Ext. 223

Whiteville
630 South Madison St.
Whiteville, NC 28472
910-642-0146 Ext. 210

Wilkes County
312 Wilkesboro Ave.
Midtown Plaza
North Wilkesboro, NC 28659
336-651-2540

Wilson County
302 Tarboro St. West
Wilson, NC 27893
252-234-1129

Yadkin County
246 East Main St.
Yadkinville, NC 27055
336-679-4079

NORTH DAKOTA

Job Service Centers

Beulah Job Service
119 E. Main St.
Beulah, ND 58523
877-268-5437
701-873-5607

Bismarck Job Service
1601 East Century Ave.
Bismarck, ND 58503
800-247-0981
701-328-5000

Devils Lake Job Service
301 College Drive South
Devils Lake, ND 58301
800-247-0982
701-662-9300

Dickinson Job Service
66 Osborn Drive
Dickinson, ND 58601
800-247-0983
701-227-3100

Fargo Job Service
1350 32nd St. South
Fargo, ND 58103
800-247-0985
701-239-7300

Grafton Job Service
927 12th St. West
Grafton, ND 58367

701-352-4450
701-477-5631

Grand Forks Job Service
1501 28th Ave. South
Grand Forks, ND 58201
800-247-0986
701-239-7300

Harvey Customer Service Office
119 9th St. West
Harvey, ND 58341
701-324-4552

Jamestown Job Service
1307 12th Ave. NE
Jamestown, ND 58402
800-247-0988

Minot Job Service
3416 North Broadway
Minot, ND 58702
800-482-0017

New Town Job Service
204 Main St.
New Town, ND 58763
701-627-4390

Oakes Customer Service Office
924 South 7th St.
Oakes, ND 58474
701-742-2546

Rolla Job Service
103 East Main Ave.
Rolla, ND 58367
877-516-0600
701-477-5631

Valley City Job Service
325 2nd St. NW
Valley, ND 58072
800-831-6374
701-845-8860

Wahpeton Job Service
524 2nd Ave. North
Wahpeton, ND 58702
888-671-9229
701-671-1550

Williston Job Service
422 1st Ave. West
Williston, ND 58801
800-247-0989
701-774-7900

OHIO

Bearing the Burden Ministries, Inc.
P.O. Box 212
Brookville, Ohio 45309
937-903-8519
http://www.btbmi.com/
   Bearing the Burden Ministries is primarily a correctional ministry and consultancy to churches and organizations that desire to begin or improve a jail/prison/re-entry outreach as well as pastoral care chaplaincy ministry to those without a pastor or church.

Community Shelter Board
115 West Main St.
Columbus, OH 43215
614-221-9195
info@csb.org
www.csb.org
   This organization offers emergency shelter, equip with internet access, telephones, employment leads, job training resources, and other community resources.

CURE
P.O. Box 14080
Columbus, OH 43214
TOLL FREE 877-826-8504
Cure-ohio@cure-ohio.org
http://www.cure-ohio.org
   CURE is a grassroots organization from top to bottom. It does not hire professional leaders. Instead, its leaders come from the ranks of people formerly in prison and family members of

friends of prisoners. This organization offers assistance to ex-offenders.

Justice Watch
1120 Garden St.
Cincinnati, OH 45214
513-241-0490
http://www.justicewatchinc.org/contact.html
   Works to eliminate classism and racism from prisons and opposes death penalty. Operates Garden St. Transitional House for parolees.

Opening Doors of Ohio, Inc.
1689 Hardin Lane
Powell, Ohio 43065-9646
614-543-0417
http://www.openingmoredoors.org/openingdorrs@columbus.rr.com
   Ministering to ex offenders and their families.

The Missing Link
P.O. Box 40031
Cleveland, OH 44140-0031
440-282-1683
   Links troubled youth and ex-offenders with life changing programs including Christian residential programs.

One-Stop Career Centers

Accent Allen County Job Center
1501 S. Dixie Highway

Lima, OH 45802-4506
419-999-0360

Accent Paulding County Job Center
250 Dooley Drive, Suite B
Paulding, OH 45879
419-399-3345

Adams and Brown Counties Work-
    force Connections
19221 State Route 136
Winchester, OH 45697
937-695-0316

Airport Employment One-Stop
    Northern Kentucky
Cincinnati-Northern Kentucky Inter-
    national Airport
Terminal 1
Cincinnati, OH 45275
859-767-9675

Ashland CDJFS/Employment and
    Training Connection
15 W Fourth St.
Ashland, OH 44805
419-282-5052

Ashtabula County Job Service
2247 Lake Ave.
Ashtabula, OH 44004
440-994-1234

Auglaize County One-Stop
801 Middle St.
Wapakoneta, OH 45895
419-739-7225

Belmont County Connections
302 Walnut St.
Martins Ferry, OH 43078
740-633-5627
1-877-516-5627

Brown County One-Stop (Satellite
    Office)
406 W. Plum St.
Georgetown, OH 45121
937-378-6041, Ext. 261

Butler County Workforce One
4631 Dixie Highway
Fairfield, OH 45014
513-785-6500

Carroll County Connections
55 East Main St.
Carrollton, OH 44615
330-627-3804

Clermont County Workforce One
756 Old State Route 74
Cincinnati, OH 45245
513-943-3000

Clinton County Works
1025 S. South St. Suite 500
Wilmington, OH 45177
937-382-7762

Columbiana County One-Stop
7860 Lincole Place
Lisbon, OH 44432
330-420-9675

Coshocton County Opportunity
    Links
725 Pine St.
Coshocton, OH 43812
740-622-1020
740-295-7516

COWIC/JOB LEADERS
1111 E. Broad St. Suite 201
Columbus, OH43205
614-559-5052

Crawford County Jobs Plus
225 E. Mary St.
Bucyrus, OH 44820
419-562-8066

C-TEC Champaign Technology and
    Employment Center
1512 U.S. Highway 68 Bay 14
Urbana, OH 43078
937-484-1581

Darke County Job Center Network
603 Wagner Ave.

Greenville, OH 45331
937-548-4132

Delaware Area Career Center
4565 Columbus Pike (U.S. 23)
Delaware, OH 43015
740-548-6665

Delaware Job Network
140 N Sandusky St., 2nd Floor
Delaware, OH 43015
740-833-2326

The Employment Center
1575 N. High St., Suite 100
Hillsboro, OH 45123
937-393-1933

Employment Connection
11699 Brookpark Rd.
Parma, OH 44130
216-898-1366

Employment Connection Downtown
1020 Bolivar Rd.
Cleveland, OH 44115
216-664-4673

Employment Connection Fairfax
8111 Quincy Ave.
Cleveland, OH 44104
216-391-5867

Employment Connection Glenville
12212 St. Clair Ave.
Cleveland, OH 44108
216-541-2267

Employment Connection Mt. Pleasant
13815 Kinsman Rd.
Cleveland, OH 44120
216-561-5650

Employment Connection Old Brooklyn
4261 Fulton Pkwy
Cleveland, OH 44144
216-635-4159

Employment Connection Virgil E.
 Brown

1641 Payne Ave., Room 160
Cleveland, Oh 44114
216-987-7944

Employment Connection Westshore
9830 Lorain Ave.
Cleveland, OH 44102
216-939-2599

The Employment Network
42495 North Ridge Rd.
Elyria, OH 44035
440-324-5244

The Employment Source
1260 Monroe St., Suite 35
New Philadelphia, OH 44663
330-364-9777

Fairfield County One-Stop
239 W. Main St.
Lancaster, OH 43130
740-689-2494
1-800-450-8845

Fayette Works
1270 U.S. Route 62 SW
Southern State Community College,
 Room 104
Washington C.H., OH 43160
740-333-5115 Ext. 5720

Fulton County Job Center
604 S. Shoop, Suite 110
Wauseon, OH 43567
419-337-9215

Gallia County Work Opportunity
 Center
848 Third Ave.
Gallipolis, OH 45631
740-446-3222

Greene Works Employment and
 Training Center
581 Ledbetter Rd.
Xenia, OH 45385
937-562-6097(Direct)
937-562-6565 (Main)

Guernsey County Opportunity
Center
9900 Brick Church Rd., Route 660
Cambridge, OH 43725
740-432-9317

Hancock County Job Service
7746 CR 140, Suite B
Findlay, OH 45840
419-422-3679

Hardin County One-Stop Employment Services
1021 W. Lima St.
Kenton, OH 43326
419-674-2312

Harrison CDJFS
520 N. Main St.
Cadiz, OH 43907
740-942-2171

Henry County Job Center
104 E Washington St. Room 203-
215
Napoleon, OH 43545
419-592-0946 Ext. 106

Hocking County One-Stop Jobs
389 W. Front St.
Logan, OH 43138
740-380-1545

Jackson CDJFS One-Stop Training
and Technology Center
25 E. South St.
Jackson, OH 45640
740-286-4181

Jefferson County Community Action
Council
114 N. Fourth St.
Steubenville, OH 43952
740-282-0971 Ext. 139

The Job Center
1111 S. Edwin C. Moses Blvd.
Dayton, OH 45408
937-225-5627

The Job Center
1040 E. Tallmadge Ave.
Akron, OH 44310
330-633-1050

Job Leaders
1111 East Broad St.
Columbus, OH 43205
614-559-5052

The Job Store Fremont (Operated by
Terra Community College)
2511 Countryside Drive
Fremont, Oh 43420
419-335-5386

The Job Store Norwalk (Operated by
Terra Community College)
185 Shady Lane Drive
Norwalk, OH 44857
419-668-8126 Ext. 3335

The Job Store Ottawa Community
Resource Center (Operated by
Terra Community College)
8043 W. State Route 163
Oak Harbor, OH 43449
419-898-3688 Ext. 270
800-665-1677 Ext. 270

Jobs One-Stop
160 Island Rd.
Circleville, OH 43113
740-420-7339 Ext. 369

Jobs One-Stop
150 E. Second St.
Chillicothe, OH 45601
740-779-2946

Jobs, Inc.
18065 Woodsfield Rd.
Caldwell, OH 43724
740-732-2392

Lake County Department of Job and
Family Services Lake 1 Stop
177 Main St.
Painesville, OH 44077
440-350-4000 Ext. 4320

Lake County Employment and Training Division
177 Main St.
Painesville, OH 44077
440-350-4000 Main
440-918-4000 Lake County West
440-428-4838 Lake County East

Licking County Opportunity
998 Main St.
Newark, OH 43055
740-670-8700
888-895-2790
888-408-WORK

Logan County Work Plus Center
Department of Job and Family Services
211 E. Columbus Ave.
Bellefontaine, OH 43311
937-599-5165

Madison Works
200 Midway St.
London, OH 43140
740-852-8801

Mahoning County One-Stop
141 Boardman-Canfield Rd.
Boardman, OH 44512
330-965-1787

Mahoning County One-Stop Satellite Site
345 Oak Hill
Youngstown, OH 44502
330-740-2600 Ext. 8885

Marion Corrections Workforce Development Center
622 Leader St.
Marion, OH 43302
740-387-8560

Marysville Employment Resource Center
940 London Ave, Suite 1500
Marysville, OH 43040
937-645-2018 Ext. 2226

Medina County Workforce Development
3721 Pearl Rd.
Medina, OH 44256
330-723-9675

Meigs County One-Stop Employment Training Center CDJFS
175 Race St.
Middleport, OH 45760
740-992-2117
1-800-992-2608 Ext. 127

Mercer County One-Stop Employment and Training Center CDJFS
220 West Livingston St., Room B 272
Celina, OH 45822
419-586-6409

Miami County Job Center Network
2040 N. County Rd. 25A
Troy, OH 45373
937-440-3465

Millersburg Employment and Training Connection
Holmes CDJFS
85 N. Grant St.
Millersburg, OH 44654
330-674-1111

Monroe County Job and Family Services (Jobs etc. Your One-Stop Employment)
100 Home Ave., Suite 124
Woodsfield, OH 43793
740-472-1602

Morgan County Workforce Development One-Stop Center
155 E. Main St., Third Floor
McConnelsville, OH 43756
740-962-2519 Ext. 1315

Morrow County Job Training Office
619 W. Marion Rd.
Mt. Gilead, OH 43338
419-949-2673(Direct)
419-949-8480(Main)

Muskingum County Opportunity
Center
503 Main St.
Zanesville, OH 43701
740-454-6211
888-408-9675 Ext. 3

Northwest Ohio Job Center
1300 E. Second St., Suite 202
Defiance, OH 43512
419-784-3777

Opportunity Knox Employment
Center
17604 Coshocton Rd.
Mt. Vernon, OH 43050
740-397-7177

Perry County One-Stop
212 S. Main St.
New Lexington, OH 43764
740-342-3551
1-800-551-3551

Pike Employment and Training System
941 Market St.
Piketon, OH 45661
740-289-2371
866-829-1185

Portage Workforce Connection
1081 W. Main St.
Ravenna, OH 44266
330-296-2841

Preble County Job Center Network
1500 Park Ave.
Eaton, OH 45320
937-456-6224

Putman County ACCENT/CDJFS
1225 E. Third St.
Ottawa, OH 45875
419-774-5300

Salem Public Library
821 E. State St.
Salem, OH 44460
330-332-0042

Scioto County Workforce
Connections
433 Third St.
Portsmouth, OH 45662
740-354-7545

Seneca One-Stop Career and Resource
Center
3362 S. Township Rd. 151
Tiffin, OH 44883
419-447-5011 Ext. 443
800-825-5011 Ext.443

Shelby County Job Center Network
227 S. Ohio Ave.
Sidney, OH 45365
937-498-4981 Ext. 297

The Source North West Ohio
1301 Monroe St.
Toledo, OH 43604
419-213-6300

Springfield Work Plus Center
1345 Lagonda Ave.
Springfield, OH 45503
937-327-1961 Ext. 1962

Stark County — The Employment
Source
822 30th St., NW
Canton, OH 44709
330-433-9675

Trumbull County One-Stop
280 North Park Ave., Suite 1
Warren, OH 44481
330-675-2179

Van Wert County One-Stop
114 East Main St.
Van West, OH 45891
419-238-4931

Vinton CDJFS One-Stop
Employment and Training Center
30975 Industrial Park Rd.
McArthur, OH 45651
740-596-2584

Warren County Workforce One
300 East Silver St.
Lebanon, OH 45036
513-695-1130

Washington Morgan Community Action
218 Putman St.
Marietta, OH 45750
740-373-3745

Williams County Job Center
228 South Main St.
Bryan, OH 43506
419-636-5047

Wood County Job Solutions
1928 E. Gypsy Lane
Bowling Green, OH 43402
419-352-4172
419-373-6970

Wooster Employment and Training Connection
358 W. North St.
Wooster, OH 44654
330-264-5060

Work Place at Geauga County CDJFS
12480 Ravenwood Drive
Chardon, OH 44024
440-285-9141 Ext. 220

The Work Station
70 N. Plains Rd, Suite C
The Plains, OH 45780
740-797-1405

Workforce Development Resource Center
120 N. Third St.
Ironton, OH 45638
740-532-3140

Wyandot County Job Solutions and Family Services
120 E. Johnson St.
Upper Sandusky, OH 43351
419-294-4977

Your Job Store
5500 Milan Rd., Suite 386B
Sandusky, OH 44870
419-624-6451

OKLAHOMA

Big Five Community Services
1502 North 1st St.
P.O. Box 1577
Durant, OK 74702
580-924-5331
www.biglive.org

Helps clients overcome barriers to employment and provides employment and job training opportunities.

Case Recovery Ministry/New Starts Prison Ministry
P.O. Box 19352
Oklahoma City, OK 73144-0352
405-420-3192
Revrick73010@aol.com

Provides services for ex-offenders and their families.

Community Action Project of Tulsa County
717 S. Houston, Suite 200
Tulsa, OK 3200
www.captc.org
webmaster@captc.org

CAP offers programs that provide support in housing, employment, education, childcare, tax preparation, assistance, social services, emergency aid, medical services, and advocacy.

Criminal Justice and Mercy Ministry
OK Methodist Conference
1501 NW 24th St.

Oklahoma City, OK 73106
405-530-2015
abasler@ukumc.org
   Provides services to ex-offenders and their families.

CURE
P.O. Box 9741
Tulsa, OK 74157
okcure@okcure.org
http://www.okcure.org
http://groups.yahoo.com/group/OKCURE
   CURE is a grassroots organization from top to bottom. It does not hire professional leaders. Instead, its leaders come from the ranks of people formerly in prison and family members of friends of prisoners. This organization offers assistance to ex-offenders.

Exodus House Oklahoma City
433 NW 26th
Oklahoma City, OK 73103
405-525-2300
   This program is administered by the United Methodist Church and provides transitional housing for recently released individuals and their children. Services provided include on-site substance abuse treatment, referrals for mental hygiene counseling, anger management group counseling and computer instruction. Job referrals are made, although no formal job development is available. People with a history of sexual offenses or a tendency toward violence are not accepted for residency at Exodus House.

Exodus House Tulsa
2624 E. Newton St.
Tulsa, OK 74110
918-362-0805
ehousetulsa@prodigy.net

Workforce Oklahoma Centers

Ada Center
1628 East Beverly St, Suite 115
Ada, OK 74820
580-332-1533

Altus Center
1115 North Spurgeon St.

Altus, OK 73521
580-482-3262

Antlers Center
204 Southwest 4th St.
Antlers, OK 74523
580-298-6601

Ardmore Center
201 A St. S.W.
Ardmore, OK 73401
580-223-3291

Bartlesville Center
6101 SE Nowata Rd, Suite C100
Bartlesville, OK 74006
918-331-3400

Chickasha Center
301 South 2nd St.
Chickasha, OK 73018
405-224-3310
Chickasha/Ft. Cobb

Caddo Kiowa Technology Center
100 Campus Rd.
Ft. Cobb, OK 73038

Claremore Center
1810 North Sioux Ave.
Claremore, OK 74017
918-341-6633

Clinton Center
1120 Frisco Ave.
Clinton, OK 73601
580-323-1341

Duncan Center
1927 West Elk Ave.
Duncan, OK 73533
580-255-8950

Durant Center
4310 West Highway 70
Durant, OK 74701
580-924-1828

Enid Center
2613 North Van Buren

Enid, OK 73701
580-234-6043

Guymon Center
225 East Highway 54
Guymon, OK 73942
580-338-8521

Holdenville Center
115 Rodgers Drive
Holdenville, OK 74848
405-379-5452

Hugo Center
107 South Third St.
Hugo, OK 74743
580-326-7502

Idabel Center
2202 SE Washington
Idabel, OK 74745
580-286-6667

Kay County One-Stop Career Center
1201 West Grand Ave.
Ponca City, OK 74601
580-765-3372

Lawton Center
1711 SW 11th St.
Lawton, OK 73501
580-357-3500

LeFlore County Center
106 Rogers Ave.
Poteau, OK 74953
918-647-3124

McAlester Center
1201 Wade Watts Ave.
McAlester. OK 74501
918-423-6830

Miami Center
121 North Main
Miami, OK 74354
918-542-5561

Muskogee Center
717 South 32nd St.

Muskogee, OK 74401
918-682-3364

Norman Center
1141 East Main
Norman, OK 73071
405-701-2000

Oklahoma City Center
7401 NE 23rd
Oklahoma City, OK 73141
405-713-1890

Okmulgee Center
1801 East 4th St.
Okmulgee, OK 74447
918-756-5791

Pryor Center
219 NE 1st St.
Pryor, OK 74361
918-825-2582

Reno Center
416 Hudiburg Circle, Suite B
Oklahoma, City, OK 73108
405-639-3640

Rockwell Center
Francis Tuttle Tech-Campus Center
  Bldg.#1
12777 North Rockwell
Oklahoma City, OK 73142
405-470-3200

Sallisaw Center
HC 61 Box 12
Sallisaw, OK 74955
918-775-5541

Sapulpa Center
1700 South Main
Sapulpa, OK 74066
918-224-9430

Seminole Center
229 N. 2nd St.
Seminole, OK 74868
405-382-4670

Shawnee Center
2 John C Burton Blvd.
Shawnee, OK 74804
405-275-7800

Southside Oklahoma City
   Center
4509 South I-35 Service Rd.
Oklahoma City, OK 73129
405-670-9100

Stillwater Career Center
711 East Krayler Ave.
Stillwater, OK 74075
405-624-1450

Stilwell Center
219 West Oak

Stilwell, OK 74960
918-696-6608

Tahlequah Center
1755 South Muskogee Ave.
Tahlequah, OK 74464
918-456-8846

Tulsa Center
14002 E. 21st St., Suite 1030
Eastgate Metroplex
Tulsa, OK 74134
918-796-1200

Woodward Center
1117 11th St.
Woodward, OK 73801
580-256-3308

OREGON

Better People
4310 N.E. Martin Luther King Blvd.
Portland, Oregon 97211
503-281-2663
www.betterpeople.org
   Better People is a program that combines job placement and retention services with a therapeutic approach called Moral Reconation Therapy

CURE
1631 NE Broadway #460
Portland, OR 97232
503-977-9979 Portland Media area
TOLL FREE 1-866-357-
   CURE(2873) statewide
http://www.orgeoncure.org/
   CURE is a grassroots organization from top to bottom. It does not hire professional leaders. Instead, its leaders come from the ranks of people formerly in prison and family members of friends of prisoners. This organization offers assistance to ex-offenders.

Hepatitis C Awareness Project
P.O. Box 41803

Eugene, Oregon
Http://www.madimi.com/hepc.html
   Newsletter, information packet. Offers seminars, workshops, and support groups both in and out of prison for those impacted by Hepatitis C.

Steps-to-Success
1415 SE 122nd Ave.
Portland, Oregon 97233
503-258-0432
www.steps-2-success.org
   Employment services to enable job seekers to gain the skills and qualifications necessary to obtain permanent jobs.

One-Stop Career/Work Source Centers

Baker City
1575 Dewey Ave.
Baker City, OR 97814
541-523-6331

Benton Work Force Development
   Center

545 SW 2nd St.
Corvallis, OR 97333
541-967-2171

Bend Vocational Rehabilitation
1230 NE Third, Suite A-152
Bend, OR 97701
541-388-6336

Burns Employment Department
90 West Washington
Burns, OR 97720
541-573-5251

Business Health Care and Division
6500 Pacific Blvd. WH 120
Albany, OR 97321
541-917-4923

Canyon City
120 S Washington St.
Canyon City, OR 97820
541-575-0744

Central City Concern-Employment
  Access Center
2 NW 2nd Ave.
Portland, OR 97209
583-226-7387

Central Oregon Inter-Governmental
  Council
103 North G St.
Lakeview, OR 97630
541-947-5702

Clackamas County One-Stop Resource Center
506 High St.
Oregon City, OR 97045
971-673-6400

Clatsop County One-Stop Center
450 Marine Drive, Suite 110
Astoria, OR 97103
503-325-4821

Columbia County One-Stop
500 N. Highway 30, Suite 320

St. Helens, OR 97051
503-397-4995

Community Services Consortium
120 NE Avery St.
Newport, OR 97365
541-265-8505

The Dalles
700 Union St., Suite 105
The Dalles, OR 97058
541-295-5435

Douglas Employment Department
846 SE Pine St.
Roseburg, OR 97470
541-440-3344

Douglas Work Links DHS One-
  Stop
1937 W. Harvard Ave.
Roseburg, OR 97471
541-440-3301

Douglas Works Link Umpqua
Community College Work Force
  Training Center
2555 N.E. Diamond Lake Blvd
Roseburg, OR 97470
541-440-4668

East Linn Work Force Development
  Center
44 Industrial Way
Lebanon, OR 97355
541-259-5787

Employment Department
16339 Lower Harbor Rd.
Brookings, OR 97415
541-469-9838

Enterprise
104 Litch St.
Enterprise, OR 97828
541-426-4972

Florence
3180 Hwy 101 N

Florence, OR 97439
541-997-1913

Gorge, Mid Columbia Council of
Governments
1113 Kelly Ave.
The Dalles, OR 97058
541-298-4101

Grants Pass
1545 Marbeck Rd.
Grants Pass, OR 97527
541-476-1187

Hanscam Center
16399 Lower Harbor Rd.
Harbor, OR 97415
541-469-5306
1-800-481-5777

Hermiston
950 SF Columbia Drive
Hermiston, OR 97838
541-567-3381

Klamath
801 Oak Ave.
Klamath Falls, OR 97601

La Grande One-Stop
1901 Adams Ave.
La Grande, OR 97630
541-947-5702

Lincoln City
801 SW Hwy 101
Lincoln City, OR 97367
541-994-6992

Linn Work Force Development Center
139 4th Ave.
Albany, OR 97321
541-967-2171

Malheur County One-Stop Center
375 SW 2nd Ave.
Ontario, OR 97914
541-889-5394

MTC Works
3600 East 2nd St., Suite B

Tillamook, OR 97141
503-842-3244

North Curry Families and Children's
Center
1403 Hwy 101
Port Oxford, OR 97465
541-332-9191

Oregon Employment Department
1645 NE Forbes Rd., Suite 100
Bend, OR 97701-4990
541-388-6070

Oregon Employment Department
243 SW Third St., Suite B
Madras, OR 97741
541-475-2382

Oregon Employment Department
2075 Sheridan Ave.
North Bend, OR 97459
541-756-8459

Pendleton
408 SE 7th St.
Pendleton, OR 97801
541-276-9050

Polk Center
580 Main St., Suite B
Dallas, OR 97338
503-831-1950

Portland Metro Beaverton/Hillsboro
241 SW Edgeway Drive
Beaverton, OR 97006
503-526-2700

Portland Metro East
19421 SE Stark St.
Portland, OR 97033
503-669-7112

Portland Metro Tualatin
7995 SW Mohawk St.
Tualatin, OR 97062
503-612-4200
877-877-0813

Prineville
2321 NE 3rd St.
Prineville, OR 97754
541-447-8076

Redmond
2158 SE College Loop, Building 2
and 3
Redmond, OR 97756
541-504-2955

Salem Center
605 Cottage St. NE
Salem, OR 97301-2419
503-378-8389

South East Works
6927 SE Foster Rd.
Portland, OR 97206
503-772-2300

Springfield Main St. Center
101 30th St.
Springfield, OR 97478
541-726-3525

UTE 1Stop
760 N.W. Hill Place
Roseburg, OR 97471
541-672-7761

Woodburn Center
120 East Lincoln St.
Woodburn, OR 97071
503-982-2817

Work Source Lane
4000 E. 30th Ave.
Eugene, OR 97405-0640
541-463-5223

The Workforce Network
2510 Oakmont Way
Eugene, OR 97401
541-686-7601

Yamhill Center
270 NE Norton Lane
McMinnville, OR 97128
503-472-5118

PENNSYLVANIA

Bebashi-Care Outreach
1217 Spring Garden St. 1st Floor
Philadelphia, PA 19123
215-769-3561
www.bebashi.org
bell@critpath.org
   This organization offers referrals, counseling, and testing for people with AIDS who are newly released from Pennsylvania state prisons.

CURE
P.O. Box 26708
Elkins Park, PA 19077
215-548-8267
beteasley@comcast.net
   CURE is a grassroots organization from top to bottom. It does not hire professional leaders. Instead, its leaders come from the ranks of people formerly in prison and family members of

friends of prisoners. This organization offers assistance to ex-offenders.

Family and Corrections Network
(FCN)
93 Old York Rd.
Suite 1#510
Jenkintown, PA 19046
215-576-1110
http://www.fenetwork.org/fen@fenet-work.org
   FCN is an organization for and about families of prisoners. We offer information, training and technical assistance on children of prisoners, parenting programs for prisoners, prison visiting, incarcerated fathers and mothers, hospitality programs, keeping in touch, returning to the community, the impact of the justice system on families, prison marriage.

Jubilee Ministries
235 South 12th St.
Lebanon, PA 17042
717-274-7528
http://www.jub.org

    This ministry strives to demonstrate the love of God to the economically disadvantaged by helping to meet their physical, emotional, and material needs regardless of race, color, creed, age, or gender. Jubilee also provides Christian discipleship to those incarcerated or in after-care programs who are committed to seeking reconciliation with God and establishing a personal growing relationship with Jesus Christ as Savior and Lord.

Justice and Mercy
P.O. Box 223
Shillington, PA 19607
610-208-0406
http://www.justicemercy.org/

    Justice and Mercy is a nonprofit, volunteer organization dedicated to decreasing the effects of crime in our communities, increasing public safety, and ministering to and restoring both crime victims and offenders. These goals are achieved by educating and informing the public at large, advocating cost-effective and practical reforms within the criminal justice system and by supporting and encouraging wise public policy.

National Incarcerated Parents and
    families Network
P.O. Box 6745
Harrisburg, PA 17112
http://www.incarceratedparents.org/

    The National Incarcerated Parents and Families Network(NIPFN) offers effective, re-ality-based training for people seeking to work with incarcerated parents in correctional fa-cilities and with the family of these individuals in re-entry back into their lives and back into the communities.

One-Stop/PA Career Link Centers

Adams County
150 V Twin Drive

Gettysburg, PA 17315
717-334-1173

Allegheny East
2040 Ardmore Blvd.
Pittsburg, PA 15221
412-436-2225

Allegheny West
Rte. 60 and Park Manor Drive
Robinson Plaza 2, Suite 410
Pittsburgh, PA 15205
412-809-3500

Alle-Kiski
1150 5th Ave., Suite 200
New Kensington, PA 15068
724-334-8600

Armstrong County
77 Glade Drive
Kittanning, PA 16201
724-548-5693

Beaver County
2103 9th Ave.
Beaver Falls, PA 15010
724-728-4860

Bedford County
1 Corporate Drive, Suite 103
Bedford, PA 15522
814-623-6107

Berks County
501 Crescent Ave.
Reading, PA 19605-3050
610-988-1300

Blair County
3001 Fairway Drive
Altoona, PA16602
814-940-6200

Bradford County
218 Main St. Unit 1
Towanda, PA 18848-1844
570-265-2171

Bucks County
1260 Veterans Hwy

Bristol, PA 19007
215-781-1073 Ext. 222
Butler County

Pullman Commerce Center
112 Hollywood Drive, Suite 101
Butler, PA 16001
724-431-4000

Cambria County
445 Schoolhouse Rd.
Johnstown, PA 15904
814-533-2493 Ext. 243

Cameron County
301 Chestnut St.
Emporium, PA 15834
814-486-3729

Capitol Region
349 Wiconisco St.
Harrisburg, PA 17110-2125
717-783-3270

Carbon County
69 Broadway
Jim Thorpe, PA 18229-1936
570-325-2701

Centre County State College
1300 Benner Pike, Suite 2
State College, PA 16801
814-272-5465

Chester County
250 East Harmony St.
Coatesville, PA 19320-5409
610-384-9393

Clarion County
22 South Second Ave.
Clarion, PA 16214
814-223-1550

Clearfield County, Clearfield
1125 Linden St.
Clearfield, PA 16830
814-765-8118

Clearfield County, DuBois
20 N. Sixth St.

DuBois, PA 15801
814-371-0250

Clinton County
8 North Grove St., Suite F
Lock Haven, PA 17745
570-893-4022

Columbia and Montour Counties
351 Tenny St.
Bloomsburg, PA 17815
570-387-6288

Crawford County
210 Chestnut St.
Meadville, PA 16335-1856
814-337-5574

Cumberland County
1 Alexandra Court
Carlisle, PA 17015
717-243-4431

Delaware County
701 Crosby St., Suite B
Chester, PA 19013
610-447-3350

Delaware County Community College
901 S. Media Line Rd.
Media, PA 19063
610-723-1220

Elk County
301 Depot St.
St. Marys, PA 15857
814-834-2857

Elk County Workforce Development
    Office
651 Montmorenci Rd.
Ridgeway, PA 15853
814-773-3162

Erie County
1309 French St. Lovell Place
Erie, PA 16501-1999
814-455-9966

Fayette County
135bWayland Smith Drive

Uniontown, PA 15401
724-434-5627

Franklin County
600 Norland Ave.
Chambersburg, PA 17201-4205
717-264-4584

Fulton County Employment and
   Training Services
122 West Market St.
McConnettsburg, PA 17233
717-485-5131

Greene County
4 West High St.
Waynesburg, PA 15370-1324
724-852-2900

Honesdale
Team Honesdale
925 Court St.
Honesdale, PA 18431
570-253-1163

Huntington County
54 Pennsylvania Ave.
Huntington, PA 16652-1299
814-641-6408

Indiana County
300 Indian Springs Rd.
Indiana, PA 15701
724-471-7220

Jefferson County
602 East Mahoning St.
Punxsutawney, PA 15767-2316
814-938-0504

Lackawanna County
135 Franklin Ave.
Scranton, PA 18503
570-963-4671

Lancaster County
1016 North Charlotte St.
Lancaster, PA 17603-2764
717-299-7631

Lawrence County
102 Margaret St.
New Castle, PA 16101
724-656-3165

Lebanon County
243 Schneider Drive
Lebanon, PA 17046-4875
717-274-2554

Lehigh Valley
1601 Union Blvd.
Allentown, PA 18109-0490
610-437-5627

Luzerne County
Hazleton Center
75 North Laurel St.
Hazleton, PA 18201
570-459-3854

Luzerne County
32 East Union St.
Wilkes Barre, PA 18711
570-826-2401

Lycoming County
145 West Third St.
Williamsport, PA 17701
570-601-5465

McKean County
40 Davis St.
Bradford, PA 16701
814-363-9100

Mercer County
217 West State St., Cocoa Building
Sharon, PA 16146
724-347-9257

Mifflin County
6395 SR 103 North, MCJDC
Plaza, Building 58
Lewistown, PA 17044
717-248-4942

Mon Valley
570 Galiffa Drive, Donora Industrial
   Park

Donora, PA 15033
724-379-4750

Monroe County
Route 611 Merchants Plaza
Tannersville, PA 18372-0789
570-620-2850

Monroeville
Forbes Rd. Career and Technology
   Center
607 Beatty Rd.
Monroeville, PA 15146
412-373-8100

Montgomery County
1855 New Hope St.
Norristown, PA 19401-3146
610-270-3429

North Umberland County
2 East Arch St.
Shamokin, PA 17872
570-644-6570

Northwest
235 West Chelten Ave.
Philadelphia, PA 19144-3893
215-560-5151

Oil Region
255 Elm St., Suite 1
Oil City, PA 16301-1412
814-678-5050

Philadelphia
Nueva Esperanza Career Link
4261 North 5th St.
Philadelphia, PA 19140
215-324-0746

Philadelphia
Suburban Station PA Career Link
1617 JFK Blvd., Suite 200
Philadelphia, PA 19103
215-557-2592

Philadelphia North
990 Spring Garden St.

Philadelphia, PA 19123
215-560-5465

Philadelphia Northeast
3210 Red Lion Rd.
Academy Plaza Shopping Center
Philadelphia, PA 19114
215-281-1038

Pike County Workforce Development Agency
837 Route 6
Shohola, PA 18458
570-296-2909

Pittsburgh
2600 East Carson St.
Pittsburg, PA 15203
412-390-2327

Pittsburg/Allegheny County
425 6th Ave, 22nd Floor
Pittsburg, PA 15219
412-552-7100, Ext 7033

Pittsburgh Downtown
425 6th Ave., 22nd Floor
Pittsburgh, PA 15219
412-552-7100
412-552-7068

Potter County
279 Rt. 6 West
Coudersport, PA 16915
814-274-9330

Sayre VA Outpatient Clinic-Sayre
1537 Elmira St.
Sayre, PA 18840
607-733-7131

Schuylkill County at Pottsville
   Center
201-203 East Arch St.
Pottsville, PA 17901
570-622-5253

Somerset County
218 North Kimberly Ave., Suite 4

Somerset, PA 15501-1461
814-445-4161

Somerset County Office of Veterans Services
300 North Center Ave., Suite
380
Somerset, PA 15501-1497
814-445-1551

Susquehanna County
180 Main St.
Great Bend, PA 18821
570-724-1939

Tioga County
56 Plaza Lane
Wellsboro, PA 16901-1763
570-724-1939

Union/Snyder County
713 Bridge St., Suite 11
Selinsgrove, PA 17870
570-374-5751 Ext. 131

Warren County
2 Market St.

Warren, PA 16365-2540
814-723-2350

Washington County
90 West Chestnut St., Suite 150LL
Washington, PA 15301
724-223-4500

Westmoreland County
151 Pavillion Lane
Youngwood, PA 15697-1814
724-755-2330

West Pittsburgh Partnership
37 Wabash Ave.
Pittsburg, PA 15220
412-922-2740 Ext.100

Wyoming County
115 State Route 92 South
Tunkhannock, PA 18657-9803
570-836-6840

York County
841 Vogelsong Rd.
York, PA 17404-0868
717-767-7600 Ext.240

PUERTO RICO

Agencia Municipal de Oportunidad
de Empleo (AMOE-Carolina)
Carr 859, Bo. San Anton
Carolina, PR 00985-0899
787-752-4090

Area Local Guaynabo–Toa Baja
Calle Marginal Kenedy, Metro Office
Park, Edif, Universal Life (2ndo
Piso), Bo. Pueblo Viejo Guaynabo,
PR 00969
787-782-9898
787-793-5876

Centro Gestión Unica, Mayagüez
63 Calle Martínez Nadal

Mayagüez, PR 00681
787-265-3737
787-265-3738
787-883-9052

Centro de Gestión Unica, Noroeste
Carr. #2, Bo. Corrales, Km. 122.4
Aguadilla, PR 00603
787-882-1545
787-891-1500
787-891-1501

Cabo Rojo
Calle Barbosa # 30
Cabo Rojo, PR
787-851-5655

Guanica
Calle 25 de Julio #67
Guanica, PR
787-821-0998

Guayanilla
Calle Rufina # 16 A
Guayanilla, PR
787-835-2100

Hormigueros
Calle Julio Pérez Irizarry # 23
Hormigueros, PR
787-849-1705

Lajas
Centro Comercial Municipal
Lajas, PR
787-899-7015

Maricao
Calle Suzuaregui #9
Maricao, PR
787-838-3997

Peñuelas
Calle Dr. Loyola #705
Peñuelas, PR
787-836-3997

Sabana Grande
Calle San Isidro # 18
Sabana Grande, PR
787-873-3141

Salinas
Santos P. Amadeo
Salinas, PR 00751
787-824-1060
787-824-1070

Yauco
Calle Mattei Lluveras # 70
Yauco, PR
787-856-2222

Adjuntas
9 Calle Antonio Cesar González
Adjuntas, PR 00601
787-829-3060

Aguada
Calle Paz
Aguada, PR
787-868-8405

Aguadilla
Carr# 2 Km 122-4
Aguadilla, PR 00603
787-819-1501
787-819-1503

Aguas Buenas
Calle Pedro Albizú Campos Final
Aguas Buenas, PR
787-732-1505

Aibonito
Edificio Guayacan Suite
Aibonito, PR 00705
787-735-4545

Añasco
Calle 65 Infanteria # 95
Añasco, PR
787-735-4545
787-826-5045

Arecibo
Avenida Jose de Diego #108
Arecibo, PR 00613-9933
787-879-4439

Arroyo
Bo. Guasitas, Km 131.4
Arroyo, PR 00714
787-839-0030

Barceloneta
Centro de Gobierno Juan Cancel Ríos
Barceloneta, PR
787-846-2035

Barranquitas
Calle Barceio #58
Barranquitas, PR 00794
787-857-0093

Bayamón
Calle Palmer Esquina Dr. Veve

Bayamón, PR 00960
787-787-6750

Caguas
Calle Goyco #65
Caguas, PR 00726
787-746-2616

Camuy
50 Muñoz Rivera, Oeste
Camuy, PR 00627
787-262-1005

Canóvanas
Calle Autonomía #78
Canóvanas, PR 00729
787-256-6724

Cataño
Centro Gubernamental Hector L.
  Santiago
Cataño, PR
787-788-5620

Cayey
215 Calle Barbosa, Esq. Gallart
Cayey, PR 00736
787-263-4747

Ceiba
Severiano Fuentes Fria
Ceiba, PR 00735
787-885-5680

Centro de Gestión Unica, Caguas,
  Gurabo Trujillo Alto
P.O.Box 8518
Caguas, PR 00726
787-744-5329

Centro de Gestión Unica, Salinas
Sur-Central Celle Santos P
Amadeo # 29
Salinas, PR 00769
787-803-0119

Centro de Gestión Unica, San Germán
La Avenida Los Atléticos
Esquina Golondria, Suite 201
Edificio 3M

San Germán, PR 00683
787-892-3185

Ciales
Calle José de Diego #53
Ciales, PR
787-871-3115

Coamo
Calle José I. Quintón #33
Coamo, PR 00769
787-825-8801

Comerío
P.O. Box 1588
Comerío, PR 00960
787-785-5524

Consorcio Guaynabo–Toa Baja
Edificio City Hall 5 Piso
Guaynabo, PR 00969
787-720-4040

Consorcio de La Montaña
Calle José de Diego Final
Cidra, PR 00703
787-739-1370

Consorcio Norte Central Dorado/
  Manatí
Carr. 670 KM 4
Manatí, PR 00674
787-884-4055

Corozal
Calle Gandara #1
Corozal, PR
787-859-4295

Culebra
Calle Manuel Vázquez Alayón
Culebra, PR
787-742-0283

Dorado
Centro de Gobierno Luis Muñoz
  Marín
Dorado, PR
787-796-6340

Fajardo
Calle Unión #168
Fajardo, PR 00738
787-860-6087
787-860-4005

Florida
Calle Arizmendi #93
Florida, PR
787-822-2333

Guayama
Calle Hostos 44 Norte
Guayama, PR 00784
787-866-0049

Gurabo
2ndo Piso, Casa Alcaldia
Gurabo, PR 00778
787-737-7524

Hatillo
155 Calle Comercio
Hatillo, PR 00659
787-898-1015

Isabeta
Calle Corchado #69
Isabela, PR
787-872-0030

Jayuya
57 Calle Guillermo Estévez
Jayuya, PR 00664
787-828-4052

Juana Díaz
Calle Tomás Carrión Maduro #73
Juana Díaz, PR 00795

Juncos
Calle Argarín #3
Juncos, PR
787-561-0101

Lares
4 Calle Gardera
Lares, PR 00669
787-897-5540

Las Marias
77 Ave. Marias Brugman #2
Las Marisa, PR 00670

Las Piedras
Calle José T. Pinero #77
Las Piedras, PR
787-912-8266

Loíza
Calle García de la Noceda
Loiza, PR 00722
787-886-1620

Luquillo
Calle 10 Bo. Fortuna
Luquillo, PR 00773
787-889-1112

Manatí
Centro Commericial Puerta del Sol
Manatí, PR
787-884-3088

Maunabo
Calle Santiago Iglesias
Maunabo, PR
939-329-0022

Mayagüez
63 Calle Rafael Martínez Nadal
   Nortc
Mayagüez, PR 00680
787-529-3296
787-265-3737
787-265-3738

Moca
Carr# 111 Km 3.9
Moca, PR
787-877-0855

Morovis
Calle Comercio #13
Morovis, PR
787-862-5814

Naguabo
Naguabo Shopping Center

Naguabo, PR
787-874-1609

Naranjito
Calle Georgetti # 125 Altos
Naranjito, PR 00719
787-869-2675

Northeast Consortium of Rio Grande
Marginal Carr, 3 Km 23.9
Rio Grande, PR 00745
787-888-3030

Orocovis
Calle Ramos Antonini # 2
Orocovis, PR
787-867-5731

Patillas
Calle Riefkhol Altos
Patillas, PR
939-307-0000

Ponce
Calle Isabel 6163
Ponce, PR 00733
787-840-0457

Quebradillas
47 B Calle Eduardo Abraham
Quebradillas, PR
787-895-1030

Rincón
Calle Santa Rosa #1
Rincón, PR
787-823-0505

Sebastián
Calle Muñez Rivera #3
San Sebastián, PR
787-896-8790

Salinas
Calle Luis Muñoz Rivera #102 Altois
Salinas, PR 00751
787-824-1060

San Juan
Avenida Ponce de León # 1205
Santurce, PR 00907
787-289-0470
787-289-0474
787-289-0460

San Lorenzo/Central
Calle José de Diego #110
San Lorenzo, PR 00754
787-937-0000

Santa Isabel
Calle Hostas #16
Santa Isabel, PR 00757
787-845-4065

Toa Alta
Calle Muñoz Rivera #70
Toa Alta, PR
787-870-5987

Trujillo Alto
Western Auto Plaza
Trujillo, PR 00976
787-283-0805

Utuado
100 Calle Dr. Cuoto
Utuado, PR 00641
787-894-2088

Vega Alta
Calle Luis Muñoz Rivera #64
Vega Alta, PR
787-883-6478

Vieques
Coliseo Luis González Camareno
Vieques, PR 00765
787-741-0468

Villalba
Calle Barcelo #26
Villaba, PR
878-847-0246

RHODE ISLAND

CrossRd.s
160 Broad St.
Providence, RI 02903
401-521-2255

This program assists ex-offenders in job development, including case management, counseling, respite services and information and referral, along with other programs, call to find out about other services.

CURE
HMLopez@cori.edu

CURE is a grassroots organization from top to bottom. It does not hire professional leaders. Instead, its leaders come from the ranks of people formerly in prison and family members of friends of prisoners. This organization offers assistance to ex-offenders.

Justice Services Program-Travelers Aid
    Society of Rhode Island
177 Union St.
Providence, RI 02903
401-521-2255, 24-hour helpline
401-521-SAFE. No collect calls

This travel Aid Program assists ex-offenders in job development. Originally an on-site program at ACI (adult Correctional Institute) called Making It Work, the program continues to help prisoners make the transition from prison to community life, specifically through employment services. Other core services: crisis intervention, case management, counseling, respite services, and information and referral. The program is for Travelers Aid-clients, and becoming a client requires a simple intake process.

PAWTUCKET Network Center
175 Main St.
Pawtucket, RI 02860
401-721-1800

PROVIDENCE Network One-Stop
    Center
1 Reservoir Ave.
Providence, RI 02907
401-462-8900

WEST WARWICK Network Center
1330 Main St.
West Warwick, RI 02893
401-828-8382

WOONSOCKET Network Center
219 Pond St.
Woonsocket, RI 02895
401-235-1201

These organizations provide educational, training, and employment assistance to ex-offenders.

Women in Transition, Inc.
PO Box 20135
Cranston, RI 02920
401-462-1767

This program is a resource for women who are beginning to transition back into community life. They provide case management, counseling, life skills training, parenting classes, job development and housing assistance.

SOUTH CAROLINA

Alston Wilkes Society
3519 Medical Dr.
Columbia, SC 29203
803-799-2490
www.alstonwilkessociety.org

This organization offers a variety of post-release services to former prisoners. They operate two co-ed facilities that house inmates from the Federal Bureau of Prisons. These facilities are located in Columbia and Greenville, South Carolina.

Higher Ground Foundation
P.O. Box 1602
Altoona, PA 16603
814-742-7500
prisonmail@gmail.com
    This ministry focuses on helping prisoners, ex-offenders and others experience a life-changing transformation through seminars and workshops.

One-Stop Workforce Centers

Abbeville
353 Highway 28 Bypass
Abbeville, SC 29620
864-459-5486

Aiken
1571 Richland Ave. East
Aiken, SC 29802-2418
803-641-7640

Aiken Technical College
2276 Jefferson Davis Hwy
Aiken, SC 29802
803-593-9954 Ext. 1283

Allendale
Employment Security Commission
3489 Allendale-Fairfax Highway
Fairfax, SC 29827
803-584-3263

Anderson
309 West Whitner St.
Anderson, SC 29624(29622)
864-226-7273

Andrews
102 East Main St.
Andrews, SC 29510
843-264-5178

Baptist Hill/Charleston Adult Education
5117 Baptist Hill Rd.
Younges Island, SC 29449
843-938-6325

Barnwell
248 Wall St.

Barnwell, SC 29812
803-259-7116

Beaufort WF Center
164 Castle Rock Rd.
Beaufort, SC 29906 (29901)
843-524-3351

Bennettsville
460 Highway 9 West
Bennettsville, SC 29512
843-479-4081

Berkeley One-Stop Career Center
107 East Main St.
Moncks, SC 29461
843-899-8736

Bishopville
123 S. Nettles St.
Bishopville, SC 29010
803-483-2021

Bluffton One-Stop Center
9 Oak Forest Drive
Bluffton, SC 29910
843-757-1624

Camden
205 E. Dekalb St.
Camden, SC 29020
803-432-5153

Charleston
176 Lockwood Drive
Charleston, SC 29403
843-953-8400

Cheraw
318 Front St.
Cheraw, SC 29520
843-320-9760

Chester
764 Wilson St.
Chester, SC 29706
803-337-8147

Chesterfield
201 N. Page St.

Chesterfield, SC 29709
843-623-5270

Coastal
200 A Victory St.
Anderson, SC 29526
843-234-9675

Colleton
101 Mable T. Willis Blvd.
Walterboro, SC 29488
843-538-8980

Dillon County
401 West Main St.
Dillon, SC 29536
843-774-1420

Dorchester One-Stop Career Center
2885 West 5th North St.
Summersville, SC 29484
843-574-1814

East Cooper Community Outreach
(ECCO)
1145 Six Mile Rd.
Mount Pleasant, SC 29466
843-849-9220

Edgefield
400 Church St., Edgefield
Neighborhood Center
Edgefield, SC 29824
803-637-4029

Florence
1558 West Evans St.
Florence, SC 29501
843-669-4271

Gaffney
133 Wilmac Rd.
Gaffney, SC 29342
864-489-3112

Georgetown
2704 Highmarket St.
Georgetown, SC 29440
843-546-8581

Greenville County, McAlister
Square
225 S. Pleasantburg Drive, Suite C
16-17
Greenville, SC 29607
864-467-8080

Greenville
Employment Security Commission
706 Pendleton St.
Greenville, SC 29602
864-242-3531

Greenwood
519 Monument St.
Greenwood, SC 29648
864-223-1681

Hampton
12 Walnut St. East
Hampton, SC 29924
803-943-3291

Hartsville Employment and
Security
1319 S. Fourth St.
Hartsville, SC 29550
843-332-1554

Jasper
7774 West Main St.
Ridgeland, SC 29936
843-726-3750

Kingstree
530 Martin Luther King Jr. Ave.
Kingstree, SC 29556
843-354-7436
843-354-7436

Lake City/Florence School District 3
209 Graham Rd.
Lake City, SC 29560
843-374-0970 Ext. 1058

Lancaster
705 N. White St.
Lancaster, SC 29721
803-285-6966

Laurens County
18 Hazel Drive
Clinton, SC 29325
864-833-0142

Lexington County
714 S. Lake Dr., Suite 140
Lexington, SC 29072
803-359-6131

Liberty
317 Summit Drive
Liberty, SC 29657
864-843-9512

Manning
3351 Hwy 521
Manning, SC 29102
803-473-2086

Marion ESC
1305 North Main St.
Marion, SC 29571
843-423-8288

McCormick
109 West Augusta St.
McCormick, SC 29835
864-465-3649

Midlands (Columbia)
700 Taylor St.
Columbia, SC 29202
803-737-0253

Myrtle Beach
9714 North Kings Highway, Magnolia
  Town Centre, Suite 144
Myrtle Beach, SC 29572-0020
843-839-5900

Newsberry
833 Main St.
Newsberry, SC 29108
803-276-2110

Orangeburg
Employment Security Commission
1804 Joe Jeffords Hwy

Orangeburg, SC 29116
803-534-3336

Palmetto Youth Connections
45 Simons St.
Charleston, SC 29403
843-793-1193

Piedmont Technical College
620 North Emerald Rd.
Greenwood, SC 29648
864-941-8395

Rock Hill
1228 Fincher Rd.
Rock Hill, SC 29731
803-328-3881

St. George Adult Learning
    Center/Dorchester County Adult
    Education
121 South Metts St.
St. George, SC 29477
843-873-7372
843-563-5954

Saluda County
407 West Butler Ave.
Saluda, SC 29138
864-445-2047

Spartanburg
Employment Security Commission
364 South Church St.
Spartanburg, SC 29304
864-573-7525

Sumter
31 E. Calhoun St.
Sumter, SC 29151
803-774-1300

Trident One-Stop Career System
1930 Hanahan Rd., Suite 200
North Charleston, SC 29406
843-574-1800

Union
440 Duncan Highway

Union, SC 29379
864-427-5672

Upstate Career Source
110 Commerce St.
Spartanburg, SC 29306
864-562-4168

Voorhees One-Stop Career Center
1000 Kincaid Bridge Rd.

Winnsboro, SC 29180
803-635-2292

York Technical College Workforce
　Development Center
452 S. Anderson Rd.
Rock Hill, SC 29730
803-327-8006

SOUTH DAKOTA

CURE
804 Nunda Place
Sioux, SD 57107
605-334-5473
Lschr@q.com

　CURE is a grassroots organization from top to bottom. It does not hire professional leaders. Instead, its leaders come from the ranks of people formerly in prison and family members of friends of prisoners. This organization offers assistance to ex-offenders.

South Dakota Prisoner Support
　Group
P.O. Box 3285
Rapid City, SD 57709
605-399-1830
http://groups.yahoo.com/group/South-DakotaPrisonerSupportGroup/

　The PSG was formed to support people on the inside, ex-offenders, family, and friends, and to draw attention to racist injustice, medical neglect, and illegal conditions inside S.D. prisons and jails.

One-Stop Career Centers

Aberdeen Department of Labor Office
420 South Roosevelt St.
Aberdeen, SD 57402-4730
605-626-2340

Black Hills Career Learning Center
730 East Watertown St.

Rapid City, SD 57701-4178
605-394-5120

Brookings Department of Labor
　Office
1310 Main Ave. South, Suite 103
Brookings, SD 57006-3893
605-688-4350

Brookings Learning Center
1310 South Main Ave.
Brookings, SD 57006
605-688-4370

Cornerstone Career Learning Center
420 South Roosevelt
Aberdeen, SD 57402-4730
605-626-2298

Cornerstone Career Learning Center
33 3rd St. SE, Suite 202
Huron, SD 57350
605-353-7175

Hot Springs Department of Labor
　Office
2500 Minnekahta Ave.
Hot Springs, SD 57747-1199
605-745-5101

Huron Department of Labor Office
380 Illinois Ave. SW
Huron, SD 57350
605-353-7155

Madison Department of Labor
    Office
223 S. Van Eps Ave., Suite 101
Madison, SD 57042-2817
605-256-5300

Mitchell Department of Labor Office
1321 North Main
Mitchell, SD 57301-7186
605-995-8060

Mobridge Department of Labor
    Office
1415 East Grand Crossing
Mobridge, SD 57601-2905
605-845-2971

North Sioux City Department of
    Labor Office
504 River Drive
North Sioux, SD 57049
605-242-5445

Pierre Department of Labor Office
116 West Missouri Ave.
Pierre, SD 57501-4506
605-773-3372

Pine Ridge Department of Labor
    Office
Billy Mills Hall
Pine Ridge, SD 57770-0400
605-867-5843

Rapid City Department of Labor
    Office
111 New York St.
Rapid City, SD 57701-1832
605-394-2296

The Right Turn
124 East Dakota
Pierre, SD 57501-2341
605-773-4755

Sioux Falls Department of Labor Office
811 East 10 St., Department41

Sioux Falls, SD 57103-1650
605-367-5300

Sisseton Department of Labor Office
205 East Oak St., Suite 120
Sisseton, SD 57262-1500
605-698-3964

Spearfish Department of Labor
    Office
1300 North Ave.
Spearfish, SD 57783-1525
605-642-6900

Vermillion Career Center
1024 West Cherry St.
Vermillion, SD 57069-1742
605-677-6900

Volunteers of America Dakotas
1309 West 51st St.
Sioux Falls, SD 57105
605-334-1414

Watertown Area Career Learning
    Center
2001 9th Ave. SW, Suite 100
Watertown, SD 57201
605-882-5080

Watertown Department of Labor
    Office
2001 9th Ave SW, Suite 200
Watertown, SD 57201-4029
605-882-5131

Winner Department of Labor Office
313 South Main St.
Winner, SD 57580-1728
605-842-0474

Yankton Department of Labor
    Office
3113 Spruce St., Suite 124
Yankton, SD 57078-5320
605-668-2900

TENNESSEE

Breakaway Outreach
P.O. Box 3452
Cleveland, TN 37320
423-559-9649
http://www.breakawayoutreach.com/

Breakaway Outreach is a faith-based organization dedicated to helping kids Breakaway from a troubled past by communicating the life-changing message of Jesus Christ so that every juvenile offender, and young person at-risk for delinquency, has the opportunity to hear and respond to that message

CURE
2019 9th Ave. North
Nashville, TN 37208
tscruggs@bqcmt.org

CURE is a grassroots organization from top to bottom. It does not hire professional leaders. Instead, its leaders come from the ranks of people formerly in prison and family members of friends of prisoners. This organization offers assistance to ex-offenders.

Dismas House
320 East St.
PO Box 41736
Memphis, TN 37212
901-526-3701
And
Dismas House
1226 Byrne Ave.
Cooksville, TN 38502
931-520-8448

Knox County
1316 Forest Ave.
Knoxsville, TN 37923
1513 16th Ave. South
Nashville, TN 37212
615-297-4511 or 615-297-9287
www.dismas.org

Dismas House is a supportive community shared by recently released inmates, college stu-dents, and local volunteers. Typical length of stay is four to six months. Residents are expected to find employment and leave the community with a stable income, sense of self-worth and hope for a sober and productive future.

Karat Place
829 North Parkway
Memphis, TN 38105
901-525-4055
Gibs55@bellsouth.net

Provides transitional housing for women who have recently been released from incarceration and some job development and placement assistance. Rent is free until employment is secured and then the rate is 30 percent of the resident's earned wages.

Project Return
1200 Division St. Suite 200
Nashville, TN 37203
615-327-9654
www.projecttreturninc.org

Project return offers a number of programs, services provided include employment assistance and training, life skills workshops, direct aid(bus passes, emergency food boxes), information and referral to support services, and on-going follow-up and job counseling.

Second Chance
444 North Main St.
Memphis, TN 38103
901-545-0343

This program is a private/public partnership between the city of Memphis and local businesses designed to connect people with criminal histories (no more than one felony conviction) looking for work with employers who are willing to hire them. To graduate from the program an applicant must keep a job for six months to a year, maintain a good work record and remain drug free.

One-Stop Workforce/Tennessee Career Centers

Alcoa
366 Glascock St., Suite 120
Alcoa, TN 37701
865-379-5525

Athens
410 N. Congress Parkway
Athens, TN 37303
423-745-2028

Bolivar
602 A Tennessee St.
Bolivar, TN 38008-2329
731-658-6442

Bristol
1712 W. State St.
Bristol, TN 37620
423-989-6600

Brownsville
140 S. Wilson
Brownsville, TN 38012-0413
731-772-3490

Camden
60 N. Church Ave.
Camden, TN 38320
731-584-1711
731-584-6058

Carthage
120 Pauline Gore Way
Carthage, TN 37030
615-735-0377

Chattanooga
5600 Brainerd Rd., Suite A5
Chattanooga, TN 37411
423-894-5354

Cheatham County Workforce Essentials
202 N. Main St., Unit 4
Ashland City, TN 37015
615-792-2520

Clarksville-Montgomery County
350 Pageant Lane, Suite 406
Clarksville, TN 37040
931-648-5530

Clay County
500 Dow Ave.
Celina, TN 38551
931-520-8733

Collierville
942 W. Poplar, Suite 4
Collierville, TN 38017-2546
901-853-4752

Columbia
119 Nashville Hwy. Ste 106
Columbia, TN 38401-2710
931-380-2500

Cookeville
3300 Williams-Enterprise Drive
Cookeville, TN 38506
931-526-9701

Covington
973 Highway 51 N.
Covington, TN 38019
901-475-2529

Crossville
60 Ridley St.
Crossville, TN 38555
931-484-7456 Ext. 114

DeKalb County
527 West Main St.
Smithville, TN 37166
615-597-6197

Dickson County
446 Highway 46 South, Suites D and E
Dickson, TN 37055
615-446-0229

Dresden
35 South Poplar, Suite B
Dresden, TN 38225
731-364-2554

Dyersburg
439 McGaughey St.
Dyersburg, TH 38024
731-286-8300

Elizabethton
386 Highway 91, Suite #1
Elizabethton, TN 37643
423-547-7515

Fayette County
121 West Court Square
Somerville, TN 38068
901-466-7656

Fentress County
308 South Main St.
Jamestown, TN 38556-3739
931-879-8040

Gallatin
175 College St.
Gallatin, TN 37 066
615-451-5800

Gatlinburg
405 Reagan Drive
Gatlinburg, TN 37738-0641
865-436-5131

Giles County
125 South Cedar Lane
Pulaski, TN 38478
931-363-9550

Heart of Knoxville Career and Resource Center
1610 Magnolia Ave.
Knoxville, TN 37917
865-329-3166

Henderson County
67 West Church St.
Lexington, TN 38351-0590
731-968-8159

Hickman County
130 Progress Center Plaza
Centerville, TN 37033
931-729-5941

Houston County
155 W. Front St.
Erin, TN 37061
931-289-4127

Humboldt
1481 W. Mullins St.
Humboldt, TN 38343
731-784-3552

Humphreys County Workforce Essentials
711 Holly Lane
Waverly, TN 37185
931-296-5872

Huntington
470 Mustang Drive
Huntington, TN 38344
731-986-8217

Jacksboro
1016 Main St.
Jacksboro, TN 37757
423-566-3300

Jackson
362 Carriage House Drive
Jackson, TN 38305
731-668-2040

Johnson County, Department of
Labor and Workforce Development
358 Hospital Rd.
Mountain City, TN 37683
423-727-9181

Kingsport
1140 E. Center St.
Kingsport, TN 37660
423-224-1800

Knoxville
1610 University Ave., Suite 101
Knoxville, TN 37921
865-594-5500

Lawrence County
702 Main Ave.

Lawrenceville, TN 38464
931-762-8705

Lenoir City
100 West Broadway, Suite 141
Lenoir City, TN 37771
865-986-5506

Lewis County
35 South Ave.
Hohenwald, TN 38462
931-796-3319

Macon County
607 Highway 52 Bypass E.
Lafayette, TN 37185
931-296-5872

Marshall County
980 South Ellington Parkway
Lewisburg, TN 37091
931-359-9726

Maury County
119 Nashville Highway, Suite 106
Columbia, TN 38401
931-490-3800

McMinnville/Warren Counties
107 Lyon St.
McMinnville, TN 37110
931-473-2153

Memphis
444 North Main St., 2nd Floor
Memphis, TN 38105
901-545-2240

Memphis Housing Authority
700 Adams Ave.
Memphis, TN 38105
901-544-1367

Memphis Meritan Center
4700 Poplar Ave., Suite 445
Memphis, TN 38117
901-766-0600 Ext. 1600

Mendenhall
5368 Mendenhall Mall

Memphis, TN 38115
901-365-3205 Ext. 110

Millington Career and Transition Assistance Center
5722 Integrity Drive
Millington, TN 38054
901-873-3462

Murfreesboro
1313 Old Fort Parkway
Murfreesboro, TN 37129
615-898-8081

Nashville South Office
3763 Nolensville, TN 37211
615-741-3556

Nashville/Trousdale County Career
Advancement Center
716 McMurray Blvd.
Hartsville, TN 37074
615-374-9501

Newport
440 Eastern Plaza Way
Newport, TN 37821
423-623-1108

Northeast Tennessee
2515 Wesley St.
Johnson City, TN 37601
423-610-0222

Oak Ridge
599 Oak Ridge Turnpike, Suite B
Oak Ridge, TN 37830
865-483-7474

Oneida
180 Eli Lane
Oneida, TN 37841
423-569-9348

Paris
1023 Mineral Wells Ave., Suite F
Paris, TN 38242-4938
731-644-7355

Perry County
113 Factory St., Suite 1

Lin den, TN 37096
931-589-5012

Poplar
1295 Poplar Ave.
Memphis, TN 38174
901-543-7535 Ext. 2549

Putman County
3300 Williams Enterprise Drive
Cookeville, TN 38506
931-526-9701

Raleigh
2850 Old Austin Peay Highway,
    Suite 132
Memphis, TN 38128
901-543-7842

Ripley
301 C Lake Drive
Ripley, TN 38063
731-635-3479

Robertson County
299 10th Ave. East
Springfield, TN 37172
615-384-1097

Rockwood
1082 North Gateway Ave.
Rockwood, TN 37854
865-376-3082

Rogersville
1112 E. Main St.
Rogersville, TN 37857
423-272-2661

Rosa L. Parks Blvd.
2200 Rosa L. parks Blvd.
Nashville, TN 37228
615-253-8920

Savannah
1080 Wayne Rd.
Savannah, TN 38372-0970
731-925-5095

Sevierville
740 Old Knoxville Hwy.

Sevierville, TN 37862-3139
865-429-7001

Shelbyville/Bedford Counties
301 N. Main St.
Shelbyville, TN 37160-0083
931-685-5000

Stewart County Workforce Essentials
1356 Donelson Parkway
Dover, TN 931-232-5035
931-232-5035

Talbott
6057 W. Andrew Johnson Hwy.,
Alpha Square, Suite 6A
Talbott, TN 37877
423-317-1060

Tazewell
1731 Main St.
Tazewell, TN 37879
423-526-5620

Tullahoma-Coffee County
111 East Lincoln St.
Tullahoma, TN 37388
931-454-1905

Union City
126 E. Main St.
Union City, TN 38261
731-884-2621

Vonore
59 B. Excellence Way
Vonore, TN 37885
423-884-2400

Wartburg
104 S. Kingston St.
Wartburg, TN 37887
423-346-3060

Wayne County
211 Dexter L. Woods Blvd.
Waynesboro, TN 38485
931-722-9214

White County
826 Valley View Drive

Sparta, TN 38583-1500
931-738-0830

Williamson County
225 Noah Drive, Suite 360
Franklin, TN 37064
615-790-3311

Wilson County
155 Legend Drive, Suite M

Lebanon, TN 37087
615-444-9355

Wilson County
813 North Cumberland St.
Lebanon, TN 37087
615-444-9355

TEXAS

ACLU of Texas Prison and Jail Accountability Project
P.O. Box 12905
Austin, TX 78711-2905
512-478-7300
http://www.aclutx.org/projects/prisons. php
Write for their free 49-page national Prisoner Resource Guide (also available on their website). Contains summaries of the law on common prisoner problems and extensive listings of advocacy groups for Texas prisoners.

Anarchist Black Cross
P.O. Box 667233
Houston, TX 77266-7233
Write for their ABC information and Resource Guide (Available for download on their website). Contains essays on the politics of the ABC and addresses for local chapters that do prisoner support.

Bridging the Gap Ministries
P. O. Box 131747
Tyler, TX 75713-1747
903-539-6797
http://www.bridgingthegap.freeservers.co m/bridgingthe gap@flash.net
Provides services for ex-offenders and their families.

Crime Prevention Institute-Targeted Project Re-Enterprise
8401 Shoal Creek Blvd.

Austin, TX 78763-0541
512-502-9704
Post-Release services include supportive resources, job placement services, employment monitoring and incentives, follow up and information and referral services.

CURE
4121 Burning Tree Lane
Garland, TX 75042
972-276-9865
txcure@bxcure.org
www.bxcure.org
Cure is a grassroots organization from top to bottom. It does not hire professional leaders. Instead, its leaders come from the ranks of people formerly in prison and family members of friends of prisoners. This organization offers assistance to ex-offenders.

Diocese of Beaumont Criminal Justice Ministry
P.O. Box 3948
Beaumont, TX 77704-3948
409-838-0451
http://www.dioceseofbmt.org/hdavis@di oceseofbeaumont.org
P.O. Box 3948
Beaumont, TX 77704-3948
409-838-0451
Provides services for ex-offenders and their families.

Encompassing Reentry Ministries and Outreach

P.O. Box 851587
Mesquite, TX 75185-1587
http://prisonministry.net/ermojcook@en-compassingreentry.org
Provides services to ex-offenders and their families.

Mercy Heart
4805 NE Loop 820
Fort Worth, TX 76137
817-514-0290
http://www.mercyheart.org/info@mercy-heart.org
Mercy Heart is a faith-based organization that assists families and children of inmates through and beyond the transitions of incarceration toward mental, emotional, material and spiritual well-being through chapel programs in the local church.

Morning Star Jail/Prison Ministry
2251 El Paso
Grand Prairie, TX 75051
http://www.morningstar-baptist.org/se-tatliberty1@aol.com
This ministry provides services for ex-offenders and their families.

Open, Inc.
P.O. Box 472223
Garland, TX 75047-2223
972-271-1971 or 1-800-966-1966
www.openinc.org
info@openinc.org
Open, Inc. sells 99 Days and Get Up, Man I Need a Job and other pre-release guides for $4.95 each.

Saints of Christ Prison Ministry
P.O. Box 111275
Houston, TX 77293-0275
281-449-2703
Provides Services to ex-offenders and their families.

Welcome Home House
921 N. Peak St.
Dallas, TX 75204
214-887-5204

This organization offers a recovery program for parolees that include a structured drug free environment.

One-Stop Career Centers

American G.I. Forum NVOP
611 N. Flores St.
San Antonio, TX 78205-1206
210-354-4892

Brazos Valley Workforce Solutions
3991 East 29th St.
Bryan, TX 77805
979-595-2801 Ext. 2101

Cameron Workforce Solutions
301 Mexico Blvd., Suite F8
Brownsville, TX 78520
956-547-5040

Cameron Workforce Solutions
601 E. Harrison St.
Harlington, TX 78550-9147
956-423-9266

Caprock Community Action
701 E. Lee St., Caprock
Community Action Building
Floydada, TX 79235
806-983-3134

Caprock Community Association
224 South Berkshire, Caprock Community Action Building
Crosbyton, TX 79322-2548
806-675-7307

Center for Workforce Preparedness
1359 Lomaland Drive
El Paso, TX 79935-5201
915-887-2000

Dallas Stemmons Workforce Center
2707 N. Stemmons Freeway
Dallas, TX 75207-2281
214-920-3663 Ext. 3351

Farm Worker Center
201 East 9th Ave.

El Paso, TX 79901
915-532-1059

Greater Texarkana Workforce Center
1702 Hampton Rd.
Texarkana, TX 75503
903-794-4163

Heart of Texas Workforce Center
1416 S. New Rd.
Waco, TX 75503
254-754-5421 Ext. 5277

Towne Market Workforce Center
3402 N. Buckner Blvd., suite 308
Dallas, TX 75228
972-288-2703

Ysleta Del Sur Pueblo Tribal Empowerment Department
11100 Santo Sanchez
Socorro, TX 79927
915-872-8648
915-872-8648

Workforce Solution Centers by City/County

Abilene
400 Oak St.
Abilene, TX 79602-1520
325-795-4200

Alice
601 E. Main St., Floor 3
Alice, TX 78332-4975
361-668-0167
1-800-388-5813

Alpine
710 E. Holland Ave.
Alpine, TX 79830-5006
432-837-9800
866-280-9800

Amarillo
1206 W. 7th St.
Amarillo, TX 79101-2006
806-372-5521

Angelina County
210 N. John Redditt Rd.
Lufkin, TX 75904-2620
936-639-1351

Athens
205 N. Murchison St., Suite 101
Athens, TX 75751-2110
903-677-3521

Austin
6505 Airport Blvd., Ste 101 A
Austin, TX 78752
512-454-9675

Austin East
3401 Webberville Rd-ACC
Eastview Campus, Bldg. 1000
Austin, TX 78702-3004
512-223-5400

Austin South
4175 Freidrich Ln., Suite 200
Austin, TX 78744-1017
512-381-4200

Bandera
702 Buck Creek
Bandera, TX 78003
830-796-3739 Ext. 226

Bastrop
53 Loop 150 West
Bastrop, TX 78602-9662
512-303-3916

Bay City
3501 Ave. F
Bay City, TX 77414
979-245-4808

Baytown
6952 Garth Rd.
Baytown, TX 77521
281-837-0079

Beaumont
304 Pearl St.
Beaumont, TX 77701-2248

409-839-8045 Ext 3222
409-719-4791

Beeville Center
202 N. Saint Mary's St.
Beeville, TX 78102-4607
361-358-8941

Big Springs
501 S. Main St., Suite 235
Big Springs, TX 79720-3039
432-263-8373
800-749-8373

Boerne
1414 E. Blanco
Boerne, TX 78006
830-249-9229

Bonham
1205 B East Sam Rayburn Drive
Bonham, TX 75418
903-640-0222

Borger
901 Opal, Room 102
Borger, TX 79007
806-274-7171

Bowie
800 Highway 59 N.
Bowie, TX 76230-3603
940-872-2424

Brownfield
801 Tahoka Rd.
Brownfield, TX 79316-4315
806-637-4234

Brownsville
851 Old Alice Rd.
Brownsville, TX 78520-8551
956-546-3141

Brownwood
2202 Highway 377 South
Brownwood, TX 76801-3912
325-646-1591

Burnet
1001 W. Buchanan Drive, Suite 1

Burnet, TX 78611-2324
512-756-6769

Caldwell
119 S. Main St., Suite C
Caldwell, TX 77836-1565
979-567-1570

Cameron
605 W. 4th St.
Cameron, TX 76520-2406
254-697-3373

Camp Wood
104 E. 4th St.
Camp Wood, TX 78833
830-597-3356

Canton
1760 N. Trade Days Blvd.
Canton, TX 75103-9772
903-567-4706

Carrizo Springs
307 W. Nopal St.
Carrizo Springs, TX 78834-3211
830-876-3533

Carthage
424 W. Sabine St.
Carthage, TX 75633-2460
903-693-2272

Center
1121 Hurst St., Suite 2
Center, TX 75935
936-598-2468
800-256-9095

Childress
210 Commerce St.
Childress, TX 79201
940-937-6171

Cleburne
202 Hyde Park, Suite 200
Cleburne, TX 76033-8772
817-641-6201

Clifton
702 S. Ave. G

Clifton, TX 76634-2463
254-675-2024

Columbus
104 B Shult Dr.
Columbus, TX 78934
979-732-3299

Concho Valley, San Angelo
202 Henry O. Flipper St.
San Angelo, TX 76903-7008
325-653-2321 Ext. 1274

Conroe
2018 IH 45 N
Conroe, TX 77301
936-441-0037

Corpus Christi
400 Main St.
Corpus Christi, TX 78401
361-903-7885

Corpus Christi
520 North Staples
Corpus Christi, TX 78401-2414
361-882-7491

Corpus Christi
5858 S Padre Island Drive, Suite 1
Corpus Christi, TX 78412
361-882-7491 Ext.402

Corsicana
720 N. Beaton St.
Corsicana, TX 75110
903-874-8276

Cotulia
707 Buckley
Cotulia, TX 78014-2538
830-879-3053

Crystal City
613 W. Zavala
Crystal City, TX 78839-2506
830-374-2308

Cuero
1137 N. Esplanade

Cuero, TX 77954-0348
361-277-8870

Dalhart
412 Denver St., Suite 502
Dalhart, TX 79022
806-244-1834

Dallas
2707 North Stemmons Freeway, Suite 150
Dallas, TX 75207
214-920-3663
972-709-5377

Dallas, MLK Center
2922 Martin Luther King Jr. Blvd.
Dallas, TX 75215
214-421-2460

Dallas, Towne Market
3402 N. Buckner Blvd., Suite 308
Dallas, TX 75238
972-288-2703 Ext. 4307

Decatur
1810 S FM 51, Suite B
Decatur, TX 76234-3700
940-627-3919

Del Rio
1927 Bedell
Del Rio, TX 78840
830-774-4741

Denison
2415 S. Austin Ave., Suite 105
Denison, TX 75020-7742
903-463-9997

Denton
1300 Teasley Lane
Denton, TX 76205-7946
940-382-6712

Dumas
500 E. 1st St.
Dumas, TX 79029-0576
806-935-3351

Eagle Pass
1200 Perry St.
Eagle Pass, TX 78852
830-773-1191

Edinburg
2719 W. University
Edinburg, TX 78539-7889
956-380-0008

Edna
903 S. Wells St.
Edna, TX 77957-3744
361-782-7526

East El Paso
1359 Lomaland Drive
El Paso, TX 79935-5201
915-887-2000

El Paso
5070 Doniphan Drive, Suites F and G
El Paso, TX 79932-1455
915-887-2758

El Paso
9740 Dyer St., Suite 109-113
El Paso, TX 79924
915-887-2820

El Paso
300 E. Main St.
El Paso, TX 79901-1372
915-313-3000 Ext. 3023

Emory
209 E. Quitman St.
Emory, TX 75440
903-473-8757

Ennis
2705 N Kaufman St., Suite B
Ennis, TX 75120
972-875-9121

Fabens
206 Southeast 8th St.
Fabens, TX 79838
915-764-4285

Falfurrias Satellite Office
1200 E. Highway 285
Falfurrias, TX 78355
361-325-9095

Falls County
230 Coleman St.
Marlin, TX 76661-2854
254-883-5678

Floresville
1106 10th St., Hwy 181
Floresville, TX 78114-2110
830-393-0405

Fort Bliss
Bldg. 2494 Ricker Rd.
Ft. Bliss, TX 79906
915-566-8649

Fort Stockton
300 N. Main
Fort Stockton, TX 79735-5620
432-336-6382

Fredericksburg
221 Friendship Lane
Fredericksburg, TX 78624-5054
830-481-0088

Freestone County
517 Main St.
Teague, TX 75860-1625
254-739-2887

Gainesville
900 N. Grand Ave.
Gainesville, TX 76240-3522
940-665-1121

Galveston
4700 Broadway St. B101
Galveston, TX 77551-4241
409-770-9915

Garland
217 N.10th St.
Garland, TX 75040
972-276-8361

Garland Day Labor Center
2007 Saturn Rd.
Garland, TX 74041-1641
972-864-1739

Giddings
234 W. Austin
Giddings, TX 78942-3208
979-542-1548

Gilmer
405 East Marshall
Gilmer, TX 75644-5724
903-797-3655

Goliad
329 W. Franklin St.
Goliad, TX 77963-4214
361-645-2703

Gonzales
1617 E. Sarah DeWitt Drive
Gonzales, TX 78629-3568
830-672-2146

Granbury
919 E. Hwy 377, Suite 8
Granbury, TX 76048-1436
817-573-4282

Grand Prairie
801 West Freeway, Suite 500
Grand Prairie, TX 75051
972-264-5881

Greenville
2500 Stonewall St., Suite 201
Greenville, TX 75401-4212
903-454-9350 Ext. 3600

Hallettsville
727 South Promenade
Hallettsville, TX 77964
361-798-1046

Harlingen
505 South P St.
Harlingen, TX 78550
956-425-6461

Hearne
303 Post Oak St.
Hearne, TX 77859-2556
979-279-0940
800-386-7200

Hebbronville
1310 W. Viggie St.
Hebbronville, TX 78361
361-527-4632

Henderson
1424 S. Main St.
Henderson, TX 75652
903-657-9553

Hereford
121 West Park Ave.
Hereford, TX 79045
806-364-8600

Hill County
233 Main St.
Hillsboro, TX 76645-3322
254-582-8588

Hobby
8231 Broadway
Houston, TX 77061-1201
713-847-6118

Hondo
1802 Ave. M
Hondo, TX 78861-1775
830-426-8111

Houston
4424 Interstate 45N, Suite A
Houston, TX 77022
713-692-7755

Houston
600 Jefferson, Suite 950
Houston, TX 77002
713-210-4050
70 SM 1960 West #A
Houston, TX 77090
281-260-2950 Ext. 255

Houston Astrodome
9315 Stella Link Rd.
Houston, TX 77025-4012
713-661-3220

Houston Cypress Station
70 FM 1960 West
Houston, TX 77090
281-891-2850

Houston Downtown
600 Jefferson St., Ste 125
Houston, TX 77002
713-658-0966

Houston East End
5104 Harrisburg Blvd.
Houston, TX 77011
713-228-8848

Houston Northeast
4217 East Tidwell Rd.
Houston, TX 77093
713-697-3437

Houston Northline
4424 North Freeway
Houston, TX 77022
713-692-7755

Houston Northshore
14355 E. Wallisville Rd.
Houston, TX 77049-4134
281-458-1155

Houston Southwest
12710 Bissonnet St.
Houston, TX 77099
281-564-2660

Houston Spring Ranch
10405 Katy Freeway, Suite G
Houston, TX 77024
713-465-1677

Houston Willowbrook
17517 Hwy 249
Houston, TX 77064
281-807-9462

Houston County
1512 A Loop 304
Crocket, TX 75835
936-544-7859

Humble
9668 FM 1960 Bypass Rd. W
Humble, TX 77338-4040
281-446-4837

Huntsville
901 Normal Park Dr. #7
Huntsville, TX 77320-3770
936-291-3336

Jacksonville
2027 N. Jackson St., Suite A
Jacksonville, TX 75766-5137
903-586-3688

Jasper County
150 W. Gibson St.
Jasper, TX 75951-4544
409-384-9031
877-384-9031

Jefferson
208 Walnut St.
Jefferson, TX 75657
903-665-1024

Katy Mills
5000 Katy Mills Circle, Suite 659
Katy, TX 77494
281-644-1030

Kenedy
491 N. Sunset Strip
Kenedy, TX 78119-2051
830-583-3332

Kerryville
1701 Sidney Baker
Kerryville, TX 78028-5343
830-257-3171

Killeen
300 Cheyenne Drive
Killeen, TX 76542-1300
254-200-2000

Kingsville
1417 E. Corral Ave.
Kingsville, TX 78363-4120
361-592-1086

La Grange
811 E. Travis St.
La Grange, TX 78945-2314
979-968-8553

Lake Jackson
491 This Way
Lake Jackson, TX 77556
979-297-6400

Lampasas
1305 S. Key Ave.
Lampasas, TX 76550-3515
512-556-4055

Laredo
2389 E. Saunders St.
Laredo, TX 78041
956-765-1804

Leon County
204 East St. Mary's St.
Centerville, TX 75833
903-536-4243
800-386-7200

Levelland
1102 Austin St.
Levelland, TX 79336
806-894-5005

Liberty
2131 Highway 146 Bypass
Liberty, TX 77575
936-336-8063

Limestone County
507 E. Yeagua St.
Groesbeck, TX 76642-1578
254-729-8775

Littlefield
1700 Hall Ave.
Littlefield, TX 79339
806-385-7897

Llano
119 W. Main St.
Llano, TX 78643-1931
325-248-0275

Lockhart
117 N. Main St.
Lockhart, TX 78644
512-398-3491

Longview
2430 S. High St., Suite A1
Longview, TX 75602-3432
903-758-1783

Lubbock
1218 14th Ave.
Lubbock, TX 79401
806-765-5038

Madison County
300 W. School Rd.
Madisonville, TX 77864-3280
936-348-5111
800-386-7200

Mansfield Workforce Center
1275 North Main St., Suite 103
Mansfield, TX 76063
817-804-2690

Marshall
4300 E. End Blvd. South
Marshall, TX 75672
903-935-7814

McAllen Business Resource
3101 W. Business 83
McAllen, TX 78501
956-928-5000

McKinney
1713 W. Louisiana St.
McKinney, TX 75070
972-542-3381

Mesquite
2110 N. Galloway Ave., Suite 116
Mesquite, TX 75150-5737
972-329-1948

Midland
3510 N. A St.
Midland, TX 79705-542B
432-687-3003

Mineral Wells
2307 E. Hubbard St.
Mineral Wells, TX 76067-5616
940-325-2595

Monahans
308 S. Calvin
Monahans, TX 79756
432-238-7523

Mount Pleasant
1902 W. Ferguson Rd.
Mount Pleasant, TX 75455
903-572-9841

Muleshoe
203 Main St.
Muleshoe, TX 79347-3853
806-272-7540

Nacogdoches County
2103 South St.
Nacogdoches, TX 75964-6177
936-560-1441

Navasota
513 La Salle St.
Navasota, TX 77868-2435
936-870-3614
800-386-7200 Ext. 3615

New Braunfels
183 S. Interstate 35
New Braunfels, TX 78130-4817
830-629-2010

North Richland Hills
7001 Blvd. 26, Suite 501
North Richland Hills, TX 76180
817-548-5200

Odessa
2626 JBS Parkway, Building D
Odessa, TX 79761-1957
432-367-3332

Orange
320 Green Ave.
Orange, TX 77630-5875
409-882-0302

Palestine
500 E. Murchison St.
Palestine, TX 75801-2369
903-729-0178

Pampa Workforce Center
1327 N. Hobart St.
Pampa, TX 79065-7153
806-665-0938

Paris
5210 SE Loop 286
Paris, TX 75460
903-784-4356

Pasadena
103 Pasadena Town Square Mall
Pasadena, TX 77506
713-472-1608

Pearsall
107 E. Hackberry St.
Pearsall, TX 78061-4453
830-334-4464

Pecos
1000 S. Eddy St.
Pecos, TX 79772
432-445-9664

Pharr
1100 E. Business 83
Pharr, TX 78577-0977
956-702-0977

Pittsburg
211 Mill St.
Pittsburg, TX 75686-1315
903-856-5643

Plainview
1001 N. I-27, Suite 228
Plainview, TX 79072
806-293-8566

Plano
820 Jupiter Rd., Suite 100
Plano, TX 75074-7464
469-229-0099

Pleasanton
206 N. Smith St.
Pleasanton, TX 78204
830-281-6630

Polk County
1241 West Church St., Suite 300
Livington, TX 77351
936-327-5421

Port Arthur
3901 Twin City Hwy.
Port Arthur, TX 77642-2118
409-962-1236

Port Lavaca
1800 State Highway 35, Suite H
Port Lavaca, TX 77979-5111
361-552-1563

Presidio
100 Market St.
Presidio, TX 79845
432-229-1170

Quitman
405 S. Hart St., Dogwood Plaza
Quitman, TX 75783
903-763-5421

Raymondville
100 N. Expressway 77, Unit H2
Raymondville, TX 78580-4000
956-689-3412

Refugio
414-B North Alamo
Refugio, TX 78377-2601
361-526-9211

Richardson
1222 E. Arapaho Rd., Suite 336
Richardson, TX 75081-2451
972-234-5391

Rio Grande City
5408 Brand St., Suite 1
Rio Grande, TX 78582-4613
956-487-9100

Rockdale
313 Main St.
Rockdale, TX 76567-2908
512-446-6440 Ext. 6012

Rockport Satellite Office
619 North Live Oak Room A 4
Rockport, TX 78382
361-727-2684

Rock Springs
203 W. Austin St.
Rock Springs, TX 78880
830-683-5248

Rockwell
102 s 1st St., Suite C
Rockwell, TX 75087-3650
972-722-1573

Rosenburg
117 Lane Dr., #7
Rosenburg, TX 77471-2263
281-344-0279

Round Rock
1611 Chisholm Trail, Suite 600
Round Rock, TX 78681-2946
512-244-2207

San Antonio
4535 East Houston St.
San Antonio, TX 78220-1701
210-581-0190

San Antonio
1499 Hillcrest Drive
San Antonio, TX 78228-3900
210-438-0586

San Antonio
7008 Marbach Rd.
San Antonio, TX 78227-1940
210-436-0670

San Antonio
6723 S. Flores St., Suite 100
San Antonio, TX 78221-1741
210-928-3985 Ext. 1763

San Antonio, VA Benefits
5788 Eckert Rd.
San Antonio, TX 78240-3900
210-699-5077

San Antonio
4615 Walzem Rd.
San Antonio, TX 78218-1610
210-822-7640

San Marcos
202 S. CM Allen Pkwy
San Marcos, TX 78666
512-392-1291

Sealy
3701 Outlet Center Drive #140
Sealy, TX 77474
979-627-0241

Sequin
1500 E. Court St.., Suite 444
Sequin, TX 78155-5268
830-379-4244

Silsbee
1205 Highway 327 E.
Silsbee, TX 77656-6607
409-385-9644

Sinton
1113 E. Sinton St., Suite D
Sinton, TX 78387-2928
361-364-3284

Snyder
1912 37th St.
Snyder, TX 79549
325-574-1739

Southplains Community Action
Hwy 84 Multipurpose Center
Post, TX 79356
806-495-2329

Stephenville
2165 W. South Loop, Suite 2
Stephenville, TX 76401-3912
254-965-5100

Sulphur Springs
1716 Posey Lane
Sulphur Springs, TX 75482-4502
903-885-7556

Sweetwater
606 Broadway
Sweetwater, TX 79556-4626
325-235-4324

Tarrant County
140 W. Mitchell St.
Arlington, TX 76010-1801
817-804-2647

Tarrant County
1400 Circle Drive
Fort Worth, TX 76119-8142
817-804-2647

Tarrant County
6000 Western Place, Suite 700
Fort Worth, TX 76107-4618
817-737-0311

Tarrant County
2100 N. Main St., Suite 100
Fort Worth, TX 76164-8572
817-626-5262

Tarrant County, Eastside Workforce
    Center
4701 E. Lancaster St.
Fort Worth, TX 76103-3835
817-531-7800 Ext. 5210

Taylor
516 North Main St.
Taylor, TX 76574
512-365-8750

Temple
102 E. Central Ave, Suite 300
Temple, TX 76501-4300
254-771-2555 Ext. 4413

Temple
2420 S. 37th St.
Temple, TX 76504-7168
254-773-1607 Ext. 4018

Terrell
109 Tejas, Suite 300
Terrell, TX 75160-6582
972-563-7271

Texas City
3549 Palmer Highway
Texas City, TX 77590-6513
409-949-9055

Tulia
310 W. Broadway Ave.
Tulia, TX 79088-2245
806-995-2421

Tyler
4100 Troup Hwy
Tyler, TX 75703-1927
903-561-8131

Uvalde
216 W. Main St.
Uvalde, TX 78801-5506
830-278-4491

Vanhorn
2520 W. Broadway
Vanhorn, TX 79855
432-283-8327

Vernon
1700 Wilbarger St., Room B7
Vernon, TX 76384
940-552-5211

Victoria
120 S. Main St., Suite 110
Victoria, TX 77901-8144
361-578-0341

Wake Village
911 N. Bishop
Wake Village, TX 75501
903-794-9490

Waller
40644 Business Highway 290
Waller, TX 77484
936-931-3987

Washington County
2448 Becker Drive
Brenham, TX 77833-5714
979-836-9997

Waxahachie
1712 W. 287 Business
Waxahachie, TX 75165-4707
972-937-8114

Weatherford
126 College Park Drive
Weatherford, TX 76086-6212
817-594-0049

Weslaco
1600 North Westgate, Suite 400
Weslaco, TX 78596
956-969-6100

West Hidalgo
901 W. Travis
Mission, TX 78572
956-519-4300
956-519-4347

Westheimer
8373 Westheimer
Houston, TX 77063-2703
713-953-9211

Wharton
1506 N. Alabama Rd.
Wharton, TX 77488-3202
979-531-0730

Wichita Falls
4309 Jacksboro Hwy
Wichita Falls, 76302-2700
940-322-1801

Winnie
111 W. Pine St.
Winnie, TX 77665
409-296-2000

Woodville
205 North Charlton
Woodville, TX 75979-4803
409-283-3400

Yoakum
307 Crittenden St.

Yoakum, TX 77995
361-741-5100

Zapata
146 1st Ave.
Zapata, TX 78076
956-765-1804

UTAH

Behind the Wire Prisoner Information
  Network
235 West 100 South
Salt Lake City, UT 84101
801-335-0234
  *Began in 1995, when a small group of Utah
State prisoners, their families, and other allies
organized a coalition to give voice and information to Utah's incarcerated and ex-offenders.*

Department of Workforce Services Employment Centers

American Fork Employment Center
751 East Quality Drive, Suite 100
American Fork, UT 84003
801-492-4500

Beaver Employment Center
875 North Main
Beaver, UT 84003
435-438-3580

Blanding Employment Center
544 North 100 East
Blanding, UT 84511
435-678-1400

Brigham City Employment Center
1050 South 500 West
Brigham City, UT 84302
435-734-4060

Business Services Center
1385 South State St.
Salt Lake City, UT 84115

888-920-9675
801-468-0097

Cedar City Employment Center
176 East 200 North
Cedar City, UT 84720
435-865-6530

Clearfield Employment Center
1290 East 1450 South
Clearfield, UT 84015
801-776-7800

Davis Applied Technology Center
  Satellite Office
550 East 300 South
Kaysville, UT 84037
801-593-2442

Delta Employment Center
44 South 350 East
Delta, UT 84624
435-864-3860
866-748-1471

Emery County Employment Center
550 W. Hwy 29
Castle Dale, UT 84513
435-381-6100
877-505-8296

Heber City Employment Center
69 North 600 West, Suite C
Heber City, UT 84032
435-654-6520

Junction Employment Center
550 North Main

Junction, UT 84740
435-577-2443

Kanab Employment Center
468 East 300 South
Kanab, UT 84741
800-576-3938

Loa Employment Center
18 South Main
Loa, UT 84747
435-836-2406

Logan Employment Center
180 North 100 West
Logan, UT 84321
435-792-0300

Metro Employment Center
55 South Main, Suite #3
Manti, UT 84642
435-835-0720

Metro Employment Services
720 South 200 East
Salt Lake City, UT 84111
801-536-7000

Midvale Employment Center
7292 South State St.
Midvale, UT 84047
801-567-3800

Moab Employment Center
457 Kane Creek Blvd.
Moab, UT 84532
435-719-2600

Nephi Employment Center
625 North Main
Nephi, UT 84648
435-623-1927

Ogden Employment Center
480 27th St.
Ogden, UT 84401
801-626-0300

Panguitch Employment Center
665 North Main

Panguitch, UT 84759
435-676-1410

Park City Employment Center
1960 Sidewinder Drive, Suite 202
Park City, UT 84060
435-649-8451

Price Employment Center
475 West Price River Drive #256
Price, UT 84501
435-636-2300

Provo Employment Center
1550 North Freedom Blvd.
Provo, UT 84604
801-342-2600

Richfield Employment Services
115 East 100 South
Richfield, UT 84701
435-893-0000

Roosevelt Employment Center
140 West 425 South, Suite 330-13
Roosevelt, UT 84 066
435-722-6500

Roy Employment Center
1951 West 5400 South
Roy, UT 84067
801-776-7200

St. George Employment Center
162 North 400 East, Building B
St. George, UT 84770
435-674-5627

Salt Lake Downtown Employment
158 South 200 West
Salt Lake City, UT 84101
801-524-9000

South County Employment Center
5735 South Redwood Rd.
Taylorville, UT 84123

South Davis Employment Center
763 West 700 South
Woods Cross, UT 84087

Spanish Fork Employment Center
1185 North Chappel Drive
Spanish Fork, UT 84660
801-794-6600

Tooele Employment Center
305 North Main St., Suite 100
Tooele, UT 84074
435-833-7310

Vernal Employment Center
1050 West Market Drive
Vernal, UT 84078-4100

West Valley Employment Center
2750 South 5600 West, Suite A
West Valley City, UT 84120
801-840-4400

VERMONT

Vermont Catholic Charities, Inc.
351 North Ave.
Burlington, VT 05401
802-658-6110 Ext 312
www.vermontcatholic.org/vcc/vcc.html
sratte@vermontcatholic.org
    *This organization assists former prisoners
with employment and transitional housing.*

One-Stop Career Centers

Barre Resource Center
5 Perry St., McFarland House State
    Office Bldg
Barre, VT 05641
802-476-2600

Brattleboro Resource Center
232 Main St., State Office Building
Brattleboro, VT 05301-0920
802-254-4555

Burlington Resource Center
63 Pearl St.
Burlington, VT 05401-4331
802-863-7676

Middlebury Resource Center
1590 Route 7 South, Suite 5
Middlebury, VT 05753
802-388-4921

Morrisville Resource Center
63 Professional Drive

Morrisville, VT 05661-0429
802-885-2167

St. Johnsbury Office of Dept of Labor
1197 Main St., Suite 1
St. Johnsbury, VT 05819-0129
802-748-3177

Springfield Resource Center
56 Main St., Suite 101
Springfield, VT 05156-2900
802-885-2167

Vermont Department of Labor
150 Veterans memorial Drive, Suite 2
Bennington, VT
05201-1945
802-442-6376

Vermont Department of Labor
Newport Resource Center
100 Main St.
Emory E. Hebard State Office Bldg.,
    Suite 210
Newport, VT 05855
802-334-6545

Vermont Department of Labor
Rutland Resource Center
88 Merchants Row
Rutland, VT 05701
802-786-5837

Vermont Department of Labor
St. Albans Career Resource Center

20 Houghton St., Room 101
St. Albans, VT 05478-2246
802-524-6585

White River Junction Resource Center
220 Holiday Drive
White River Junction, VT 05001-0797
802-295-8805

VIRGIN ISLANDS

Organizations by Region

St. Johns

Bureau of Health Insurance and Medical Assistance
Morris Decastro Clinic
Cruz Bay, St. Johns, VI 00831
340-776-6400

Department of Human Services
Cruz Bay
St. Johns, VI 00831
340-776-6334

Myrah Keating Clinic Community Health Center
Myrah Keating Smith Clinic
Cruz Bay, St. John, VI 00831
340-693-8900

St. Croix

Bureau of Health Insurance and Medical Assistance
Charles Harwood Clinic
St. Croix, VI 00820-4370
330-773-1311 Ext. 4197

Department of Education
Division of Curriculum, Assessment and Technology
2133 Hospital St.
Christiansted St. Croix, VI 00820
340-773-1095 Ext. 7051

Department of Human Services
Children, Youth and Families Intervention Program

6179 Anna Hope Christiansted
St. Croix, VI 00820
340-773-5303

Department of Human Services
Division of Preschool Services/Headstart
6179 Anna's Hope
St. Croix, VI 00820
340-773-1972

Department of Labor
Division of Training
2203 Church St.
Christiansted, St. Croix, VI 00820-4612
340-773-1994

Division of Community Health Services
Ingeborg Nesbitt Clinic
Frediksted St. Croix, VI 00840
340-772-1992

St. Croix One-Stop Center
Sunny Isle Store #4
Christiansted, St. Croix, VI 00823
340-773-1440

St. Croix Church St. Resource Center
Store 4 Sunny Isle
Christiansted, St. Croix, VI 00820
340-773-1994 Ext. 210

St. Thomas

Bureau of Nutrition Services
Department of Health Office of the Commissioner

St. Thomas, VI 00802
340-776-8311 Ext.2266

Department of Human Services
Children, Youth, and Families Intervention Services
1303 Hospital Ground, Knud Hansen
Complex Building A
St. Thomas, VI 00802
340-774-4393

Department of Human Services
Elderly Social Services
1303 Hospital Ground
St. Thomas. VI 00802
340-773-2323 Ext. 2044

Department of Human Service
Intake and Emergency Services
1303 Hospital Ground, Knud
Hansen Complex Building A
St. Thomas, VI 00802
340-774-0930 Ext. 4265

Department of Human Services
Senior Community Service Employment
1303 Hospital Ground
St. Thomas, VI 00802
340-774-5265 Ext 4329

Division of Community Health Services
Morris DeCastro Clinic, Cruz Bay
St. John, VI 00831
340-776-6400

Division of Community Health Services
Roy L. Schneider Hospital
St. Thomas, VI 00802
340-774-1758
774-9000 Ext. 4704

Human Services
Division of Preschool Services
1303 Hospital Ground, Knud
Hansen Complex Building A
St. Thomas, VI 00802
340-774-5370

St. Thomas One-Stop Center
53A and 54B Kronprindsens Gade
Affiliate One-Stop
St. Thomas, VI 00803
340-776-3700

Territorial Court/Family Division
P.O. Box 70
St. Thomas, VI 00804
340-774-6680
340-692-6435

V.I. Department of Labor
P.O. Box 302608
St. Thomas, VI 00803
340-776-3700

Women, Infant $ Children (WIC)
28-29 Norre Gade
St. Thomas, VI 00802
340-776-1770

VIRGINIA

Caregivers Choices
1600 Duke St. Suite 300
Alexandria, VA 22314
1-703-224-2200
http://www.mentoring.org/
   This is an innovative project that connects

*children of incarcerated parents to quality
mentoring programs.*

Child Welfare League of America
2345 Crystal Drive
Suite 250
Arlington, VA 22202

703-412-2400
http://www.cwla.org/

The Juvenile Justice Division focuses on achieving the goal of reducing the incidence of juvenile delinquency nationwide and reducing the reliance on incarceration of accused or adjudicated delinquent youth.

CURE
P.O. Box 6010
Alexandra, VA 22306
703-765-6579
FAX: 703-765-6549
virginiacure@cox.net
www.vacure.org
VirginiaPrisoners@yahoogroups.com

CURE is a grassroots organization from top to bottom. It does not hire professional leaders. Instead, its leaders come from the ranks of people formerly in prison and family members of friends of prisoners. This organization offers assistance to ex-offenders.

Great Dads
P.O. Box 7537
Fairfax Station, VA 22039
703-830-7500
http://www.greatdads.org

Great dads provides in-prison training to fathers on effective parenting. Great Dads provides to fathers the 6 basics of being a Great Dad seminar which gives them practical training amd motivates them to turn their heart to their children and to Jesus Christ.

Offender Aid and Restoration of Arlington County
1400 Uhle St. Suite 704
Arlington, VA 22201
703-228-7030

Provides direct referrals, employment and vocational guidance, skills training, job placement, and counseling.

Offender Aid and Restoration of Charlottesville/Albemarle
750 Harris St. Suite 207
Charlottesville, VA 22903

434-296-2441

Provides job assistance and emergency assistance for offenders and families.

Offender Aid and Restoration of Richmond
1 N. 3rd St. Suite 200
Richmond, VA 23219
804-643-2746
www.oarric.org
info@oarric.org

Post-Release services are provided to former prisoners released from a jail in the greater Richmond area and to parolees released from a state or federal prison with plans to return to the Richmond area.

Prison Fellowship Ministries (PFM)
44180 Riverside Parkway
Lansdowne, VA 20176
http://www.pfm.org/

To seek transformation of prisoners and their reconciliation to God, family, and community through the power and truth of Jesus Christ, PF's ministries include in-prison, Inner Change Freedom Initiative, Operation Starting Line, Angel Tree, and Communities of Care.

Richmond Community Action Program, Inc./VA C.A.R.E.S
1021 Oliver Hill Way
Richmond, VA 23219
804-788-0050
www.rcapva.org

Post-release services include like skills training, consumer education, social skills and family relationship workshops, and emergency assistance in locating counseling, housing, employment, clothes, and transportation. Transition specialists work with clients to begin the process of making long-range plans for education, employment, and literary housing.

The Salvation Army
615 Slaters Lane
Alexandra, VA 22313

Have transitional housing in some cities for ex-offenders.

One-Stop Career Centers

Albemarle Career Center
1600 5th St., Suite A
Charlottesville, VA 22902
434-972-4010

Alexandria Job Link
1900 North Beauregard St., Suite 300
Alexandria, VA 22311
703-838-4316

Alexandria Workforce Center, VEC
5520 Cherokee Ave., Suite 100
Alexandria, VA 22312-2319
703-813-1300

Arlington Employment Center
3033 Wilson Blvd., Suite 400B
Arlington, VA 22201
703-228-1400

Bristol Virginia Workforce Center
192 Bristol East Rd.
Bristol, VA 24209
276-642-7450

Buena Vista Career Café
2141 Sycamore Ave.
Buena Vista, VA 24416
540-264-0208

Cedar Bluff VEC Field Office
12061 Governor GC Peery Highway
Cedar Bluff, VA 24609-9803
276-964-4007

Charlotte Court House Workforce
    Center
400 Thomas Jefferson Highway
Charlotte Court House, VA 23923
434-542-5605

Charlottesville Workforce Center
2211 Hydraulic Rd.
Charlottesville, VA 22901
434-977-2662

Chatham Workforce Center
13995 U. S. Highway 29, Suite 400

Chatham, VA 24531
434-432-4257

Chesterfield Capitol Area Workforce
    Center
7333 Whitepine Rd.
Chesterfield, VA 23237
804-271-8510

Covington Workforce Center
106 North Maple Ave.
Covington, VA 24426
540-962-0983

Culpeper Career Resource Center
210 E. Stevens St., Suite 300
Culpeper, VA 22701
540-727-1055
Culpeper VEC

529 Meadowbrook Shopping Center
Culpeper, VA 22701
540-829-7430

Danville Workforce Career Center
707 Piney Forest Rd., Piney Forest
    Shopping Center
Danville, VA 24540
434-792-3061

Eastern Shore Workforce Center
25036 Lankford Highway Unit
16, Chesapeake Square Shopping
    Center
Onley, VA 23418
757-302-2029

Emporia Workforce Center, VEC
1746 East Atlantic St.
Emporia, VA 23847-0391
434-634-2326
866-270-9193

Falls Church Skill Source Center
6245 Leesburg Pike, Suite 315
Falls Church, VA 22044
703-533-5400
Farmville VEC

223 Sunchase Blvd.
Farmville, VA 23901
434-392-8871

Fisherville VEC Field Office
1076 Jefferson Highway
Staunton, VA 24401
540-332-7750

Franklin Center
50 Claiborne Ave.
Rocky Mount, VA 24151
540-483-0179

Franklin Workforce Development
   Center
Paul D. Camp Community College
100 North College Drive, Room 222
Franklin, VA 23851
757-569-6082
757-569-6081

Fredericksburg Regional Workforce
   Center
3501 Lafayette Blvd.
Fredericksburg, VA 22404
540-898-3806

Galax Workforce Center
963 East Stuart Drive
Galax, VA 24333
276-236-5105

Giles County Partnership for Excellence Foundation
211 Main St., Suite 101
Narrow, VA 24124
540-726-8201

Goodwill Industries of the Valleys-
   Workforce Development Center
106 Town Center Drive
Dublin, VA 24084
540-674-1721

Harrisonburg VEC Office
1909 A East Market St.
Harrisonburg, VA 22801
540-434-8946

Hopewell Workforce Center, VEC
5240 Oak Lawn Blvd.
Hopewell, VA 23860
804-541-6548
804-541-6541

Lake Anne Skill Source Affiliate Center
11484 Washington Plaza West, Suite 110
Reston, VA 20190
703-787-4974

Luray Work Force Job Center
1230 East Main St.
Luray, VA 22835
540-743-4320

Loudoun Workforce Resource Center
102 Heritage Way, NE 1st Floor Rear
   Entrance
Leesburg, VA 20176
703-777-0150

Madison Department of Social Services
101 South Main St.
Madison, VA 22727
540-948-5521

Marion Workforce Center
1590 North Main St.
Marion, VA 24354
276-781-7431

Martinsville Workforce Career Center
Henry County
730 E. Church St.
Martinsville, VA 24112
276-656-2352

Metro Richmond North
8093 Elm Drive
Mechanicsville, VA 23111-1160
804-559-3133

Norfolk VEC
5145 East Virginia Beach Blvd.
Norfolk, VA 23502
757-455-3960

Northern Neck One-Stop Center
14243 Historyland Highway

Warsaw, VA 22572
804-333-3675

Norton VEC Field Office
1725 Park Ave. S.W.
Norton, VA 24273
276-679-9413

Opportunity, Inc. One-Stop Workforce Center
861 Glenrock Rd., Suite 223. Circle
East Bldg.
Norfolk, VA 23502
757-461-7537

Peninsula Worklink
600 Butler Farm Rd., Suite D
Hampton, VA 23666
757-865-5874

People Incorporated of Virginia
1173 West Main St.
Abingdon, VA 24210
276-466-6527
276-466-5587

People Incorporated of Virginia
800 Martin Luther King Jr. Blvd.
Bristol, VA 24266
276-466-5587

People Incorporated of Virginia
122 Price St.
Lebanon, VA 24266
276-889-0999

Petersburg Workforce Center
114 North Union St.
Petersburg, VA 23803
804-862-6155

Powhatan County Public Library
2270 Mann Rd.
Powhatan, VA 23139
804-598-5670

Radford Workforce Center
206 Third Ave.
Radford, VA 24141-4767
540-831-5980

Region 2000 Career Center
2323 Memorial Ave., Suite 25
Lynchburg, VA 24501
434-455-5940

Roanoke Workforce Center
1351 Hershberger Rd.
Roanoke, VA 24012
540-204-9660

Sandston Capital Area Workforce
Center
5410 Williamsburg Rd.
Sandston, VA 23150
804-226-0885

Shackiefords Job Assistance Center
1399 Centerville Rd.
Shackiefords, VA 23156
804-785-2470

South Boston Workforce Center
SVHEC 820 Bruce St.
South Boston, VA 24592
434-572-5551

South County Skill Source Center
8350 Richmond Highway, Suite 327
Alexandra, VA 22309
703-704-6286

South Hill Employment Commission
910 North Mecklenburg Ave.
South Hill, VA 23970
434-447-8700

Stopp Organization
Center for Employment Training
125 Tynes St.
Suffolk, VA 23434
757-539-8081

Stuart Career Center
Patrick County Adult Ed.
108 E. Blue Ridge St.
Stuart, VA 24171
276-694-6542

Warrenton Workforce Career Resource Center

70 Main St., Suite 43
Warrenton, VA 20186
540-341-3350

Williamsburg Workforce Center
5235 John Tyler Highway
Williamsburg, VA 23185
757-253-4738

Winchester VEC Office
100 Premier Place

Winchester, VA 22602
540-722-3415

Woodbridge Employment Commission
13370 Minnieville Rd.
Woodbridge, VA 22192

Wytheville Workforce Center
800 East Main St., Suite 200
Wytheville, VA 24382
276-228-4051

WASHINGTON (State)

Catholic Community Services,
  Katherine's House
253-856-7716

Provides transitional housing and case management for homeless, single women coming out of Regional Justice Center or chemical dependency programs.

Central Area Motivation Program
Re-Entry Program
722 18th Ave. Central District
Seattle, WA 98122-4704
206-812-4940
www.campseattle.org

This organization offers an ex-offender program designed to transition clients back into the work force.

Compass Center
77 South Washington St.
Seattle, WA 98104
206-357-3100
www.compasscenter.org
info@compasscenter.org

The Compass center is Lutheran organization comprised of four shelters for those in immediate need, a transitional center for women, and transition housing. Services provided include mail services, the Compass Center Bank, hygiene center, and chaplaincy.

Downtown Emergency Service Center
517 Third Ave.
Seattle, WA 98104

206-464-1570

Shelter priority given to women, men over 60, mentally ill, physically or developmentally disabled. Chemically dependant persons who are willing to engage in services to treat their addiction will also have priority.

First Ave. Service Center
2015 3rd Ave.
Seattle, WA 98121
206-441-8405

Day center provides assistance for basic needs of homeless people, such as food, clothing, hygiene facilities, mail, and referrals. Offers assistance for offenders including advocacy, community service assignments and contacts for jail and parole.

Interaction/Transition
935 16th Ave.
Seattle, WA 98122
206-324-3932
i-t@mindspring.com

Assists ex-offenders who are serious about making a successful transition from life in prison to life in the community. Operates a low cost housing facility with transitioning support services.

Justice Works
P.O. Box 1489
Lake Stevens, WA 98258

Focuses on racism in Criminal Justice System in Washington state. Newsletter, corre-

spondence classes, court watch and advocacy on specific reform issues, and transition support for ex-offenders.

M-2 Job Therapy
205 Ave. "C"
Snohomish, WA 96291-0293
877-625-6214

Provides a wide range of employment services for ex-offenders, including job referrals and resume assistance in Snohomish County.

Pioneer Human Services
7440 West Marginal Way S
Seattle, WA 98108
206-768-1990
www.pioneerhumanserv.com

Offers a sheltered workshop to help society disadvantaged individuals, ex-offenders, and recovering drug/alcohol abusers obtain work training, an orientation to the job world, employment references, and transitional employment.

Salvation Army-Northwest Divisional
　Headquarters
P.O. Box 9219
Seattle, WA 98109
206-587-0503
www.nwarmy.org

Oversees a wide range of service programs including support services for offenders and their families, coordinates shelter beds for ex-offenders.

Salvation Army-William Booth Center
811 Maynard Ave S
Seattle, WA 98134
206-287-0125

Dormitory shelter for Department of Corrections male inmates and limited number of sex offenders; $70 fee per week for bed and locker; application fee and recommendation required.

Worksource Centers by County

ADAMS COUNTY

Central Basin Worksource Center
309 E. 5th Ave.

Moses Lake, WA 98837
509-766-2559

ASOTIN COUNTY

Rural Resources Clarkston Affiliate
1013 Bridge St.
Clarkston, WA 99403
509-758-5461

BENTON COUNTY

Columbia Basin Worksource Center
815 N. Kellogg, Suite D
Kennewick, WA
99336
509-734-5900

CHELAN COUNTY

Skill Source Wenatchee Affiliate
233 N. Chelan
Wenatchee, WA 988801
509-663-3091
800-999-8694

Wenatchee Valley College Affiliate
1300 5th St.
Wenatchee, WA 98801
509-682-6890

Wenatchee Worksource Affiliate
215 Bridge St.
Wenatchee, WA 98801
509-665-6605

CLALLAM COUNTY

Clallam County Worksource Center
228 W. 1st St., Suite A
Port Angeles, WA 98362-2639
360-457-9407

CLARK COUNTY

Vancouver Worksource Center
5411 E. Mill Plain Blvd., Suite 15
Vancouver, WA 98661-7046
360-735-5000

COLUMBIA COUNTY

Walla Walla Worksource Center
1530 Stevens
Walla Walla, WA 99362
509-527-4393

COWLITZ COUNTY

Cowlitz Worksource Center
305 S. Pacific Ave., Suite A
Kelso, WA 98626
360-577-2250

DOUGLAS COUNTY

Skill Source Wenatchee Affiliate
233 N. Chelan
Wenatchee, WA 988801
509-663-3091
800-999-8694

Wenatchee Valley College Affiliate
1300 5th St.
Wenatchee, WA 98801
509-682-6890

Wenatchee Worksource Affiliate
215 Bridge St.
Wenatchee, WA 98801
509-665-6605

FERRY COUNTY

Colville Worksource Center
956 S. Main, Suite B
Colville, WA 99114
509-685-6158
800-451-1549

Rural Resources Republic Affiliate
72 N Clark St.
Republic, WA 99166
509-775-2009
800-451-1549

FRANKLIN COUNTY

Columbia Basin Worksource Center
815 N. Kellogg, Suite D

Kennewick, WA
99336
509-734-5900

GARFIELD COUNTY

Rural Resources Clarkston Affiliate
1013 Bridge St.
Clarkston, WA 99403
509-758-5461

GRANT COUNTY

Central Basin Worksource Center
309 E. 5th Ave.
Moses Lake, WA 98837
509-766-2559

Mattawa Opportunities Affiliate
403 Broadway
Mattawa, WA 99349
509-932-4297

GRAYS HARBOR COUNTY

Grays Harbor Worksource Center
511 W. Heron
Aberdeen, WA 98520
360-533-9318

ISLAND COUNTY

Whidbey Island Worksource Center
31975 SR 20, Suite 3
Oak Harbor, WA 98277
360-675-5966

JEFFERSON COUNTY

Clallam County Worksource Center
228 W. 1st St., Suite A
Port Angeles, WA 98362-2639
360-457-9407

Jefferson County Affiliate
207 W Patison
Port Hadlock, WA 98339
360-379-5036

KING COUNTY

Auburn Affiliate
2707 I St. NE
Auburn, WA 98002
253-804-1177

Bellevue College Worksource Connection
3000 Landerholm Circle SE
Bellevue, WA 98007
425-564-4054

Downtown Seattle Affiliate
2024 3rd Ave.
Seattle, WA 98121
206-436-8600

North Seattle Affiliate
600 Washington St. Grays Harbor
    College-Riverview Education Center
Raymond, WA 98577
360-875-9470

Rainer Affiliate
2531 Rainer Ave. South
Seattle, WA 98144-5328
206-721-6000

Redmond Worksource Center
7735 178th Place NE
Redmond, WA 98052
425-861-3737

Renton Worksource Center
500 SW 7th St., Suite 100
Renton, WA 98057
206-205-3530

South Seattle Community College
    Affiliate
6000 16th Ave. SW
Seattle, WA 98106-1499
206-764-5304

KITSAP COUNTY

Kitsap Community Resources
1211 Bay St.

Port Orchard, WA 98366
360-473-2159

Kitsap County Worksource Center
1300 Sylvan Way
Bremerton, WA 98310
360-337-4810 Ext 0

KITTITAS COUNTY

Kittitas County Worksource Center
309 East Mountainview Ave.
Ellenburg, WA 98926
509-925-5311

KLICKITAT COUNTY

Columbia Gorge Worksource Center
107 West Jewett Blvd.
White Salmon, WA 98672
509-493-1210

Goldendale Affiliate
116 East Main
Goldendale, WA 98620
509-773-5503

LEWIS COUNTY

Lewis County Worksource Center
151 NE Hampe Way
Chehalis, WA 98532
360-748-2360

LINCOLN COUNTY

Colville Worksource Center
956 S. Main, Suite B
Colville, WA 99114
509-685-6158
800-451-1549

MASON COUNTY

Mason County Worksource Center
2505 Olympic Hwy N., Suite 420
Shelton, WA 98584
360-427-2174

OKONOGAN COUNTY

Okanogan County Worksource Center
126 South Main
Omak, WA 98841
509-826-7310
800-887-8057

PACIFIC COUNTY

Long Beach Affiliate
2601 Ave. North
Long Beach, WA 98631
360-642-6213
800-269-6126

Pacific County Affiliate
600 Washington St Grays Harbor
    College-Riverview Education Center
Raymond, WA 98577
360-875-9470

PEND OREILLE COUNTY

Colville Worksource Center
956 S. Main, Suite B
Colville, WA 99114
509-685-6158
800-451-1549

Rural Resources Newport Affiliate
420 West Hwy #2
Newport, WA 99156
509-447-5614

PIERCE COUNTY

Fort Stellacoom Affiliate
9401 Farwest Drive SW
Lakewood, WA 98498-1999
253-964-6500

Lakewood Affiliate
5712 Main St. SW
Lakewood, WA 98499
253-984-5400

Lakewood Affiliate, Clover Park Technical College

4500 Steilacoom Blvd. SW
Lakewood, WA 98499
253-589-5510

Pierce Worksource Center
1305 Tacoma Ave South, Suite 201
Tacoma, WA 98402
253-593-7300

Tacoma Affiliate, Bates Technical College
1101 South Yakima Ave.
Tacoma, WA 98405-4895
253-680-7240

Tacoma Community College Affiliate
6501 South 19th St., Building 7
Tacoma, WA 98466-6100
253-566-5191

Tacoma Community House Affiliate
1314 South L. St.
Tacoma, WA 98415
253-383-3951

Tacoma Housing Authority Affiliate
1724 E. 44th St.
Tacoma, WA 98404
253-207-4447

Vadis Affiliate
1701 Elm St.
Summer, WA 98390
253-863-5173

Worksource Business Connection
4650 Steilacoom Blvd. SW. Building 19
Lakewood, WA 98499
253-583-8800

SAN JUAN COUNTY

Skagit Worksource Center
2005 E. College Way
Mount Vernon, WA 98273
360-416-3600

SKAGIT COUNTY

Skagit Worksource Center
2005 E. College Way

Mount Vernon, WA 98273
360-416-3600

SKAMANIA COUNTY

Columbia Gorge Worksource Center
107 West Jewett Blvd.
White Salmon, WA 98672
509-493-1210

Stevenson Affiliate
704 SW Rock Creek Drive
Stevenson, WA 98648
509-427-4464

SNOHOMISH COUNTY

Everett Worksource Center
3201 Smith Ave., Suite 114
Everett, WA 98201
425-258-6330

Lynnwood Worksource Center
20311 52nd Ave. West, Suite 300
Lynnwood, WA 99114
509-685-6158
800-451-1549

Youth Center Affiliate
3331 Broadway, Suite 1001
Everett, WA 98201
425-252-6400

SPOKANE COUNTY

Next Generation Zone
130 S. Arthur
Spokane, WA 99202
509-532-3040

Spokane Affiliate, Goodwill Industries
130 E. Third Ave.
Spokane, WA 99202
509-838-4246

Spokane Community College Affiliate
1810 N. Green St., Bldg.6
Spokane, WA 99217-5399
509-533-7249

Spokane County Career Path Services
130 S Arthur
Spokane, WA 99202
509-532-3160

Spokane Falls Community College
 Affiliate
3410 W. Ft. George Wright Drive
Spokane, WA 99224
509-533-3521

Spokane Worksource Center 130 S.
 Arthur St.
Spokane, WA 99202
509-532-3120

STEVENS COUNTY

Colville Worksource Center
956 S. Main, Suite B
Colville, WA 99114
509-685-6158
800-451-1549

THURSTON COUNTY

Thurston County Worksource Center
1520 Irving St. SW
Tumwater, WA 98512
360-704-3600

WAHKIAKUM COUNTY

Cowiltz Worksource Center
305 S. Pacific Ave., Suite A
Kelso, WA 98626
360-577-2250

WALLA WALLA COUNTY

Blue Mountain Action Council
342 Catherine St.
Walla Walla, WA 99362
509-529-4980

Walla Walla Community College
 Affiliate
500 Tausick Way

Walla Walla, WA 98648
509-527-4279

Walla Walla Worksource Center
1530 Stevens
Walla Walla, WA 99362
509-527-4393

WHATCOM COUNTY

Whatcom Worksource Center
101 Prospect St.
Bellingham, WA 98227
360-676-1521

WHITMAN COUNTY

Pullman Affiliate
350 SE Fairmont Rd.

Pullman, WA 99163-5500
509-332-6549

YAKIMA COUNTY

Sunnyside Worksource Center
1925 Morgan Rd.
Sunnyside, WA 98944
509-836-5405

Toppenish Affiliate
706 Rentschler Lane
Toppenish, WA 98948
509-865-7630

Yakima Worksource Center
306 Division
Yakima, WA 98902
509-574-0105

WASHINGTON, D.C.

Altar of Ed Ministries
2800 Ontario Rd. NW, Suite 506
Washington DC 20009
202-232-0866

Ex-offenders in need of help with re-entry may contact Jim Wilder for assistance.

Center for Neighborhood Enterprise
1625 K. St., NW
Suite 1200
Washington DC 20006
202-518-6500
http://www.cneonline.org/info@cneon-line.org

The Center for Neighborhood Enterprise's mission is to empower neighborhood leaders to promote solutions that reduce crime and violence, restore families, revitalize low-income communities, and create economic enterprise.

Our Place, DC
801 Pennsylvania Ave., SE, Ste 460
Washington DC 20003
202-548-2400

www.ourplacedc.org
ourplace@ourplacedc.org

Post-release services include a support center offering employment and housing resources, a safe and nurturing environment, and referrals to other support services necessary to obtain and retain employment.

One-Stop Career Centers

Business Resource Center
64 New York Ave., N.E., 3rd Floor
Washington, DC 20002
202-671-2144

Franklin One-Stop Career Center
1500 Franklin St., N.E.
Washington, DC 20018
202-576-3091 Ext. 3092
202-576-3077

Naylor Rd. One-Stop Center
2626 Naylor Rd., S.E.
Washington, DC 20020

South Capital One-Stop Career Center
4049 South Capitol St., S.W.

Washington, DC 20032
202-645-4000

WEST VIRGINIA

CURE
C/o Catholic Charities West Virginia
P.O. Box 386
Princeton, WV 24740
304-425-7515
mvcc@citlink.net

CURE is a grassroots organization from top to bottom. It does not hire professional people. Instead, its leaders come from the ranks of people formerly in prison and family members of friends of prisoners. This organization offers assistance to ex-offenders.

Workforce Career Centers by City/County

Beckley
200 Value City Center
Beckley, WV 25802
304-256-6792

Charleston
1321 Plaza East
Charleston, WV 25325
304-558-0342

Clarksburg
321 West Main St.
Clarksburg, WV 26302
304-627-2125

Elkins
1 Pleasant Ave., Suite #2
Elkins, WV 26241
304-637-0255

Fairmont
320 Adams St., Suite 107
Fairmont, WV 26555
304-363-0654

Huntington
2699 Park Ave., Suite 240

Huntington, WV 25704
304-528-5525

Logan
214 Dingess St.
Logan WV 25601-1619
304-792-7010

Martinsburg
891 Auto Parts Pl., Suite 1314
Martinsburg, WV 25403
304-267-0030

Moorefield, South Branch
1929 State Rd. 55
Moorefield, WV 26836
304-530-3917

Morgantown
304 Scott Ave.
Morgantown, WV 26508
304-285-3120

New Martinsville
257 North State Route #2
New Martinsville, WV 26155
304-455-0902

Parkersburg
304 Lakeview Center
Parkersburg, WV 26101
304-420-4531
304-420-4531

Point Pleasant
307 R 8th St.
Point Pleasant, WV 25550
304-675-0857

Princeton, Mercer County Job Service
195 Davis St., Suite 102
Princeton, WV 24740

304-487-2248
304-487-2248
Payne, Putman County

19 Putman Village Shopping Center
Payne, WV 25569
304-757-7270

Summersville
830 Northside Drive, Suite 123
Summersville, WV 26651
304-872-0820

Weirton
100 Municipal Plaza, Suite 300
Weirton, WV 26062
304-794-2000

Welch
110 Park Ave.
Welch, WV 24801
304-436-3131

Wheeling
1275 Warwood Ave.
Wheeling, WV 26003
304-232-6280
866-956-2669

Williamson
241 East 2nd Ave.
Williamson, WV 25661
304-235-6012

WISCONSIN

CURE
P.O. Box 183
Greendale, WI 53129
414-384-1000 Ext. 32
Harthouse9@yahoo.com

CURE is a grassroots organization from top to bottom. It does not hire professional leaders. Instead, its leaders come from the ranks of people formerly prisoners and family members of friends of prisoners. This organization offers assistance to ex-offenders.

Madison Urban Ministries (MUM)
2300 S. Park St. Suite 5
Madison, WI 53713
608-256-0906
www.emum.org
mun@emum.org

MUM is an interfaith organization with a restorative justice project that supports people with criminal histories in their attempts to re-enter society. Services offered including housing, transportation, employment referrals, counseling, substance/alcohol treatment, family reunification, and child support issues.

Job Centers by City/County

Adams County
401 North Main St.
Adams, WI 53910
608-339-9559

Ashland
101 Main St. West
Ashland, WI 54806
715-682-7220

Barron County
331 South Main St., Suite 6
Rice Lake, WI 54868
715-234-6826

Berlin
742 Green Tree Mall
Berlin, WI 54923
920-361-3400

Black River Falls Workforce Connections
808 Red Iron Rd.
Black River Falls, WI 54615
715-284-7117

Burnett County
7410 County Rd. K
Siren, WI 54872-9043
715-349-2150

Chippewa County
770 Scheidier Rd., Suite 2
Chippewa Falls, WI 54729
715-723-2248

Clark County
501 Hewett St.
Neillsville, WI 54456
715-743-4631

Dane County
1819 Aberg Ave.
Madison, WI 53704
608-245-5390

Dodge County
143 E. Center St.
Juneau, WI 53039
920-386-4083

Door County
1300 Egg Harbor Rd., Suite 124
Sturgeon Bay, WI 54235
920-743-6915

Dunn County
401 Technology Drive East
Menomonie, WI 54751
715-232-7360

Eau Claire County
221 West Madison St., Suite 140-A
Eau Claire, WI 54703
715-836-2901

Fenimore, Southwest Wisconsin
  Technical College
1800 Bronson Blvd.
Fennimore, WI 53809
608-822-3262 Ext. 2333

Fond du Lac
349 North Peters Ave.
Fond du Lac, WI 54935
920-929-3900

Grant County
8820 Hwy 35 and 61 South
Lancaster, WI 53813
608-723-2153

Green Bay/Northeast Wisconsin
701 Cherry St.
Green Bay, WI 54301
920-448-6760

Hayward
15618 Windrose Lane
Hayward, WI 54843
715-634-3011

Independence Workforce Connections
36084 Walnut St.
Independence, WI 54747
715-284-7117
715-985-2118

Iowa County
201 South Iowa St.
Dodgeville, WI 53533
608-935-3116

Jefferson County
874 Collins Rd.
Jefferson, WI 53549
920-674-7500

Kenosha County
8600 Sheridan Rd.
Kenosha, WI 53143
262-697-4500

La Crosse County
402 8th St. North
La Crosse, WI 54601
608-789-5627

Ladysmith Workforce Connections
108 West Second St. North
Ladysmith. WI 54848
715-532-2700

Lafayette County
627 Main St.
Darlington, WI 53530
608-776-4900

Langlade County
312 Forest Ave.
Antigo, WI 54409
715-623-2117

Menasha/Fox Cities
1802 Appleton Rd.
Menasha, WI 54952
920-997-3272

Manitowoc County
3733 Dewey St.
Manitowoc, WI 54220
920-683-2888

Marathon County
364 Grand Ave.
Wausau, WI 54403-6221
715-261-2700

Marinette
1605 University Drive, Suite A
Marinette, WI 54143
715-732-7840

Marquette County Economic Support
480 Underwood Ave.
Montello, WI 53949-0099
608-297-7550

Marshfield
630 South Central Ave.
Marshfield, WI 54449
715-387-6386

Mauston Workforce Connections
111 East State St.
Mauston, WI 53948
608-847-4899

Medford Workforce Connections
624 East College Ave.
Medford, WI 54451
715-748-5621

Milwaukee YMCA
1915 North Martin Luther King Drive
Milwaukee, WI 53212
414-267-3950

MJCN-Milwaukee North
4030 North 29th St.
Milwaukee, WI 53216
414-486-5200

MJCN-Milwaukee Northwest (Maximus)
6550 North 76th St.
Milwaukee, WI 53223
414-607-7416

MJCN-Milwaukee Southeast (UMOS)
2701 S. Chase Ave.
Milwaukee, WI 54220
414-389-2888

MJCN-Southwest (Maximus)
1304 70th St.
West Allis, WI 53214
414-607-7416

Monroe County
120 E. Milwaukee St.
Tomah, WI 54660
608-374-7740

Niagara/Florence APS
705 Washington Ave.
Niagara, WI 54151
715-251-1144

Oconto NEWCAP
1201 Main St.
Oconto, WI 54153
920-834-4621

Oneida Nation Job Training Programs
2640 West Point Rd.
Oneida, WI 54155
920-496-7870

Pepin County
316 West Madison St.
Durand, WI 543736
715-672-8801

Polk County
404 Main St.

Balsam Lake, WI 54810
715-485-3115

Racine County Service Center
380 McCanna Pkwy
Burlington, WI 53105
262-767-5399

Rhinelander Northern Advantage
100 West Keenan St., Riverwalk Center
Rhinelander, WI 54501
715-365-1500

Richland County
221 West Seminary
Richland Center, WI 53581
608-647-8821

Oshkosh Area
315 Algoma Blvd.
Oshkosh, WI 54901
920-232-6200

Ozaukee County
5555 West Highland Rd.
Mequon, WI 53092
262-238-2880

Park Falls
400 South 4th Ave., City Hall
Park Falls, WI 54552
715-762-2477

Phillips
1408 Pine Ridge Rd.
Phillips, WI 54555
715-339-4555

Prairie du Chien Workforce Connections
225 N. Beaumont Rd.
Prairie du Chien, WI 53821
608-326-1100

Racine County 1717 Taylor Ave.
Racine, WI 53403
262-638-6420

Rock County
1900 Center Ave.

Janesville, WI 53546
608-741-3400

St. Croix Valley
625 Whitetail Blvd., Suite 120
River Falls, WI 54022
715-426-0388

Sauk County
522 South Blvd.
Baraboo, WI 53913
608-355-3140

Shawano County
607 East Elizabeth St.
Shawano, WI 54116
715-524-2511

Sheboygan County
3620 Wilgus Ave.
Sheboygan, WI 53081
920-208-5856

Spooner Workforce Connections
522 Service Rd. Hwy 70 East
Spooner, WI 54801
715-635-2175

Superior
1805 North 14th St., Suite 1
Superior. WI 54880
715-392-7800
715-780-0378

Tomah
120 East Milwaukee
Tomah, WI 54660
608-374-7740

Viroqua Workforce Connections
220 South Main St.
Viroqua, WI 54665
608-637-6450

Walworth County
1000 East Centralia St.
Elkhorn, WI 53121
262-741-5180

Waukesha County
892 Main St.

Pewaukee, WI 53072
262-695-7991

Waupaca Area
1979 Godfrey Drive
Waupaca, WI 54981
715-258-8832

Wautoma
205 East Main St.

Wautoma, WI 54982
920-787-3338

Wisconsin Rapids
320 W. Grand Ave., Suite 102
Wisconsin Rapids, WI 54495
715-422-5000

WYOMING

Community Action of Laramie
   County
1620 Central Ave. Suite 300
Cheyenne, WY 82001
307-635-9291
www.calc.net
info@calc.net
   *Provides workshops that address self-suffi-
ciency issues including conflict and stress management, career choices, and budgeting. It also
provides housing assistance.*

CURE
P.O. Box 2138
Casper, WY 82602
sydneys@tribcsp.com
   *CURE is a grassroots organization from top
to bottom. It does not hire professional leaders.
Instead, its leaders come from the ranks of people formerly in prison and family members of
friends of prisoners. This organization offers
assistance to ex-offenders.*

Workforce Centers

Afton Workforce Services
350 South Washington, Suite 5
Afton, WY 83110
307-886-9260

Casper Workforce Center
851 Werner Court, Suite 120
Casper, WY 82601-1308
307-234-4591

Cheyenne Workforce Center
1510 East Pershing Blvd.
Cheyenne, WY 82002
307-777-3700

Cody Workforce Center
1026 Blackburn Ave., Suite 1
Cody, WY 82414-8464
307-587-4241

Diamondville/Kemmerer Workforce
   Center
20 Adaville Rd.
Diamondville, WY 83116
307-877-5501

Douglas Workforce Center
311 N. Russell, Suite B
Douglas, WY 82633
307-358-2147

Evanston Workforce Center
98 Independence Drive
Evanston, WY 82930
307-789-9802

Gillette Workforce Center
1901 Energy Court, Suite 230
Gillette, WY 82718
307-682-9313

Jackson Workforce Center
155 West Gill St.
Jackson, WY 83001
307-733-4091

Lander Workforce Center
455 Lincoln St.
Lander, WY 82520
307-335-9224

Laramie Workforce Center
112 South Fifth St.
Laramie, WY 82070
307-742-2153

Newcastle Workforce Center
2013 West Main St., Suite 102
Newcastle, WY 82701
307-746-9690

Powell Workforce Center
231 W. 6th
Powell, WY 82435
307-754-6436

Rawlins Workforce Center
1703 Edinburgh
Rawlins, WY 82301
307-324-3485

Riverton Department of Workforce
  Services
P.O. Box 1610

Riverton, WY 82501
307-856-9231

Rock Springs Workforce Center
2451 Foot Hill Blvd., Suite 100
Rock Springs, WY 82901
307-382-2747

Sheridan Workforce Center
61 South Gould
Sheridan, WY 82801
307-672-9775 Ext. 222

Torrington Workforce Center
1610 East "M" St.
Torrington, WY 82240-3508
307-532-4171

Wheatland Workforce Center
956 Maple St., Suite 6
Wheatland, WY 82201
307-322-4741

Worland Workforce Center
1200 Culberson St., Suite F
Worland, WY 82201-2920
307-347-8173